British Seashells

To Simon Butler and Karen Pulford

What is it? A learned man
Could give it a clumsy name.
Let him name it who can,
The beauty would be the same.

Alfred Lord Tennyson; *The Shell*

British Seashells

A Guide for Collectors and Beachcombers

Paul Chambers

Original Victorian illustrations by George Sowerby

First published in Great Britain in 2009 by
REMEMBER WHEN
An imprint of
Pen & Sword Books Ltd
47 Church Street
Barnsley
South Yorkshire
S70 2AS

ISBN 978 1 84468 051 1

A CIP catalogue record for this book is available from the British Library

Typeset by Phoenix Typesetting, Auldgirth, Dumfriesshire
Printed and bound by KNP

Pen & Sword Books Ltd incorporates the Imprints of Pen & Sword Aviation, Pen & Sword Maritime, Pen & Sword Military, Wharncliffe Local History, Pen & Sword Select, Pen & Sword Military Classics, Leo Cooper, Remember When, Seaforth Publishing and Frontline Publishing.

For a complete list of Pen & Sword titles please contact
PEN & SWORD BOOKS LIMITED
47 Church Street, Barnsley, South Yorkshire, S70 2AS, England
E-mail: enquiries@pen-and-sword.co.uk
Website: www.pen-and-sword.co.uk

Contents

Introduction

A STROLL ALONG a British beach is like participating in an endless treasure hunt in which the gold and jewels are the myriad of sea creatures that live among the sand and rocks, or are washed onto the shore from deeper waters. This book concerns itself with the most obvious and desirable of these natural jewels: the seashells.

Britain is home to over 400 different species of seashell, most of which are described in the pages that follow. However, this book is much more than just an identification guide. It is a celebration of the cultural and historical significance of Britain's wonderful and varied seashells. I have spent almost three decades indulging my passion for British seashells, and in writing this book I had two objectives in mind. The first was to produce a general guide to the many sorts of seashell that may be deliberately or idly picked up during a sojourn to the beach. The second was to glorify the magnificence of our British seashells by highlighting their historical, cultural and scientific significance.

This is because I am not just passionate about the pleasing shape and striking colours that our shells may adopt, but also by their association with humankind, be it through fishermen, scientists, collectors or holidaymakers. As well as physically collecting the shells themselves, I have spent many years gathering small snippets of information associated with them and have devoted much time to researching their natural history and the history of those people who are connected to them. In the coming chapters, you will find an individual entry for almost all the known British species of seashell (though some very rare and deep water shells are omitted) which will not only permit you to identify the shell concerned, but will provide you with a flavour of its journey from an anonymous mollusc to an acknowledged part of our magnificent British marine fauna.

It should be noted that this approach is not original. Many Victorian conchologists (a conchologist is someone who collects and studies shells; they should not be confused with a malacologist who studies the whole molluscan animal) displayed a similar enthusiasm for their seashells, treating them almost as though they were personalities in their own right. In recent times, our attitude towards nature has become somewhat dispassionate and clinical. This book is aimed at recapturing some of the enthusiasm and quirkiness displayed by our Victorian forebears, many of whom could write keenly about the most mundane-looking shell. Each and every British seashell, no matter how trivial, has something to say for itself. I hope that this book may, in some small measure, provide them with a voice.

Paul Chambers

Acknowledgements

MY PROFOUND THANKS go to all the people who were kind enough to offer me their time, advice and knowledge during the time it took to research and write this book. In particular, I would like to thank the staff at the following institutions for allowing me access to their records and for their patience when answering my many questions: British Library; British Newspaper Library; Cambridge University Library; The National Archives; Institute of Historical Research; Natural History Museum; Royal Historical Society; Society of Genealogists; University College London and Wellcome Library.

A big thank-you must go to the staff at Pen and Sword, especially Fiona Shoop, whose support and enthusiasm for this project ensured that the production process went without a hitch. I would like to thank my wonderful agents Isabel Atherton and Mandy Little (of Watson Little) for their sound advice and continued guidance. My unlimited thanks go to those who encouraged and helped me during my early beachcombing days, including John Perry, Dr Arthur Mourant, Roger Long, Karl Hairon and Tim le Gallais. Their advice and patience allowed my hobby to develop into an obsession. Finally, this project could not have been undertaken without the support of my immediate and extended family, especially my father, Martyn Chambers, and my parents-in-law, John and Elizabeth Baxter. As ever, my greatest debt is to my wife Rachel and daughter Eleanor. Their humour and ability to withstand the sight and smell of drying seashells is apparently without limit. My love for you is without end.

British Seashells

An Overview

Technically speaking, a seashell is the hard, durable part of a soft-bodied animal known as a mollusc. We are most familiar with molluscs in the form of the slugs and snails that ooze their way across our gardens, or perhaps through edible marine species such as whelks, mussels, oysters, cockles, squid and scallops, which may adorn our dinner plates. As such, the molluscs are a very broad group of animals which adopt a variety of forms and live in wide range of environments. This book concerns itself with what may loosely be termed 'British seashells' – those molluscs that have a hard external shell and which live on the beach or in the shallow seas that surround the British Isles.

Confining this book to just British seashells means that several other groups of mollusc have been omitted, including: all land-dwelling and freshwater shells; any entirely soft-bodied marine molluscs (such as sea slugs; see Chapter 17); and molluscs with a reduced or wholly internal shell (such as octopuses, squid and chitons; see Chapter 17). Overall, this book covers 402 individual species of seashell, a total which includes all those that are liable to be found on the seashore or adjacent shallow sea. As such, this is the largest modern popular presentation of British seashells and the only one to provide a cultural and historical perspective for each species.

What is a Mollusc?

The molluscs are a large and incredibly diverse group of animals. They have adopted many different forms, from primitive worm-like deep-sea species to the intelligent and dextrous octopus, and vary in size from just a millimetre to some thirteen metres in length (this is the infamous giant squid, the world's largest invertebrate). A quick flick through the illustrations in this book alone will demonstrate that even among those British species with hard shells, there is a mind-boggling array of shapes, colours, sizes and ornamentation.

For centuries, molluscs were known under a variety of names such as slugs, snails, clams, seashells, squid, octopuses, etc. The first scientists had only a loose understanding of molluscs, and confused

The French gunboat *Alecton* captures the world's largest mollusc, a giant squid, in 1861.

them with any sort of shelled animal including barnacles, foraminifera (minute single-celled organisms), brachiopods (small clam-like animals) and the enigmatic jelly-like sea squirts. By the early Nineteenth Century, much of this confusion was gone, leaving us with a clear understanding as to what is, and is not, a mollusc.

To the modern scientist, a mollusc is defined by its having an unsegmented body (i.e. a body that has no joints), a bisymmetrical shape, the presence of a head, a muscular foot, and a soft body which contains the vital organs. Thus molluscs are invertebrates, soft-bodied animals that lack a spine, and so are evolutionarily far-removed from back-boned vertebrates such as fish, amphibians, reptiles and mammals. Most marine molluscs are herbivorous, but some species are predators, scavengers or filter feeders. (There are even venomous species such as the cone shells but none is known in British waters.) Most molluscs that have a shell live on the seabed, either buried in sediment or on or under rocks, but there are species (usually without a shell) that swim freely or which drift near the sea surface at the mercy of the wind and waves. A majority of molluscs live on the beach or in the shallow sea, but they may also be found at extraordinary depths, including the deepest parts of the ocean.

Our understanding of the evolutionary history of the molluscs begins around 520 million years ago when the first fossils of their shells were found. Prior to this, they were probably worm-like animals (some molluscs, such as the caudofoveata and solenogastres, still are) which evolved shells as protection against predators and the pounding of the seas, or perhaps to allow them to gain a purchase in their chosen habitat. The mollusc fossil record is continuous from all those millions of years ago until the present day, and it is estimated that there around 100,000 living species, of which approximately 920 are known from British waters. Of this number, over half have either a reduced shell or no shell at all and are not covered by this book. Our interest is with the shelled species which for centuries have been gathered and removed from the seashore by conchologists, fishermen and tourists to be eaten, admired, catalogued or discarded. We collectively call these lifeless relics of the ocean 'seashells' (or 'sea shells'), a vernacular term that is sometimes erroneously expanded to include the remains of other coastal animals such as crabs and sea urchins.

That the British Isles is home to such a divergence of seashells is not surprising; after all, the coastlines of England, Scotland, Wales and Ireland are lengthy with varied coastal environments such as mud flats, sandy beaches, brackish estuaries, rocky coasts, lochs and jagged cliffs, as well as offshore waters that include shallow and abyssal habitats. Throughout much of this book, I shall be referring to the British seashore (i.e. that portion of a beach uncovered by the tide) in two very generalised categories: (1) seashores that are dominated by sediment (e.g. sandy beaches, gravel banks, mud flats, etc.) and (2) seashores that are dominated by rocks (e.g. rock pools, cliffs, stony ground, etc.). On sediment beaches, molluscs will often hide by

On sandy beaches much of the marine life lies buried beneath the surface.

Rocky beaches provide numerous hiding places and hard surfaces which can be utilised by molluscs.

burying themselves in the sand, mud, gravel, etc., although there are some species that will crawl about on the surface. On rocky beaches, the molluscs may live by adhering to the rock surface using their muscular foot or organic threads (e.g. limpets, winkles and mussels), or they may protect themselves by hiding under stones, among seaweed, or in rock crevices. A minority of bivalves live by tunnelling into soft rock and wood, and there are even species of mollusc that are planktonic (i.e. they spend their lives floating in the sea). A beach's habitat will usually dictate the type of species of molluscs that will be found there, something that is worth bearing in mind before setting off on a collecting expedition.

As well as habitat, molluscs are also sensitive to other environmental factors, the most important being sea temperature which, in many species, plays an important role in their ability to reproduce. Fortunately, the British Isles are ideally positioned so that they encompass several different marine provinces. The northern and eastern coasts are the coldest and play host to a range of Arctic and subarctic species, while the western and southern coasts are lapped by the warm North Atlantic Drift (a northerly arm of the Gulf Stream oceanic current) which brings with it temperate, Atlantic molluscs. Finally, Cornwall, the Scilly Isles and the Channel Islands, find themselves at the extreme

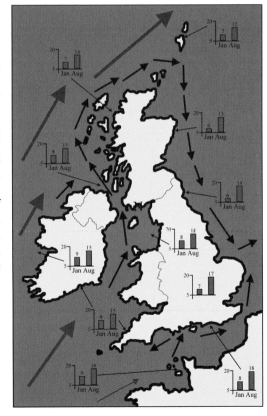

The British coastline. The red arrows indicate the warm North Atlantic Drift current. The black arrows indicate localised coastal currents. The bar charts represent winter and summer sea temperatures, in centigrade, at selected coastal locations.

northern limit of some species that are more commonly associated with southern Europe and the Mediterranean Sea. Thus, Britain's coastline, which is nearly 18,000 km long and stretches from 60°N at the Shetlands to 49°N at Jersey, is situated at a crossroads in the marine realm, attracting species from many different provinces. Put simply, Britain is a shell collector's paradise.

A Brief History of British Conchology

AS YOU FLICK THROUGH the pages that follow, it will become apparent that most (approximately two-thirds) of the species described here were first discovered by scientists working in Britain. During the late Eighteenth and Nineteenth Centuries, Britain led the world in the study of molluscs, with much of the work being undertaken by keen amateurs who would scour their local beaches for new and interesting specimens. With such a diversity of marine environments in such a small area, it is perhaps little wonder that Britain and Ireland have produced many of the world's pioneering conchologists. This section will provide a very brief outline of British involvement with the collection and study of seashells. Many of the people named below feature extensively later on in the book.

The oldest known British conchologist is John Tradescant (1570-1628), a gardener to Charles I, who founded 'The Ark' – a museum of natural history objects based in London. Tradescant's collection included seashells from Britain and abroad, and after his death it was greatly expanded by his son John. However, the contents of the Ark were broken up in the late Seventeenth Century and little is known about the whereabouts of its seashells or other exhibits. Following the turmoil caused by the English Civil War, the medics Martin Lister (1639-1712) and James Petiver (1658-1718) started large natural history collections which they chose to catalogue in quite some detail. Lister and Petiver were working at a time when there was no consensus about how to name a species but fortunately, they made drawings of all their shell specimens which are detailed enough to allow modern conchologists to give them scientific names. Although both men collected seashells from around the world, they labelled many of specimens as having come from British locations, thus providing us with the earliest records for some species.

Such piecemeal private collecting was sporadic until the 1750s, when a commercial market developed for the buying and selling of seashells. This practice began on mainland Europe but soon spread to Britain and while the dealers were mainly focused on foreign shells gathered by colonial seafarers, there was also a market for local specimens. This trade in seashells coincided with the development of Carl Linnaeus' 1758 scheme which proposed a consistent means of naming and classifying plants and animals. Linnaeus suggested each species should have two names which, together, would allow scientists and collectors to compare and contrast their specimens (thus under Linnaeus' system a dog becomes *Canis familiaris* and a cat *Felix domesticus*). Prior to Linnaeus, these animals were known under dozens of different names. The general adoption of the Linnaean system (which still operates today) allowed naturalists and collectors to identify and compare specimens from across the world. It was a big step forward and coincided with the first scientific studies of British seashells.

A sketch of an abalone shell from Martin Lister's 1685 book *Historiae Conchyliorum*.

Two pioneers in this field were the Welshman Thomas Pennant (1726-1798) and London-based Emanuel da Costa (1717-1791). Both men produced books whose aim was to list and describe all the known British seashells (although in practice their accuracy is often wanting). Neither man was especially keen on fieldwork (indeed, da Costa spent

Carl Linnaeus, the father of modern taxonomy, dressed in native costume.

a long period of time languishing in a debtors' prison) and they relied heavily on second-hand reports when compiling their lists of species. Nonetheless, Pennant's *British Zoology* (vol.4, 1777) and da Costa's *Historia Naturalis Testaceorum Britanniae* (1778) provide the first true conchology manuals for the British Isles.

At the time of Pennant and da Costa, shell collecting was more popular in Europe than Britain but during the late Eighteenth Century, wars and revolutions saw a collapse in European commercial shell dealing and brought widespread disruption to the scientific community. The relative political stability of Britain allowed the development of intensive regional collecting by amateur gentlemen scientists such as John Adams (Pembrokeshire), William Boys (Kent) and Richard Pulteney (Dorset). No one sought to pull together these many regional studies until 1803, when the prolific naturalist George Montagu (1753-1815) published his *Testacea Britannica*. Montagu was weary of hearsay reports and claimed to have taken his seashell lists from the most reliable of sources; although some foreign shells did still feature as being British (apparently unscrupulous dealers were apt to palm off foreign shells as being British). *Testacea Britannica* was a marked improvement on Pennant and others, allowing Monatgu to set a new standard which others sought to imitate. In the coming three decades there were several similar volumes covering the scientific study of British shells, some of whose quality is questionable. Amongst the better works, perhaps the most notable came from William Turton (1762-1835) who was probably the first person to make purposeful collecting trips around much of the British coast, even using an adapted oysterman's dredge to obtain deep water specimens. His two conchology books, published in 1819 and 1822, (see Bibliography) were popular and were in part responsible for an upsurge in interest in conchology that would last throughout the Victorian era.

The period between about 1820 and 1914 is sometimes referred to as 'The Golden Age of Conchology'. During this period there was a thriving commercial market in shells which was matched by a proliferation of dozens of amateur British conchologists, many of whom would devote their every waking hour to walking the seashore or dredging the seabed from boats. It is in this period that we find such extraordinary people as Edward Forbes (1815-1854) and

A cartoon depicting the conchologist Edward Forbes using the Naturalist's Dredge, a device which he helped popularise in Britain.

Sylvanus Hanley (1819-1899) who obsessively collected from all parts of the British Isles and who, in 1852, published the multivolume *History of British Mollusca*. This work set new standards in the detail and presentation of information about British shells and would remain a standard reference work well into the Twentieth Century.

Forbes and Hanley helped encourage what was an already growing craze for shell collecting among the general public. By the 1860s, collecting had become so popular that some well known locations such as Barnstaple, Guernsey and Exmouth, were stripped clean of specimens, threatening some species with localised extinction. One conchologist who visited the island of

Victorian conchologists would typically lay their shells out in a cabinet; this selection is from the collection of Joseph Sinel (1844-1929).

Herm, reported seeing 'at least two hundred excursionists, who were busily engaged in picking up shells on the famous beach there; some of them on their hands and knees, others in various recumbent attitudes, and all provided with bags and baskets.'

The shell craze was further hyped with the publication of *British Conchology*, a five volume set of books written by the lawyer John Gwyn Jeffreys (1809-1885) and which managed to combine scientific exactitude with delicate, informative historical commentary. Published between 1862 and 1869, and beautifully illustrated by the conchological artist George Sowerby (1812-1884), *British Conchology* would not be bettered during the Victorian era and it remains a useful and readable resource to this day.

The later decades of the Nineteenth Century saw the British conchological community shift away from its aristocratic practitioners towards a more professional and academic footing. Although some prolific amateur collectors remained (most notably James Thomas Marshall (1842-1922), John Tomlin (1864-1954) and James Melville (1845-1929), the practice of randomly gathering shells gave way to intensive studies of individual species, groups of species, or habitats.

The First World War marked the end of conchology's so-called 'Golden Age'. Across Europe the prolonged warfare had left people short of money and leisure time, and so intensive middle-class hobbies such as shell collecting became unfashionable. By 1930, the commercial shell market had virtually collapsed, leading to what have been described as 'the lean years' where conchology became the provenance of universities and biological stations.

It was not until the 1960s and 1970s that popular interest in the fields of natural history and the environment was renewed, leading to a gradual recovery in amateur conchology. Commercial shell dealing also began to expand and was given a huge boost by the internet, which now plays host to a number of shell auction websites and online markets. Currently, the amateur conchology sector is expanding, with many collectors coordinating their work through institutions such as the Conchological Society of Great Britain and Ireland and the Malacological Society of London. Although it seems unlikely that British conchology will again reach the heights it attained during the Nineteenth Century, it remains alive and well in the Twenty-First Century with its practitioners being better informed about the species that they collect and, more importantly, better informed on how to make sure that their hobby does not cause adverse damage to the environment.

Collection, Preservation and Identification Techniques

THE COLLECTION and preservation of seashells does not require any specialist scientific skills and can be accomplished without undue difficulty. The most basic method, beach-combing, is one that has been employed by most people when at the seaside. It involves simply wandering along a beach gathering up any empty shells that catch the eye. In most instances, such randomly gathered shells will lie in a pocket, bag or car boot for several months before being thrown away. However, those who are bitten by the conchology bug and who wish to preserve their finds, should soak their shells in freshwater overnight to remove some of the salt and dirt and then allow them to dry naturally. I do not recommend scrubbing dirty shells or soaking them in bleach or detergents, as this may remove delicate features on the shell (e.g. the periostracum, a thin skin that covers some shells) or destroy their colour. They may afterwards be kept in plastic bags (resealable ones are useful), shoe boxes or some other convenient container.

The gathering of 'dead' shells will satisfy many, but those wishing to gather live specimens (which are generally less worn and broken than dead ones) should hunt for them by digging – if on mud or sand – or by looking under stones, in crevices, among seaweed, or under overhangs. Do not over-collect, especially the rarer species (see below for further advice). Live specimens may be killed by immersion in boiling water for a few minutes and the soft parts may then either be pulled out (in the case of bivalves) or extracted with a pin (in the case of gastropods; retain the operculum). Shells that have had the live animal in them will retain a certain fishy smell for a long while afterwards. In such cases, it is better to seal the shell inside a plastic bag or airtight container to prevent complaints from other family members!

Micro-shells (those less than about 1cm) may be obtained in a living and dead state by sieving sand or mud, or by gathering seaweed, sponges, etc., from rocks and washing them in a sieve to dislodge any shells clinging there. In either case, an ordinary kitchen sieve will suffice, but specialist test sieves, such as those manufactured by Endecotts, may be needed for the smallest of species. The sieved sediment should be washed from the sieve into a bowl, baking tray, or other wide container (you need to remove as much organic material as possible, e.g. pieces of seaweed) and then dried in the air or in an oven at a very low heat (under 60°C). Once dry, the shells can be picked from the sediment using a dampened 00 gauge paintbrush. For the smallest shells, a low-powered dissecting microscope will be needed. Such small specimens usually need to be stored inside small plastic tubes or

A gentleman scientist searches a rock pool in Jersey for specimens (circa 1906).

resealable plastic bags. Specialist cardboard slides with removable glass tops (often called microfossil slides) onto which small shells may be mounted using water soluble glue, are used by some workers. All this equipment is available to order from companies that specialise in biological equipment or microscopy supplies (e.g. www.ukge.co.uk).

Gathering shells offshore is a different matter. Shells may be taken using a mask and snorkel or SCUBA equipment, but in some areas there are restrictions on this so check before entering the water. There are also size limits on some commercial species (e.g. whelks, scallops and ormers) whether gathered onshore or offshore. An alternative to diving, especially in deeper water areas, is to employ a naturalist's dredge: this is a lightweight device (although they still weigh several kilograms) that is lowered over the stern of a boat and slowly dragged along the seabed. The dredge will gather a selection of plants and animals from the sediment surface which, when brought onto a boat, may be emptied onto a large tray and sorted. Naturalist's dredges are available from several UK suppliers of biological equipment but they are potentially dangerous and must be used with the upmost care. Dredging is banned in some ecologically sensitive or commercially active areas such as estuaries, tourist beaches, nature reserves or narrow bays. Check before you start dredging. For further information on setting up a dredge see *Methods for the Study of Marine Benthos* (Elefteriou, A. and McIntyre, A., Blackwell Press, 2005).

Gathering shells is only half the task. For your collection to have any scientific value, it must be properly catalogued. It is important that you have a record of the exact location for each shell, the date it was found, and its approximate position on the beach. This, plus other information such as scientific name, habitat, associated species, and whether the animal was alive or dead, should be placed both with the specimen and also in a separate place such as a card index, computer database or ledger. Without such data, specimens will have little scientific value. If you are collecting from one specific area, it is worth considering making provision for your collection to one day be donated to a local museum or other institution, where it may be of use to future generations. Those that have the time and energy might want to make a photographic record of their specimens (or at least the good ones).

In some areas empty shells pile up into thick deposits known as shell gravel (or shell sand); these may contain dozens of small species.

As well as recording locality information, it is a good idea to keep a photographic record of your shell specimens.

A word of warning about the seashore. Many places around the British Isles have high tidal ranges and each year there are deaths or dramatic rescues as people become trapped on rocks, cliffs or islets by the incoming sea. Before setting foot on a beach, make sure that you have a watch, know what time low tide is (check the local paper or buy a tide table) and are aware of local hazards such as headlands or islets, which may become cut off by the incoming sea. Always head out at least an hour before low water and begin making your way back to dry land a few minutes after the time of low water. **Do not be tempted to linger**. Take care when lifting stones as they may be heavy, slippery, have sharp edges, or be covered in barnacles (builders' gloves are useful for this). Many beaches will be home to hostile animals such as crabs, conger eels or sea urchins which lurk underneath stones, among seaweed or in crevices and holes. Never stick your hand into a hole or under a stone, and for narrow crevices, use forceps to collect specimens rather than fingers.

In your backpack, take a range of useful equipment such as a notebook and pen, plastic bags (I use rolls of freezer bags), a permanent marker-pen, sealable jars and test tubes, a knife, forceps, a camera (with splash-proof housing), a sieve, builders' gloves, and a fork (if on a sandy beach). Naturally, you cannot carry everything with you at one time, so tailor your equipment to the sort of environment you are visiting. Exactly what you will need becomes evident with experience. In terms of safety, bring food, water, a mobile phone (in a waterproof bag), map (if necessary) and spare clothing (some of this may be left in a car). Dress appropriately for the season (including footwear), especially in the spring and autumn when the air temperature may be significantly warmer than that of the sea. Remember that exposed parts of the body such as hands and face, will become cold quickly, especially if wet.

Identifying shells is not as easy as it may at first appear. This book is not designed to be an expert guide and provides only a limited amount of identification information. This will suffice for most of the larger and more obvious species, but there are certain groups of seashell which regularly provide problems – most notably, the Rissoidea (Chapter 3), Pyramid Shells (Chapter 5), Nut Shells (Chapter 8) and various minute species.

If this book is not sufficiently detailed to get you an identification, then try a more specialist guide, such as *The Marine Fauna of the British Isles and North-West Europe* (Hayward, *et al.*, Oxford University Press, 1990). However, those who need very detailed descriptions and illustrations, should consider the following textbooks: For gastropods, use *Molluscs: Prosobranch and Pyramidellid Gastropods* (Graham, A., *The Linnean Society of London*, 1988) and for bivalves, use *British Bivalve Seashells* (Tebble, N., British Museum (Natural History), 1966). These books are out of print and are expensive to buy second-hand, but they should be obtainable using the inter-library loan service at your local library. Additional illustrations and photographs of individual species are commonly available by searching the internet.

As a general rule, when faced with an unidentified gastropod, take note of its general shape, size and colour, as these should allow you to deduce the broad group of shells to which it belongs. Then look at the ornamentation (e.g. ribs, striations, etc.), the shape of the aperture, apex, umbilicus, and any other features, such as siphonal canal, teeth, number of striations, etc. This should get you a firm identification, or perhaps narrow the possibility to a handful of species. A hand lens or binocular microscope may be needed to discern fine detail, and in some cases (e.g. *Littorina*), identification can only be achieved by dissecting the animal's body. Also check the known habitat and geographical range of various candidate species, as this can often narrow down identification choices – for example, if a species is only known from a handful of abyssal records all in the north of Scotland, then you are unlikely to have found it on the south coast of England.

Much of this advice applies to bivalves, but as well as general shape, ornamentation and colour, I suggest looking closely at the hinge area and the shape of the adductor muscle scar, as these will often narrow down your choice considerably. As with the gastropods, some species will need a microscope or a hand lens. If you are still stuck, then obtain one of the specialist guides listed above or track down an experienced or professional conchologist through your local museum or by joining a conchological society (see Appendix 2). It is best not to send specimens to museums or individuals without contacting them first, as some institutions will charge for their time.

Finally, it goes without saying that it is the shell collector's responsibility to treat our marine realm with the respect it deserves. The British seashore is a fragile environment that has suffered much abuse in recent decades. All beaches and animals are sensitive to pollution and disturbance, so keep your collecting to a minimum (especially live specimens) and leave everything exactly as you find it. This is especially true of rocks and stones which, when turned over, should always be returned to their original position. Never over-collect and consider photographing rare species rather than taking them home. All your equipment and rubbish should be taken back with you: your footprints should be the only thing left on the beach.

About this Book

THIS BOOK has been written by an amateur conchologist with the aim of informing, entertaining and perhaps enthusing, those with an interest in the British seashore. This is not a work that has any scientific pretensions, and so I have avoided using many of the rigid structures and layouts that are associated with more formal seashore guides and academic publications.

The bulk of this book consists of entries for individual seashell species. For each, I have pulled together a range of remarks, anecdotes and observations from various historical publications, as well as from more recent scientific studies. In doing so, my aim is to offer a glimpse into the historical and cultural world of our seashells, many of which brought great delight to the amateur and professional conchologists of yesteryear, but whose magic and sociological significance has been lost in more modern times.

Each species presented has two scientific names (the genus and the species; e.g. *Haliotis tuberculata*) written in italics, which is usually derived from Latin or Greek or a mixture of the two. I have attempted to find the etymology of each species' scientific name, but in a number of cases this was not possible. This is for various reasons, not least my appalling knowledge of classical languages, but also because in some cases the words are nonsensical or the etymology simply isn't known. As one modern conchologist put it 'the meaning is known only to the discoverer'.

Following the scientific name is the surname of the author who first described the shell (e.g. *Haliotis tuberculata* Linnaeus). If the genus has been altered since the time of its first discovery, then the author's surname will appear in brackets. I have attempted to track down some background information about these authors, the way in which they operated and the manner in which they discovered the species concerned. Most authors described only a few species, but some people, such as Carl Linnaeus and George Montagu, were responsible for identifying dozens. Rather than repeating the same information about these prolific authors several times in different places, I have mentioned them once or twice. If you are curious about a specific author then use the index to track down their main entries. Many shells have a common or vernacular name (e.g. pheasant shell). This is also provided with any regional or historical names being given in the main body of text.

As well as providing a discursive natural history, I have given each shell some brief notes pertaining to its distribution and habitat. In general terms the distribution of species around Britain falls into several broad categories: the **western coasts**, which includes north-west Scotland, Wales, north Devon and much of Ireland (the waters in these areas are exposed to the warm Gulf Stream and are rich in marine life); the **south-western coasts** which generally means Cornwall, south Devon, the Scilly Isles and Channel Islands, which are also exposed to the Gulf Stream but which have some additional southern European species; the **southern coasts**, which essentially means the English Channel from Dorset to Kent, which may be subject to cold winter waters and has a more restricted marine life (especially in the eastern Channel). This is also true of the **eastern coast** which may be defined as the North Sea which is similarly cold. Finally, the **northern coasts** of Scotland, including the Shetland and Orkney islands, which have influence both from the Gulf Stream but which also receive some sub-Arctic species. For more detailed information, see Chapter 18.

Basic identification notes are given which, together with the illustrations, should allow the reader to identify any shells they have or at least narrow down the range of options. In some cases, such as the very small species, more specialist guides will be necessary to secure identification (see previous section). A glossary of scientific and anatomical terms is given in Appendix One.

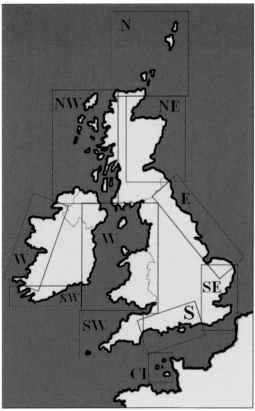

The coastal provinces of the British Isles, as approximately defined by their molluscan species. (see also Chapter 18)

True to my obsession with Victorian conchology, most of the colour illustrations reproduced here are by the historical artist George Sowerby the younger, whose beautiful images have graced such magnificent volumes as Jeffreys' *British Conchology* (van Voorst, 1862-1869), Forbes and Hanley's *A History of the British Mollusca* (van Voorst, 1853) and Sowerby's own *Illustrated Index of British Shells* (Simpkin, Marshall and Co., 1859 & 1887). These illustrations have withstood the test of time and remain accurate representations of the species they portray. However, in the case of some of the minute shells (such as the Rissoidea and Pyramid Shells), Sowerby's images may lack a certain amount of fine detail compared to the images obtainable from modern high-powered microscopes. Even today, the identification of microshells is quite a specialised process which often necessitates the use of specialist guides. This issue is discussed in the chapters concerned and in the previous section.

Just three classes of mollusc are covered by this book: Gastropoda (sea snails), Scaphopoda (tusk shells) and Pelecypoda (bivalves). These contain almost all the species of hard-shelled mollusc to be found around the British coastline. The list of species presented hereafter broadly follows the systematic order used in *The Species Directory of the Marine Fauna and Flora of the British Isles* (Marine Conservation Society, 1999) with the individual chapters roughly (but not exclusively) corresponding to the various orders of shelled mollusc (see Chapter 18). Those who require more detail about the taxonomy of British molluscs should consult the aforementioned *Species Directory* or *The Marine Fauna of the British Isles and North-West Europe* (Hayward P.J. and Ryland J.S., Clarendon Press, 1990, vol.2).

It should be noted that whereas most historical naturalists used physical characteristics to help define the evolutionary relationship between individual species or groups of species, many modern taxonomists have instead turned to the more precise science of genetics. In doing so, it has been discovered that many species which have been placed in the same family or order because they look similar to one another, are actually only genetically distantly related (i.e. they are from separate evolutionary lines; in scientific terms they are polyphyletic). In years to come, there will doubtless be extensive revisions to large areas of the molluscan family tree, but for the time being most schemes, including the one used here, remain based on physical characteristics.

I should finish by saying that finding something of interest to say about 402 individual species has been no easy task, especially as some shells have been better appreciated through the years than others. Nonetheless, there is a mass of information presented here which I trust is neither too rambling nor too eccentric in its tone. My hope is that I have created a book which may act as a companion to the many utilitarian British seashore guides currently in existence.

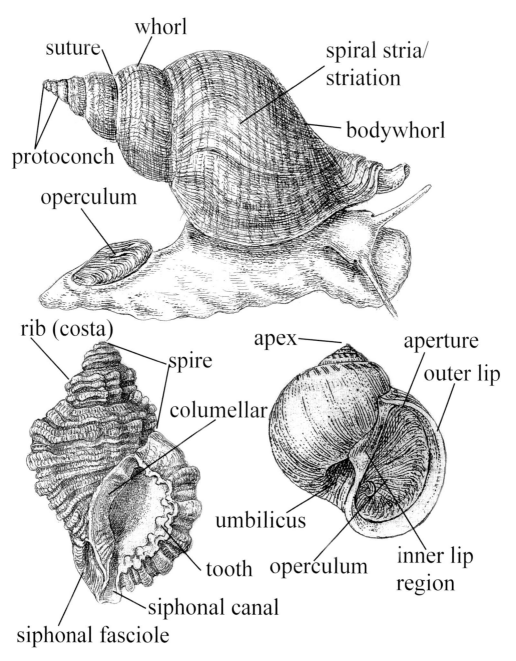

The different parts of a gastropod shell. For further information see the glossary in Appendix One.

Part One:

Gastropods and Scaphopoda

GASTROPODS (meaning 'stomach foot') are a very broad class of mollusc (meaning 'thin-shelled') that contains some 70,000 known living species worldwide. The most familiar gastropods will be the snails and slugs that slide about our gardens and hedgerows. These display the main physical characteristics possessed by all gastropods – an asymmetrical body, a distinct head with tentacles and a powerful, muscular foot. Gastropods are probably the most diverse group of molluscs and may be found on land as well as in fresh and marine water environments. Although we think of snails as having a shell, many gastropods are 'naked' (i.e. have no shell) or have a fragile internal shell. This includes the slugs, sea slugs and various specialist orders of gastropod such as the planktonic sea butterflies (Thecosomata) and sea angels (Gymnosomata).

In this section we are interested in the so-called 'sea snails' – those shallow marine or brackish water gastropods from the Subclass Prosobranchia (meaning 'gills in front', a reference to their internal biology) that possess a hard shell. This includes primitive animals such as the limpets and ormers, as well as familiar edible ones like the periwinkles and whelks. Britain is home to approximately 300 known species of shelled marine gastropod, of which 210 are covered here (very rare, subfossil and deep water forms have been excluded). For further detailed information on the shelled gastropod species of Britain, see *Molluscs: Prosobranch and Pyramidellid Gastropods* (Graham, A., Linnean Society of London, 1988).

Chapter One

Archaeogastropods

THE ORDER ARCHAEOGASTROPODA (meaning 'ancient gastropods') includes many familiar seashore species such as the ormers and top shells. They are the most biologically primitive of the gastropods, and typically possess a double-chambered heart and two gills.

Ormers and Slit Limpets

In evolutionary terms, the most primitive British seashells to be featured in this book are the ormers and slit-limpets (Superfamilies Haliotidacea; Pleurotomariacea; Fissurellacea) which do not have an enclosed shell, but instead use a broad muscular foot to adhere to rock surfaces. Ormers were known to the ancient Greeks and they have been prized for their iridescent mother-of-pearl interior as well for their edible qualities. 'It requires a good deal of beating and stewing to make it tender,' wrote one person. The slit limpets are much smaller than the ormers and inedible, and so were only noticed in comparatively recent times.

1 – *Haliotis tuberculata* **Linnaeus; Ormer, Abalone, Ear Shell**

With its distinctive flattened shape and mother-of-pearl interior, the ormer is an iconic shell that was, and remains, widely traded by commercial dealers, although it has also had industrial use in the fashion and papier-mâché industries. It is a large, unmistakable shell, and was among the animals that feature in Carl Linnaeus' original 1758 *Systema Naturae*, a book that laid down the foundations for the future scientific naming and classifying of all animals and plants.

There are historical reports of ormer shells being washed up in Devon, Sussex and Suffolk, but within modern Britain this animal is found on the Channel Islands, where it is quite common. The name 'ormer' is short for *oreille de mer* ('ear of the sea') and it has been known to English residents since at least the 1630s, when the French architect Isaac de Caus imported sacks-full of their shells from Guernsey for use in an artificial grotto at Skipton Castle, Yorkshire. To Channel Islanders, the ormer is a prized delicacy. Only the large, muscular foot is cooked and eaten, but the preparation technique is prohibitive. The foot must be tenderised at length using a mallet and then stewed in a creamy sauce for several hours. Failure to do this results in the animal being tough and inedible. The living animal hides under stones or in narrow crevices, and is only found on very low spring tides. Islanders hunt them using a short, flattened piece of iron with a hook on one end known as an ormer hook. This can prise the ormer's foot from the rock surface and then tease it from even the tightest crevice.

The Jersey and Guernsey governments have legal restrictions as to when and where the animals may be fished. These were once widely flouted, but have recently been tightened and are backed by the threat of severe fines and even a jail sentence. In the 1990s the ormer population became infected with a virus and suffered a collapse in numbers, a situation which led to a complete ban on the practice of 'ormering'. The population is currently thought to be recovering. Many historical accounts of the Channel Islands mention the ormer and it was the prospect of finding specimens that drew (and continues to draw) many conchologists and shell collectors to the islands. These days, the ormer is more rarely seen between the tide marks but it remains common offshore and empty shells may be found washed up on the beach, although they are often heavily worn.

Description: H = 10cm; W = 7cm. Large, solid, flattened, ear-shaped; mother-of-pearl interior; six to eight open holes down the outside edge; colour = reddish-brown; it is often encrusted with barnacles, bryozoans and red seaweed. Etymology: *Haliotis* = sea ear; *tuberculata* = tuberculated.

2 – *Anatoma crispata* (Fleming)

A minute, fragile shell that was first discovered in 1809 on Ross Island, Shetland, by the Reverend John Fleming (1785-1857) a renowned geologist and clergyman. Although an accomplished naturalist, Fleming was not a conchologist and only found his specimens of *Anatoma crispata* by chance when walking along a beach following a violent storm. However, neither he nor several other esteemed conchologists, recognised it as a new species until 1828, it having been generally thought of as a juvenile top shell. At just a few millimetres long, a microscope is needed to appreciate the beautiful ornamentation of this shell. It lives offshore around Scotland, usually in water greater than ten metres in depth, and is rarely recorded but, as the Reverend Fleming demonstrated, empty shells are occasionally to be found on shore and are probably best searched for by sieving sediment.

Description: H = 0.2cm. Globular, white shell with four whorls; characterised by a broad grove around the periphery which ends in a distinctive slit at the aperture. Etymology: *Anatoma* = possibly meaning dissected; *crispata* = curled.

3 – *Diodora graeca* (Linnaeus); Keyhole Limpet

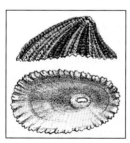

This beautiful and distinctive animal was, like the ormer, first described by Carl Linnaeus in 1758. In the Eighteenth Century it went by the name of 'thimble limpet' but is now better known as the 'keyhole limpet', because of the small keyhole-shape at the shell's apex. In life, the keyhole limpet possesses an ample and colourful mantle that laps up the outside of its shell. This is the largest and most robust of the keyhole and slit (fissurellid) limpets and is found across most of Britain with the exception of the North Sea. It may be found alive on the lower shore under stones and among rocks and boulders but adult specimens are frequently encrusted with sponges and may be hard to spot. Empty shells are not uncommon and may be found washed higher up the beach. The keyhole limpet has vivid green eggs, a characteristic that is caused by a particular type of protein related to the animal's red blood cells.

Description: H = 1.8cm; W = 3.1cm. Solid, low, conical; oval in outline; 20-30 prominent ribs crossed by numerous concentric growth lines; shell apex has a small hourglass-shaped opening; colour = white. Etymology: *Diodora* = a passageway; *graeca* = Greek.

4 – *Emarginula fissura* (Linnaeus); Slit Limpet

Although scientifically described by Carl Linnaeus in 1758, this distinctive shell was first mentioned in the Seventeenth Century when it was described by the antiquarian naturalist James Petiver as being the 'crack'd Barnstaple limpet'. This was not a very convenient name, but it was only in the early Nineteenth Century that the various *Emarginula* species received their more logical vernacular name of slit limpets. *E. fissura* is relatively common on all British coasts, but is small and is fond of living under particularly large stones on the lower shore. They are tricky to spot among seaweed and encrusting organisms. Empty shells, with their characteristic conical witch's hat shape, are generally easier to find and may sometimes be sieved from sediment.

Description: H = 0.8cm; W = 1.1cm. Fragile, conical; strongly reticulated with 20-35 vertical ribs and 20-30 horizontal ones; apex located ¾ along shell length; slit short but leading to longer, shallower channel; colour = white or off-white. Etymology: *Emarginula* = notched; *fissura* = a cleft.

5 – *Emarginula crassa* (Sowerby)

This is the largest of the British slit limpets which was first discovered in fossilised form by the talented naturalist and artist James Sowerby (1757-1822). He was the first of the Sowerby family to take an interest in the natural world, but many of his descendants showed a similar aptitude with at least 13 becoming naturalists during the Nineteenth and Twentieth Century. *Emarginula crassa* was for many years known only from fossil specimens and so was assumed to have gone extinct during the last Ice Age. Then, during the 1840s, several specimens were dredged in deep water off western Scotland. Its rarity and curiosity value as a 'living fossil' caused the shell to become a desirable commodity for collectors and commercial dealers. However, its habit of living on so-called 'foul ground' (i.e. a stony seabed over which a dredge cannot pass) meant that very few specimens could be found. 'This noble shell is never likely to become common in collections until some plan is devised for dredging in rocky ground' complained one Victorian naturalist. It remains a rarely-encountered shell and is known only from deep water along the northern and western coasts. It has not been found on the sea shore, dead or alive.

Description: H = 1.5cm; W = 3cm. Resembles *Emarginula fissura* but may be easily distinguished by its surface which is very finely striated; also the cone is more compact and the base slightly broader. Etymology: *crassa* = solid.

6 – *Emarginula rosea* Bell; Pink Slit Limpet

Only a minority of pink slit limpets have the red colouring around the aperture which gives this species its scientific and vernacular name. Such inconsistency when naming species was a source of irritation to some Victorian conchologists including John Gwyn Jeffreys, who haughtily complained that *conica* ('cone-shaped'), would have been a better choice. The first specimen of *Emarginula rosea* was discovered in Poole, Dorset, in 1824 by Professor Charles Bell (1774-1842), a man who is more famous for his work on human anatomy and especially the nervous system, but who, like most medics, took a personal interest in natural history. Relative to most other British shells, the pink slit limpet was a late discovery, something which is a reflection both of its scarcity and its restriction to the south-western coasts of England. In fact, the pink slit limpet is a typically Mediterranean species whose range just touches the extreme tip of Devon, Cornwall and the Channel Islands, where it may be found on the lower shore and in shallow water. As a matter of note, some years hence, a specimen was recovered from the stomach of a flamingo that had been accidentally killed near Nice in the south of France.

Description: H = 0.4cm; W = 0.6cm. Small, fragile, conical; apex highly curved and overhangs front margin; surface finely reticulated; colour = dirty white sometimes with red/pink area around the aperture. Etymology: *rosea* = rosy.

7 – *Puncturella noachina* (Linnaeus); Noah's Limpet

Noah's limpet gains its name from first having been collected as a fossil from Ice Age rocks in Sweden during the 1750s, and then named by the father of modern taxonomy, Carl Linnaeus. At this time, it was widely-believed that the jumbled pebbles and clays that make up many of Europe's glacial rocks were direct evidence of the occurrence of Noah's Biblical flood. It was assumed that *Puncturella noachina* had been a victim of this flood (an unusual notion given that it is aquatic) and it was thought to be extinct until the early Nineteenth Century when several living specimens were dredged from a considerable depth off the north of Scotland. Subsequent discoveries were then made from around the Scottish and northern English coastline. However, the animal has only rarely been encountered in the waters around Scotland and is normally found at depths of 30 metres or more. Like *Emarginula crassa*, it prefers a stony seabed which stops it being gathered using dredges and thus takes it out of the reach of most naturalists. Although reasonably common as a fossil, it is unlikely to be found by the average beachcomber, alive or dead.

Description: H = 0.5cm; W = 0.8cm. Small, conical; apex centrally placed and less recurved than in species of *Emarginula*; distinguished by a narrow opening which occurs behind the apex; surface is finely striated with prominent growth stages near base; colour = white. Etymology: *Puncturella* = small hole; *noachina* = after Noah.

Top Shells

The top shells (Superfamily Trochacea = 'top shell') gained their common name from the Sixteenth Century French naturalist William Rondelet who was struck by their resemblance to a child's spinning top. However, in giving them the Greek name *trochus*, Rondelet apparently picked the wrong toy (a *trochus* is a child's hoop). The error was later corrected by affording many species the name *turbo* meaning 'a top'. The top shells are a diverse and common family of shells which consists of around 500 species worldwide. The larger species are conspicuous and common on the seashore, and also relatively easily to identify. Some, such as the painted top shell (*Calliostoma zizyphinum*) possess a colourful beauty and precise symmetry that may be favourably compared with many tropical species.

8 – *Tricolia pullus* (Linnaeus); Pheasant Shell

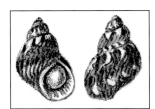

A small, but attractive shell that has brought forth praise from many conchologists for its vivid pattern of red-brown zig-zag streaks and blotches which give it some resemblance to a pheasant's feathers. It was named by Carl Linnaeus in 1758 and is notable for its gait when moving across rocks which, according to one authority, 'is like the ankle of a horse. The foot being divided in the middle, each half advances in turn; the stationary half serving as a point *d'appui*'. Although restricted to western and southern coasts, the pheasant shell is common on the lower shore where it may be looked for among red seaweeds. Its empty shell may be carried some distance by currents and becomes easily worn, removing its beautiful patterning.

Description: H = 0.9cm; W = 0.45cm. Small, solid, tall; shell is highly decorated; five–six whorls, the last two being somewhat rounded; deep sutures; white operculum; colour = white with a variable pattern of brown swirls and stripes. Etymology: *Tricolia* = three-coloured; *pullus* = dark.

9 – *Margarites helicinus* (Phipps); Pearly Top Shell

Discovered and named by the aristocratic naval officer Constantine John Phipps (1744-1792) who found it on the remote islands of Spitsbergen while making a failed attempt to sail to the North Pole. 'It is active and bold,' commented John Jeffreys, who had observed specimens crawling out of a dish of water into which he had placed them. *Margarites helicinus* prefers the cold waters of the Arctic, where it may be abundant on the sea shore, but has also been discovered offshore living hundreds of metres below the surface. In Britain, it is restricted to the northern half of the country and is uncommon south of the northern North Sea and Irish Sea. It lives among stones and seaweed on the lower shore, often gregariously, but is very small and so a sharp eye is needed. Two related Arctic species have very rarely been found in the far north of Scotland: *M. olivaceus* and *M. striatus*.

Description: H = 0.5cm; W = 0.6cm. Small, fragile; four–five rounded whorls, last of which occupies about half the total height; surface has very fine spiral striations which are more prominent of last whorl; large umbilicus; aperture oval; colour = white with green tinge. Etymology: *Margarites* = a pearl; *helicinus* = helix-like.

10 – *Calliostoma granulatum* (Born)

First described in 1778 by the Austrian naturalist Ignatius Edler von Born (1742-1791) this handsome and distinctive shell lives offshore and is most commonly encountered by trawler men in search of scallops. Specimens may occasionally be found washed up on to the shore but are likely to be worn and empty. *Calliostoma granulatum* is sometimes viewed as being the poor cousin to the painted top shell (*C. zizyphinum*) which is smaller but much more colourful. But it is considerably rarer and thus, although dull, was worth more in monetary terms to Victorian collectors than its painted cousin. There are reports of an albino version of this shell.

Description: H = 3.8cm; W = 3.8cm. Large, solid, conical; pointed apex; 10 flat-sided whorls; surface has many fine concentric striae which run the full length of the shell; colour = yellowish-white with red-brown markings. Etymology: *Calliostoma* = beautiful mouth; *granulatum* = granulated.

11 – *Calliostoma zizyphinum* (Linnaeus); Painted Top Shell

The painted top shell is one of the delights of the seashore, although its preference for muddy overhangs and narrow gulleys makes obtaining specimens a mucky business. It is was named in 1758 by Carl Linnaeus after the jujube tree (*Zizyphus*) but the correct spelling of its name gave Victorian conchologists a headache and led to many variations including *zezyphinus* and *sisyphinus* before *zizyphinum* was settled upon. Recent studies of this animal reveal that twice a day, the animal wipes the exterior of the shell clean using its mantle. This apparently compulsive behaviour was puzzling until it was discovered that by doing so, the animal is able to supplement its diet by eating all the detritus that had settled on the shell's surface. When prevented from cleaning itself, shell growth decreased by a third. It is found all around Britain on the lowest part of rocky shores among stones or in sheltered areas. One other related species, *C. occidentale*, is known from northern Britain, but it is rare and lives in deep water.

Description: H = 2.5cm; W = 2.5cm. Large, colourful, solid, conical; 10-12 flat-sided whorls; colour = light background with red-brown, purple and white streaks. Etymology: *zizyphinum* = after the jujube tree.

12 – *Gibbula cineraria* (Linnaeus); Grey Top Shell

For uncertain reasons, this average-looking shell was called the 'doh periwinkle' in historical times. It is abundant on most rocky shores around the British Isles and, while hardly the most colourful of seashells, it is a hardy animal which can survive on quite exposed coasts, and whose shell shape has been observed to become lower and broader in areas that are subject to powerful waves and tides. *Gibbula cineraria* may be found tucked in crevices, amongst stones or under seaweed, and is a favourite food of many species of fish. Empty shells may be exceptionally common in some areas where strong currents may sort and collect them into small mounds.

Description: H = 1.25cm; W = 1.3cm. Conical, solid; six–seven slightly swollen whorls; surface with irregular spiral striae; small umbilicus; colour = pale grey with oblique lines of purple. Etymology: *Gibbula* = small humped; *cineraria* = ashen.

13 – *Gibbula magus* (Linnaeus); Turban Top Shell

The turban top shell is common, large and distinctive, so much so that many conchologists cannot pass an empty specimen on the beach without picking it up, even though they may have dozens already. Like many of our larger shells, its scientific name was provided in 1758 by Carl Linnaeus, the father of taxonomy. Why he should have chosen to call it after a magician or wise man (*magus*) is not known, but it is speculated that the turreted outline may resemble the hats said to have been worn by the Persian magi as exemplified by the three wise men of the Christmas story. Although a denizen of the lower shore, where it can be found among rocks, empty shells may be washed higher onto the beach and are often covered in a thin layer of encrusting plants and animals. This makes finding a clean specimen all the more pleasing; a sentiment that has also been expressed by the Victorian naturalist Edward Forbes: 'The beauty of the hues of this shell is exceeded by the painting of the animal which rejoices in a skin of the most vivid colouring.' An albino form is also alleged to exist.

Description: H = 2.1cm; W = 2.8cm. Large, solid, stepped profile; eight whorls, slightly rounded, flattened below the suture; prominent umbilicus, striae and keel; numerous concentric striae and undulating surface below sutures; colour = white, grey or yellow. Etymology: *magus* = a magician.

14 – *Gibbula umbilicalis* (da Costa); Flat Top Shell

Once known as the 'purple-tipped top shell', the naming of *Gibbula umbilicalis* is sometimes attributed to George Montagu, although the honour actually goes to the eccentric English conchologist Emanuel da Costa (1717-1791) who first described it in 1778. This is a common, but relatively unremarkable species, which shares the same broad habitat as the grey top shell (*Gibbula cineraria*). It is has been restricted to the western coasts of Britain but in recent years, reports have occurred from the north and north-east, which suggests that its range is expanding, possibly in response to a warming of the sea which has occurred since about 1900. Its species name reflects the deep umbilicus (hole) on the underside of the shell. Live and empty shells may occur abundantly on sheltered rocky shores.

Description: H = 1.3cm; W = 1.8cm. Resembles *Gibbula cineraria* but is flattened with a rounded apex, rounded whorls, fine striations and a large umbilicus; colour = cream with broad red-purple steaks. Etymology: *umbilicalis* = with umbilicus.

15 – *Gibbula pennanti* (Philippi); Pennant's Top Shell

This species was originally discovered by Rudolph Amandus Philippi (1808-1904) who, in the 1830s, became ill and travelled to the Mediterranean Sea in expectation of dying there. Fortunately, he survived and afterwards went on to produce a series of illustrated zoological monographs on European natural history before emigrating to Chile. For many years *Gibbula pennanti*, which Philippi named after the British naturalist Thomas Pennant (1726-1798), was believed to be a colourful variety of *Gibbula umbilicus*, which it closely resembles in shape. However, during the last century, the distinctive patterning on the shell has afforded it the right to be a species within its own right. Its occurrence within the British Isles is restricted to the Channel Islands where it may be found on most rocky shores (one specimen is known from the Scilly Isles). In 1978, its presence in the Channel Islands was threatened by the Amoco Cadiz tanker disaster which saw 227,000 tonnes of crude oil spill into the ocean off Brittany. Fortunately, favourable tides and winds spared the coast from the worst effects of the pollution. This species is noted for its ability to survive in the open air and away from the sea for prolonged periods of time.

Description: H = 1.4cm; W = 1.5cm. Broadly resembles *Gibbula umbilicalis* but may be distinguished by its lighter colouring, purple banding and a more angular side profile caused by deeper sutures; colour = cream or green with purple, green or black banding. Etymology: *pennanti* = after Thomas Pennant.

16 – *Gibbula tumida* (Montagu)

First named by the astounding British naturalist George Montagu (1753-1815) in 1803 from a specimen he was sent from Dorset – probably by Robert Bryer, a correspondent of his from Weymouth. It is another widespread and common species of top shell that is known from all coasts, but one that is rarely seen onshore alive, preferring to live offshore on gravel or sand. Empty shells may be encountered on the beach, but these are rare and often greatly worn. It used to be said that specimens from the northern half of Britain were larger than those from the south, but more recent studies make no mention of this.

Description: H = 0.8cm; W = 0.8cm. Shell turreted; whorls = six–seven with numerous fine striae; colour = white/yellow background and red-brown spotting. Etymology: *tumida* = swollen.

17 – *Jujubinus exasperatus* (Pennant); Rough Top Shell

First known through the English naturalist Martin Lister's (1638-1712) Seventeenth Century catalogue of shells, where it is marked with an 'A' to denote that it is English in origin. The rough top shell was given its scientific name in 1777 by Thomas Pennant who admitted to never having seen a specimen (he used Lister's drawing for his description). The rough shell is another of those typically southern European species, whose range just touches the southern and western extremes of the British Isles. Small and easily overlooked, it lives on rocks and stones offshore, although its small size and robust nature means that empty (but often battered) specimens may be discovered on the beach. It has been noted that this animal will readily colonise new environments such as shipwrecks and artificial reefs.

Description: H = 0.8cm; W = 0.4cm. Shell solid, tall, conical and pointed; six–eight whorls with four–five ridges on each; base flattened with six–seven ridges; colour = red or pink. Etymology: *Jujubinus* = like the jujube tree; *exasperatus* = roughened.

18 – *Jujubinus miliaris* **(Brocchi)**

First described from the Mediterranean Sea by the Italian geologist Giovanni Battista Brocchi (1772-1826), this species was something of a rarity to the British conchologists who at first suspected that it was restricted to the west coast of Scotland and the Hebrides. During the early 1850s, the Liverpudlian gentlemen conchologist Robert MacAndrew (1802-1873) devoted a great deal of time to finding specimens of this animal across Britain. Thanks to him, its geographical range has been extended to most British coastal areas bar the North Sea and the eastern English Channel where it appears to be absent. It lives on the lower shore on and among rocks.

Description: H = 1cm; W = 0.9cm. Broad, conical and pointed; seven–eight whorls, flattened with six–seven coarse ridges on each; base has a keel; colour = white background with red/brown/purple patterning. Etymology: *miliaris* = millet.

19 – *Jujubinus montagui* **(Wood)**

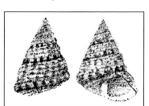

Named in honour of the naturalist George Montagu by William Wood (1774-1857), an English bookseller who developed a passion for conchology in the 1820s and who went on to publish a number of volumes on the subject. *Jujubinus montagui* is a rather dull-looking shell that lives offshore on rocky ground, but its distribution is very patchy. In some areas it is non-existent, while in others it is very common, but the populations would appear to vary through time. For example, the British conchologist John Tomlin once commented that when trawling for shell specimens off the island of Herm in the early 1900s, 'one used to get tired of picking *Jujubinus montagui* out of the dredgings'. However, two decades further on and he was to remark that not a single specimen was to be had from the exact same location. Why there should have been a collapse in the population is unknown, although Tomlin blamed commercial dredging for scallops. John Jeffreys kept live specimens in an aquarium and came to believe that they might tolerate brackish water. He experimented by placing individuals in bowls of fresh water, but dryly observed that the animal would survive for only three minutes in such circumstances. *J. montagui* is an offshore species found in the south and west and which lives on stones but whose empty shells may sometimes find their way onto the lower shore.

Description: H = 0.6cm; W = 0.75cm. Conical, tall with stepped profile; seven whorls, slightly swollen with six–seven ridges between which lie imbricated striae; colour = off-white background with brown patches on the ridges. Etymology: *montagui* = after George Montagu.

20 – *Jujubinus striatus* (Linnaeus); Grooved Top Shell

A distinctive, conical shell that was named by Carl Linnaeus in 1758. For a long while, *Jujubinus striatus* was known only from the Mediterranean Sea and was only recognised as a British species during the early Nineteenth Century, when specimens were discovered in Devon and Cornwall. It is found in western and southern regions and may be locally very common with its distribution often being linked to the occurrence of the marine plant eelgrass (*Zostera*) on which it prefers to live. The British population of *J. striatus* was badly hit in the 1930s by a fungal disease which killed large areas of eelgrass. Once prosperous populations of grooved top shell disappeared in some areas such as Salcombe, Devon, as vast acres of eelgrass were destroyed by disease. Their populations were slow to recover but are currently thought to be stable.

Description: H = 0.75cm; W = 0.8cm. Resembles *Jujubinus exasperatus* but taller with a blunt apex; seven whorls, flat-sided with eight–nine ridges on last three; base has seven–nine ridges; colour = cream with brown streaks and spotting. Etymology: *striatus* = striated.

21 – *Osilinus lineatus* (da Costa); Toothed Top Shell, Grey Winkle

A robust, hardy and plainly-patterned shell that was first noticed by the English conchologist Emanuel da Costa in 1778. It is reasonably common along our southern and western shores but, like many of our most obvious species, has been little commented on. An exception is the Somerset naturalist William Clark (1788-1869) who was a passionate observer of living molluscs. He noticed that all the specimens he obtained from Falmouth, Devon, had a distorted operculum, whereas animals from other areas did not. He accounted for this by supposing that the top shells at Falmouth were being regularly attacked by fish ripping away the operculum but unable to get at the animal itself. It was a nice theory, but more recent studies suggest that distorted opercula are the product of disease rather than aggressive fish. *Osilinus lineatus* is Britain's largest Top Shell whose surface is sometimes encrusted with barnacles. It may be found on many rocky shores and is generally common. There are records of it being sold in fish markets alongside (or instead of) the more traditional edible winkle (*Littorina littorea*).

Description: H = 2.5cm; W = 2.4cm. Large, solid and rough-looking; five–six whorls, swollen; inner lip thick and broad; colour = grey background with zig-zag pattern of red and purple. Etymology: *Osilinus* = possibly means lined mouth; *lineatus* = lined/streaked.

22 – *Dikoleps cutleriana* (Clark)

Named after Catherine Cutler (c1787-1866) who was apparently 'a lady of scientific taste and acquirements'. Miss Cutler was not a conchologist but instead, studied seaweeds in Devonshire, often working together with her friend Anne Cook Gulson (see *Aclis gulsonae*). The Bath-based conchologist William Clark frequently collected along the same coasts as Cutler and Gulson and came to mentor them both. Clark flattered Cutler with the naming of *Dikoleps cutleriana* in 1849, but was soon after forced defend its honour when John Jeffreys suggested that the correct name should be *Trochus exilis*. Clark was horrified at the prospect of Miss Cutler losing her species and wrote an open letter to Jeffreys, stating that he was 'bound to maintain her undoubted title to the appellation'. It was just one of many spats that occurred between Jeffreys and Clark which, on this occasion, resulted in victory for Clark and Cutler. This is a rare and somewhat swollen shell that may be found offshore in south-western England and Wales. It is usually only obtained using a dredge or SCUBA equipment.

Description: H = 1cm; W = 1cm. Small, globular, thin, transparent and glossy; surface with numerous fine spiral striae; three whorls with deep sutures; narrow umbilicus; colour = clear white. Etymology: *Dikoleps* = twice bent; *cutleriana* = after Catherine Cutler.

23 – *Dikoleps pusilla* (Jeffreys)

Another rare shell whose geographical range just touches the western fringe of Britain. This shell is so small and fragile that for a while it was believed to be a juvenile stage from another species of top shell. It was only after identical specimens turned up in several places, that the irrepressible lawyer-turned-conchologist John Gwyn Jeffreys (1809-1885) recognised it as being the adult shell of a hitherto unknown species. Jeffreys named it in 1847 and made much of its rarity. This quickly led to specimens being eagerly sought by Victorian conchologists who regarded any uncommon species as a prized possession. *Dikoleps pusilla* may be found on the lower shore in southern and western regions, but identification must be made using a microscope.

Description: H = 0.8cm; W = 0.75cm. Shell not so thin or globular as *Dikoleps cutleriana* but is more glossy, very smooth and almost iridescent; colour = whitish-yellow. Etymology: *pusilla* = very minute.

24 – *Skenea serpuloides* (Montagu)

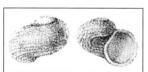

First named by George Montagu in 1808 after the talented Edinburgh natural history artist James Skene (1775-1864) who was a notable friend of Sir Walter Scott. *Skenea serpuloides* is one of Britain's smallest seashells and it will only be encountered by those conchologists that routinely scan seashore samples using a microscope. The Bath naturalist William Clark was fascinated by this and other closely-related species which he would dredge alive, from offshore sediments. He wrote of *S. serpuloides* that: 'it is active, marches with quickness, not at all shy and gave me good opportunities of observing its peculiarities'. The shell occurs all around Britain, but is more common in the south. It is sometimes found on the lowest part of the seashore among seaweed, but is more abundant offshore. Its small size necessitates the use of a microscope to identify it.

Description: H = 0.5cm; W = 0.125cm. Minute, flattened, thin, transparent and glossy; upper part is smooth but underneath contains numerous fine striae; three–four cylindrical whorls; inside the aperture is a narrow ledge; colour = white. Etymology: *Skenea* = after James Skene; *serpuloides* = a coiled snake.

<h1>Chapter Two</h1>

<h1>Patellogastropods</h1>

True Limpets

THE PATELLOGASTROPODS (Superfamily Patellacea = 'pan shells') are true limpets (as opposed to the slit limpets described in the last chapter) which are herbivorous and generally posses a solid conical shell and a flat, powerful muscular foot. Although they are biologically primitive, the limpets are highly-specialised and are ideally adapted to life between the tide marks. They may be found in some abundance on rocky shores of all kinds, including locations that are exposed to the pounding of the Atlantic sea. The limpets have long been a source of fascination to zoologists, partly because they are so common but also because most species mould their shell to the shape of the rock on which they live; a habit which forces them to return to the exact same place at each low tide. Limpets have been a source of food for humans for thousands of years, but it has also been observed that rats can dislodge them with 'a sudden jerk of the nose'. This led the Victorian conchologist James Marshall to wonder whether the populations of rats that he saw on remote islets were being kept alive by eating limpets. His theory appeared to be confirmed by the Seigneur (Lord) of the small island of Sark, who recalled finding several black rats that had drowned after getting their tongue trapped under the shell of a limpet. 'Perhaps,' speculated Marshall, 'there may be a connection between the practice of limpet-eating by colonies of rodents and the various 'Rat Islands' that are scattered around our coasts'. The idea of rats dislodging limpet seems a bit far-fetched but there are at least three 'Rat Islands' to be found around Britain. Whether they contain thriving populations of mollusc eating rodents is not recorded.

25 – *Tectura testudinalis* (Müller); Common Tortoiseshell Limpet

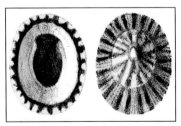

This species is one of many in this book that was first described in *Zoologiae Danicae* written in 1776 by Otto Friedrich Müller (1730-1784) and which contains many Danish seashells that would later be discovered living in Britain. Müller himself was German in origin, but he moved to Denmark to escape his impoverished upbringing. Following a spell as a tutor for the prime minister's children, he married a rich woman and settled down to the life of a gentleman scientist. Among his many achievements, Müller is credited with developing the first practical naturalist's dredge, which he used to good effect in Denmark and Norway and which is one of the reasons why he managed to describe so many new marine species, including *Tectura testudinalis*, whose geographical distribution would seem to have spread somewhat since Müller's time. *Tectura testudinalis* is a sub-Arctic species that, in the early Nineteenth Century, was known in Britain only from the shores of Scotland. By the 1850s, its range had expanded southwards to include Dublin, the Isle of Man and Tyneside, and it was speculated that it would eventually reach Wales and Cornwall. However, this small limpet has made little observable progress in the last century. It remains restricted to the Irish and northern North Sea, although its full range includes much of the sub-Arctic region, including Greenland and Canada. In Scotland, *Tectura testudinalis* may be abundant, especially on rocky shores, where it may be found on stones and boulders from the upper shore down to considerable depths offshore.

Description: H = 1cm; W = 3cm. Conical, solid; oval outline and flattened, blunt profile; apex not central but situated in forward part of shell; surface smooth with brown linear markings which anastomose in the lower half; colour = cream with brown markings. Etymology: *Tectura* = covering over; *testudinalis* = tortoiseshell.

26 – *Tectura virginea* (Müller); White Tortoiseshell Limpet

This was another of Otto Müller's 1776 Danish discoveries. *Tectura virginea* is a small, fragile limpet that looks rather understated compared to its more colourful cousin, the common tortoiseshell limpet (*Tectura testudinalis*) and is certainly more tricky to find alive as it lives on or under stones, often hidden amongst red seaweeds. Empty shells may be quite common, especially in deep rock pools where they may sometimes be found among any loose sediment that has accumulated. It is generally distributed about Britain and it is alleged that specimens from the English Channel are larger than those further north.

Description: H = 0.75cm; W = 1cm. Small, thin with minimal ornamentation; colour = white with pink and brown rays. Etymology: *virginea* = maidenly/graceful.

27 – *Helcion pellucidum* (Linnaeus); Blue-Rayed Limpet

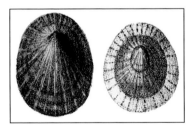

When viewed from the side, this limpet looks a bit like a streamlined cyclist's crash hat. It is small, but very colourful and for many years was assumed to live only on the fragile stalks of oarweed (*Laminaria*) until, in 1788, it was discovered that the largest specimens were to be found buried inside the seaweed's sturdy holdfast (i.e. its 'roots'). After learning of this, some Victorian naturalists took to ripping up dozens of oarweed plants in search of decent blue-rayed limpet specimens, destroying vulnerable coastal ecosystems in the process. Enacting this destruction was evidently hard work, for it led John Jeffreys to suggest that 'it is not an easy matter for a lady collector to do this. She may avail herself of the next storm and hunt for the pretty prize among the seaweeds thrown up on the beach'. Blue-rayed limpets are common on oarweed on the lowest part of rocky shores all around Britain.

Description: H = 1.5cm; W = 2cm. Elongate, rounded and smooth; colour = brown with radiating blue or bluish green streaks. Etymology: *Helcion* = possibly after a mythical bird; *pellucidum* = transparent.

28 – *Patella depressa* (Pennant); **Black Footed Limpet**

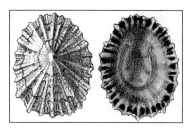

First described in 1777 by the pioneering British conchologist Thomas Pennant, the black footed limpet was historically known as the 'ware limpet'. Its modern vernacular name only arose in the mid-Nineteenth Century and is derived from the dark colour of its foot. In historical times, fishermen would knock black footed limpets from rocks, place them in their mouth alive and then chew the foot into a pulp before using it to bait their hooks. For many years, the black footed limpet was assumed to be a subspecies of the common limpet (*Patella vulgata*) but several studies have revealed that not only are the two species separate, but on many coastlines they directly compete with each other for grazing space. When a common limpet and black footed limpet go into battle, the victor tends to the larger individual whose bulk is able to keep smaller specimens at bay. This species is reasonably common on rocky shores on the southern and western coasts of Britain.

Description: H = 1.1cm; W = 3cm. Cone is low; surface covered in ribs which become indistinct towards the apex; inside porcellaneous with orange head scar; animal's foot is dark green to black in colour. Etymology: *Patella* = a pan; *depressa* = low.

29 – *Patella ulyssiponensis* (Gmelin); **China Limpet**

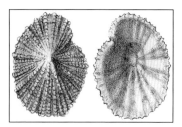

The china limpet has been known under a number of differing scientific names in recent times and is still referred to in many books under its 1798 title of *Patella aspera*. However, it was recently discovered that the species first gets a mention in 1791 by the German botanist and chemist Johann Friedrich Gmelin (1748-1804) in his updated 13th edition of Carl Linnaeus' *Systema Naturae*. Under international convention, the oldest-known scientific name for an animal (or plant) has priority, thus the china limpet is now known by Gmelin's name *Patella ulyssiponensis*. Gmelin is responsible for naming many northern European marine species and his name crops up in this book several times. It may be generally noted that the naming of European limpets has caused early conchologists something of headache. This is because many of the larger limpets are highly variable in their colour, shape and size; thus the differences between many shells were seen to be the product of natural variation, rather than their being separate species. For a long while, conchologists lumped a majority of British species, including the china limpet, under the catch-all title *Patella vulgata* (the common limpet). The Victorian naturalist Sylvanus Hanley suspected that *Patella ulyssiponensis* and *Patella vulgata* might be different species when, in the 1840s, he observed some chickens eating *P. vulgata* with relish while at the same time refusing to touch *P. ulyssiponensis*. He reasoned that if the two animals held a different flavour, then they were probably different species. *Patella vulgata* has since been split into several species, but the differences between them can be subtle, especially in worn or encrusted specimens, and telling them apart on the seashore can be problematic. The china limpet may be found on rocky shores around the entire British coastline.

Description: H = 0.5cm; W = 0.4cm. Resembles Patella vulgata but is more depressed and oblong with finer, better defined ribs; inside porcellanous with orange head-scar. Etymology: *ulyssiponensis* = from Ulyssipon.

30 – *Patella vulgata* (Linnaeus); Common Limpet

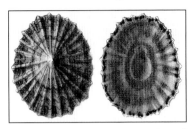

The common limpet was the first of the true limpets to receive a scientific name in Carl Linnaeus' original 1758 *Systema Naturae*. It is one of the hardiest, most conspicuous and abundant seashells in Britain and can be found brazenly clinging to rocks on even the most exposed parts of our coastline. This limpet is not exactly a delicacy to the modern human palette, but it has been used as a food source for tens of thousands of years. Many archaeologists are used to finding piles of their shells in prehistoric campsites. Even in recent times, the common limpet has been used as food, usually by impoverished coastal dwellers. But it has rarely been considered to be a delicacy. John Jeffreys recalled being the guest at an impromptu dinner party on the island of Herm in 1858: 'The hour was unfashionable, one o'clock; and the meal was served on the turf in the open air. This consisted of fine limpets, laid in their usual position and cooked by being covered by a heap of straw, which had been set on fire about twenty minutes before dinner. There was also bread and butter. We squatted round the smouldering heap, and left on the board, a couple of hundred smouldering shells.' The common limpet may be found on all of Britain's rocky coasts but do try to resist the temptation to dislodge living specimens with the blow from a foot or rock: there will be many empty shells for you collect along the strand line.

Description: W = 4.3cm; H = 3.8cm. Tall, solid with blunt apex; broad radiating ridges have smaller ridges in between; colour = generally dull grey outside and white inside. Etymology: *vulgata* = common.

31 – *Lothia fulva* (Müller)

Although first described in 1776 from Scandinavia by Otto Müller, the first official record of this shell in British waters came decades later from the geologist and biblical historian James Smith (1782–1867), who dredged a specimen from the Clyde region in the 1830s (or possibly 40s). A subsequent claim that it had earlier been found by Mary Ball (1812-1898), an Irish naturalist, are unproven because she chose not to publicise her discovery until after Smith's announcement. *Iothia fulva* is rarely found on the shore, but lives on rocky ground in water of at least a few metres depth, with some specimens having been recovered from 600 metres or more. It is generally rare in Britain and is restricted to the northern half of the country. Most records are from relatively deep water, so the chances of obtaining specimens (dead or alive) onshore are remote.

Description: H = 0.7cm; W = 0.2cm. Conical, apex located very close to anterior margin; surface covered in fine radiating and concentric lines which intersect to give a reticulate pattern; colour = yellow/orange. Etymology: *Iothia* = meaning unknown. *fulva* = deep yellow.

32 – *Lepeta caeca* **Müller**

An offshore species that was discovered in Denmark in 1776 by the dredging pioneer Otto Müller. It is a minute sub-Arctic species that is known only from a few specimens dredged off the coast of Scotland. It is a deep sea species that has no eyes and, while sometimes abundant above the Arctic Circle, it is very unlikely to be found by the average beachcomber in Britain.

Description: H = 0.8cm; W = 1.8cm. Conical; apex located two-thirds towards anterior margin; steeply conical with typical limpet-like profile; fine radiating lines crossed by very fine concentric striae; colour = off-white. Etymology: *Lepeta* = a limpet; *caeca* = blind.

Chapter Three

Mesogastropods

THE MESOGASTROPODS ('middle gastropods') were once held to be the evolutionary link between the archaeogastropods ('ancient gastropods') and neogastropods ('new gastropods'), but recent genetic studies have revealed that the situation is far more complicated than this. Although a major revision of this group is doubtless on the cards, I will refer to the mesogastropods in their traditional sense which, in simple terms, means that all the species possess one gill, one auricle and one kidney. Under this category come such common shells as the periwinkles, slipper limpets and cowries. There are estimated to be around 30,000 living species of mesogastropod, most of which are marine, but some terrestrial and freshwater species are also known. A majority are herbivorous although there are some carnivorous forms as well.

Horn, Auger and Needle Shells

The Cerithiacea (Superfamily Cerithiacea = 'horn shells') are a small group of tall, pointed and ornamented shells which includes such seaside favourites as the needle whelk and auger shell.

33 – *Bittium reticulatum* (da Costa); Needle Whelk

First described in 1778 by Emanuel da Costa from specimens that he appears to have obtained near to Falmouth at a place where he 'found it in immense quantities on sand banks thrown up by the sea'. Da Costa's description rings true, for although not commonly seen alive on the shore, there are select areas of coast where the beach may consist almost entirely of empty needle whelk shells. This may come about because the shell is small but extraordinarily robust and can thus be transported for some distance after death and be then concentrated by favourable currents. Fresh specimens are best seen using a hand lens or microscope, when their vibrant colour and ornate sculpture can be appreciated. The Victorian conchologist William Clark believed the needle whelk to be a dull animal which had a rather sad look about it. To this, his sometime adversary John Jeffreys retorted 'Oh, idle thought! In nature there is nothing melancholy!' The needle whelk is generally restricted to western and southern coastlines on sandy shores.

Description: H = 1.3cm; W = 0.3cm; 12-16 whorls; shell solid and elongate; surface covered in deep ridges and ribs which intersect to form a regular pattern of tubercles. Etymology: *Bittium* = unknown; *reticulatum* = reticulated.

34 – *Bittium simplex* (Jeffreys)

Originally discovered on the island of Guernsey in the 1850s, probably by the local conchologist Frederick Collings Lukis (1814-1863). John Jeffreys believed this to be a variety of *Bittium reticulatum* which it greatly resembles. The recovery of more specimens and its limited geographical range (see below), has led to it being elevated to the level of species. It is more typically a southern European species whose range stretches to the Channel Islands and, more rarely, to the Scilly Islands but not the British mainland. Even in the areas where it occurs, it is a rarely-encountered shell and difficult to distinguish from *Bittium reticulatum* without the use of a microscope. It lives on sand or silt in shallow water, but the empty shells are reasonably robust and may be washed onto the shore in favourable circumstances.

Description: H = 0.5mm. Resembles *Bittium reticulatum* but is without any thickened ribs (varices), is thinner and more glossy; colour = white or pale yellow with purple lines on the ridges. Etymology: *simplex* = simple/plain.

35 – *Turritella communis* (Risso); Auger Shell, Screw Shell

A very distinctive and attractive sea shell that has caught the eyes of many artists leading to it being featured in historical paintings and, in more modern times, seaside postcards and photographs. The auger shell is quite common and it is surprising that it did not catch the attention of scientists until 1826 when it was formally described by the French pharmacist Joseph Antoine Risso (1777-1845). The shell is tolerably common and may be abundant in some areas where densities of 640 individuals per square metre have been reported. In the spring months, male auger shells will gather on the seabed and arrange themselves into a star-shape in preparation for mating. This species is well-known from the fossil record, but it may be found living on mud and sand on the lowest part of the shore. It is known from sandy shores around Britain but is scarce along the south coast of England.

Description: H = 5.7cm; W = 2cm. Distinctive by its size and long, thin profile; around 20 whorls which are much rounded and ornamented with spiral striae; deep suture; colour = light brown/yellow. Etymology: *Turritella* = a small tower; *communis* = common.

36 – *Cerithiopsis barleii* (Jeffreys)

This is a rarely-encountered sea shell in Britain where its range is restricted mainly to the south-west region. It was named in 1867 by John Jeffreys for his dear friend and fellow conchologist George Barlee (1794-1861; see *Barleeia unifasciata* for more details). Its range is restricted to the south-western tip of England and along to the Pembrokeshire coast, where it lives low on rocky shores in association with the sponges on which it feeds. It resembles the other British *Cerithiopsis* species and a good hand lens or microscope is needed in order to secure a solid identification.

Description: H = 0.7cm; W = 0.2cm. Shell forms an elongate pyramid with a broad base; semitransparent and glossy; 12 whorls, the last of which forms around a third of the height; fine growth lines; colour = yellowish white with a tinge of brown. Etymology: *Cerithiopsis* = like *Cerithium*; *barleii* = after George Barlee.

37 – Cerithiopsis pulchella (Jeffreys)

Yet another species which was first described by the great British conchologist John Jeffreys, who paid particular attention to the horn shells and needle whelks. Like *Cerithiopsis barleii*, this animal is a rarity whose range is restricted to the south-west and very southern Irish Sea where it has been found offshore on rocky ground. Even its discoverer has little to say about it, other than that a friend of his once found a monstrous specimen while dredging off Land's End. There are no records of this species having been taken alive in Britain, leading some modern conchologists to believe that this typically Mediterranean species might be extinct in our region.

Description: H = 0.4cm; W = 0.25cm. Shell is cylindrical and solid; semitransparent and glossy; body whorl has 4 spiral ridges; around 10 whorls; colour = yellow-brown, occasionally with brown banding. Etymology: *pulchella* = small and pretty.

38 – Cerithiopsis tubercularis (Montagu)

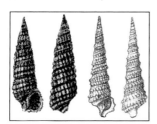

A distinctive shell that was first described by the polymath British naturalist George Montagu in his 1803 volume *Testacea Britannica*. It is sometimes confused with the needle whelk (*Bittium reticulatum*) which it resembles, although the latter is considerably larger with thickened ribs. It is widely distributed about Britain, with the exception of the southern North Sea, and may be found low on rocky shores in association with sponges (on which it feeds) or among oarweed (*Laminaria*). Dead shells are not uncommon on the shore, while live specimens may be quite active and capable of crawling at a considerable pace. Others have observed that the animal can attach itself to objects using a line of thin thread which is strong enough to hold its weight and allow it to be suspended in mid air for several seconds. A related and very rare species, *Cerithiella metula*, is known only from deep water off western Britain. Illustrated *C. tubercularis* (left) and *C. Metula* (right).

Description: H = 0.6cm; W = 0.2cm. Elongate and cylindrical; 13-14 whorls, the last of which can comprise around a third of shell height; fine rows of tubercles formed by intersecting rib and ridge ornamentation; two keels on the last whorl near the canal; size very variable. Etymology: *tubercularis* = tuberculated.

Periwinkles

The winkles and periwinkles (Superfamily Littorinacea = 'shore dwellers') are an obvious sight both on the seashore and in fish markets across the country. They are large, often brightly coloured, and may be found abundantly on rocks and among seaweed and on the middle and lower seashore. Many a child has wasted hours gathering handfuls of empty winkle shells which may accumulate in large numbers along the strand line, while their parents struggle to free the cooked animal from its shell using a pin!

Given their commonality and familiarity, it may be surprising to learn that identifying many winkle species is a very tricky process that, in some cases, can only be done by killing and dissecting the living animal. This situation has led to great confusion with different people being uncertain about how many species of winkle there are on our shores and how best to identify them. The confusion has its roots in the early Nineteenth Century, when scientists became fascinated with the variations in colour and shape that some species of shell could exhibit. The *Littorina* are especially variable and may be found in a wide variety of colours and also rough and smooth forms. Trying to determine whether these variations warranted setting up new species or not gave conchologists a problem that continued through to the Twentieth Century. The frequent reordering of *Littorina* species reached its zenith in the 1960s and 1970s when a series of careful research projects determined that the three conventionally understood species needed to be split into several new ones. But rather than doing so by shell shape as is traditional, the species were identified by the shape of their sexual organs.

The long and short of all this is that it is now very difficult to identify some species of *Littorina* without killing the animal, removing it from the shell and slicing it up with a scalpel. Rather than fret over this, as amateur conchologists sometimes do, it is perhaps best to admit defeat. I now narrow my identifications down to the two (or more) *Littorina* species to which an individual shell might belong and leave it at that. However, those among you that require a solid identification should consider finding a copy of David Reid's monograph *Systematics and Evolution of Littorina* (Ray Society, 1996).

39 – *Lacuna crassior* (Montagu); Thick Chink Shell

George Montagu first described this species in his 1803 *Testacea britannica* from specimens found in several British localities. The species is little commented on, although it has been observed to put on quite a turn of speed when the occasion arises and has been timed covering a 5cm distance in under a minute (quite fast for a small gastropod). It prefers colder waters and has spread into the northern Pacific via the Arctic Ocean. *Lacuna crassior* is relatively common in Britain but may be localised in its abundance and is best discovered by careful searching on muddy and silty shores among seaweed close to the low tide mark.

Description: W = 1.2cm; H = 0.75cm. Shell turreted, solid with an epidermis; six–seven rounded whorls with numerous spiral lines; yellow-white with brown. Etymology: *Lacuna* = a gap; *crassior* = thick.

40 – *Lacuna pallidula* (da Costa); Pallid Chink Shell

Emanuel da Costa's original specimens were sent to him in 1778 from the counties of Dorset and Kent and, based on this limited range, he suggests that it is a rare shell. However, it is not rare and da Costa's observation may be because it is more common in northern Britain than the south. The live animal hides itself among various types of seaweed on the lower shore. The shell is robust enough to withstand some mortem transportation and empty specimens may accumulate in muddy sediment.

Description: W = 1.1cm; H = 0.8cm. Thin, globular and compressed; three–four whorls, the last of which occupies 75% of overall height; aperture very large; umbilicus deep; suture deep; colour = green with no banding. Etymology: *pallidula* = pale.

41 – *Lacuna parva* (da Costa); Lesser Chink Shell

The lesser chink shell is similar to the pallid chink shell (*Lacuna pallidula*) and was described by the same person, Emanuel da Costa. The lesser chink shell has much more of a classically winkle squat and rounded shape, with the male and female sexes able to be determined by sight alone, which is something of a rarity for molluscs. (The male has a shell that is more rounded with a smaller aperture; the female aperture is larger and more angular, being squarish in outline.) It occurs around all British coasts on rocky shores where it is common.

Description: W = 0.5cm; H = 3.75cm. Shell solid, compressed and highly rounded; opaque and glossy; three–four whorls, the last of which occupies about four-fifths of the height; colour = yellow-white. It is sexually dimorphic with the female possessing an angular aperture. Etymology: *parva* = smaller.

42 – *Lacuna vincta* (Montagu); Banded Chink Shell

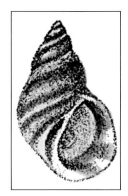

Like most British *Lacuna* species, the banded chink shell is a preferentially Arctic species, whose southerly range only just encompasses Britain. First described by the naturalist George Montagu, it is the easiest of the Chink Shells to spot and identify because of its tall shape and trademark red-brown banding. The banded chink shell may be commonly found among seaweed on rocky shores around the entire British coast and has been recovered in great quantities from inside the stomachs of seabirds. It is observed to be 'a shy but restless mollusc that has a very shambling and awkward gait'.

Description: W = 1.1cm; H = 0.75cm. Resembles *Lacuna crassior* but smaller with less pronounced ornamentation; six whorls, not turreted; aperture broad; colour yellowish with red spiral banding. Etymology: *vincta* = encircled.

43 – *Littorina littorea* (Linnaeus); Common Periwinkle

The common periwinkle was named by Carl Linnaeus in 1758 and is one of the few large gastropods to be found in numbers on the upper part of the seashore, a habit which has made it a source of food in most parts of northern Europe. Many shellfish that were once commonly eaten have, in more recent times, fallen out of culinary fashion (e.g. limpets; see *Patella vulgata*). The common periwinkle, however, remains a delicacy and has such a long association with European culture that it has entered folklore. In Scandinavia, for example, it was believed that one could foretell the weather by looking at the position of periwinkles on the shore: the higher up the beach they were, the stormier the weather would be. One only has to look at the variety of local names given to this species to see how important it has been. In the Shetlands it was called a 'wilk'; in Scarborough it was 'couvins' and in Suffolk, 'pinpatches'. The name periwinkle is supposed to be an abbreviation of 'petty winkle' although, given its dull appearance, this seems unlikely. In historical times, vast quantities of periwinkles were gathered, boiled and sold in urban fish markets. For centuries cooked 'winkles' were seen as being a food of the poor, but in truth, they were eaten at many levels of society, as is the case today (although they are more likely to be found on sale in seaside resorts rather than posh restaurants). Extracting a cooked winkle is a labour-intensive activity that requires a long pin to be inserted into the shell's aperture which can then be used to pull and unwind the animal. The periwinkle is abundant in most rocky parts of Britain except in the Channel Islands and Scilly Isles where it is rare.

Description: W = 3.1cm; H = 2.5cm. Shell solid and rough; five–six whorls, slightly tumid; numerous spiral striations; broad aperture; colour = dark brown-black with darker streaks. Etymology: *Littorina* = littoral; *littorea* = littoral.

44 – *Littorina arcana* Ellis

For many years, the *Littorina* were thought to be a genus of molluscs whose species and varieties, while often intricately defined, were relatively easy to find and indentify, even by amateur conchologists. Alas, no more. During the 1960s and 1970s it was realised that several of the well-established *Littorina* species actually consisted of two or more closely-related but genetically separate animals. There is nothing unusual in this. Many traditionally held shells have been 'split' into two or more new species. The trouble in the case of *Littorina* is that the characteristics used to identify some of these new species are based on the soft parts of the animal's body and not the features of its shell. Thus, in order to make a secure identification, one must get a live specimen, kill it and then dissect it under a microscope. *Littorina arcana* is a case in point. It was originally known under the title *Littorina saxatilis* but in 1978 it was given its own species by C. J. Hannaford Ellis. However, in order to tell *L. arcana* apart from *L. saxatilis* one has to dissect and measure the female's brood pouch and/or the male's prostate gland. This delicate task is beyond most amateur (and a few professional) conchologists, and so us beachcombers must live with the burden of not knowing whether we have picked up specimens of *L. arcana* or *L. saxatilis*. Also, because *L. arcana* has only recently been defined, its geographical range is not yet fully appreciated, although it probably occurs on rocky shores around most of Britain with the possible exception of the North Sea. (The illustration also covers *Littorina saxatilis* var. *rudis*).

Description: H = 1.6cm. The shell is identical to *Littorina saxatilis* var. *rudis* and so a safe identification can only be made by looking at the animal under a microscope. It differentiates from *L. saxatilis* as follows: the female animal lacks a brood pouch while the male has a smaller prostate gland. Etymology: *arcana* = hidden.

45 – *Littorina saxatilis* (Olivi); Rough Periwinkle

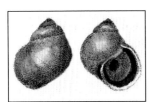

Originally thought of as being just one species, the rough periwinkle has since been subdivided into two distinct species and several varieties, the validity of which are still a matter of debate in some quarters of conchological community. Most of these species/varieties are so similar that it requires taking a microscope and detailed anatomical knowledge to effect a positive identification (see notes for *Littorina arcana* and *Littorina nigrolineata*). In truth, *Littorina saxatilis* has proved troublesome to conchologists since its first description by the Italian naturalist Guiseppe Olivi, (1769-1795) in 1782. For much of its history, *L. saxatilis* was taken to be a subspecies of *Littorina rudis* (which is now a variety of rough periwinkle, although even this is controversial, see below) before being raised to the rank of species in its own right. It has long been noted that the shell of the rough periwinkle grows larger and thicker in rougher, more exposed coastlines and in 2004, an experiment was devised which saw some young shells from a sheltered environment swapped with some from an exposed one. The sheltered shells responded to the rougher conditions by growing larger shells, thus proving that the local environment has a significant effect on the shell shape (also see notes for *L. neglecta*). It is a common species on seaweed on all British rocky shores. **(This species is generally more robust than the specimen illustrated).**

Description: W = 1.6cm; H = 1.25cm. Difficult to distinguish from several other *Littorina* species and varieties. Generally specialist knowledge is necessary to secure a definite identification. Etymology: *saxatilis* = rock-dweller.

46 – *Littorina saxatilis* var. *rudis* (Maton)

First described in 1797 by the British Royal physician and sometime naturalist William George Maton (1774-1835), this is a very contentious animal. Some modern biologists believe this to be a species in its own right which means it may occasionally be seen in textbooks as *Littorina rudis*. Others place it as a variety of *Littorina saxatilis*. Indeed, for a long while *L. saxatilis* was thought to be a variety of *L. rudis*. The differences between the two are relatively minor and it is not fully understood whether this is due to genetics or perhaps because of ecological preferences. *L. rudis* may be found on hard surfaces on the upper and middle parts of the shore all around Britain. (See *L.arcana* for illustration)

Description: W = 1.6cm; H = 1.25cm. The shell is almost identical with *Littorina arcana* and, as with *L. saxatilis*, it is almost impossible to identify this species without dissecting the animal. In general is differs from *L. saxatilis* by having a rough shell with numerous spiral ridges. Etymology: *rudis* = rough.

47 – *Littorina saxatilis* var. *tenebrosa* (Montagu)

In the 1860s, some conchologists believed that *Littorina saxatilis* had as many as nine varieties, most of which have since fallen by the wayside. One of the few survivors is the variety *tenebrosa*, first named by George Montagu in 1803, which may be distinguished from its parent species by its thinner, more slender shell shape and rounded profile. Although less controversial than *L. arcana* and *L. rudis*, you may see this in some textbooks as the separate species *Littorina tenebrosa*. It lives on the upper part of rocky shores around Britain and can tolerate lower salinity conditions.

Description: W = 1.6cm; H = 1.25cm. Shell is practically indistinguishable from *L. saxatilis*; in general the shell is considered to be thinner with deeper sutures. Etymology: *tenebrosa* = dark.

48 – *Littorina neglecta* (Bean)

Since its discovery in 1844 by the Scarborough politician William Bean (1787-1866; see *Alvania beanii* for more details), this little species has endured a turbulent time at the hands of conchologists, many of whom have lumped it in with other *Littorina* species or have refused to believe that it exists at all. Although currently recognised as a separate species, the controversy is far from over with some modern studies from north-east England suggesting that *Littorina neglecta* is nothing more than an 'ecotype' of the rough periwinkle (*L. saxatilis*). The implication from this is that *L. neglecta* is merely an example of a rough periwinkle whose shell has become thicker and larger in response to living in more exposed conditions. Doubtless genetic studies will make a useful contribution to this debate, but current consensus has it as a separate species. Its habitat and range are similar to *L. saxatilis*.

Description: H = 0.5cm. Shell is small with rounded whorls and a wide circular aperture; three–four whorls, the last of which is usually darker in colour; general colour = white or brownish. Etymology: *neglecta* = overlooked.

49 – *Littorina nigrolineata* (Gray); Black-Lined Periwinkle

Yet another controversial *Littorina* species that was first discovered in 1839 by the English zoologist John Edward Gray (1800-1875) but soon afterwards was believed to be synonymous with the rough periwinkle (*L. saxatilis*). Only in 1975 was it re-established as a full species after it was discovered that while the female rough periwinkle reproduces using a brooch pouch, the female black-lined periwinkle possesses a large 'jelly gland' for its eggs. This in turn led to observed differences in the shape of the males' penises. Naturally, such differences may only be determined using a microscope but fortunately, there are some minor physical differences between the two species' shells that can often permit identification without dissection (most notably the aperture, which is oval-shaped in *L. nigrolineata* and more defined striations on the shell surface). It is found on all British coasts among rocks and weed in the middle part of the shore.

Description: H = 2.6cm. Shell solid with rounded whorls; five–six whorls; colour = variable from pale yellow to orange with several brown or black spiral striations running round the entire shell. Etymology: *nigrolineata* = black lined.

50 – *Littorina mariae* (Sacchi and Rastelli)

This small, often colourful, periwinkle only became a species in its own right in 1966, when it was named by C. F. Sacchi and M. Rasteli after the Italian zoologist Maria Magistretti. It had been lumped together with *L. obtusata* and indeed, the two are very hard to tell apart, although adult and well-preserved specimens of *L. mariae* usually have a much larger, squarer aperture than *L. obtusata* and tend to live lower down on the shore, where it preferentially feeds upon toothed wrack seaweed (*Fucus serratus*). It is found on all British coasts and, while some older textbooks refer to this species as the flat periwinkle, this vernacular name more properly belongs to *L. obtusata*.

Description: H = 1.2cm. Requires specialist knowledge to ensure a correct identification but in general it is similar to *Littorina obtusata* but with a squarer profile, flattened spire and an enlarged aperture. Etymology: *mariae* = after Maria Magistretti.

51 – *Littorina obtusata* (Linnaeus); Flat Periwinkle

The flat periwinkle is one of the most common and colourful seashells to be found between the tide marks. It was first described by Carl Linnaeus in 1758, who named it 'blunt' after its shape. The shell colour varies considerably and is generally related to the animal's habitat; in exposed locations, where *L. obtusata* will feed more on the darker more robust seaweeds, it tends to be a darker more uniform colour (e.g. black, dark green or orange). Conversely, in more sheltered areas where the food range is greater, *L. obtusata* may be a lighter green, yellow or even patterned. Flat periwinkles are immediately attractive to the eyes of the young and, like daisies on a lawn, children may be seen gathering dozens of specimens to show their parents or to take home as souvenirs. Nor is it just the young who hold such a fascination. Necklaces made from flat periwinkles have been discovered as grave goods in Neolithic cemeteries, suggesting that the vivid colours were just as pleasing to our forebears. It is found among seaweed on rocky shores all around Britain, but is perhaps more common in the south and west. Empty shells are often abundant on the beach.

Description: W = 1.6cm; H = 1.2cm. Almost identical to *Littorina mariae*. Firm identification requires dissection of the animal but in general terms it has a more prominent spire and wider aperture. Etymology: *obtusata* = blunt.

52 – *Melarhaphe neritoides* (Linnaeus); Small Periwinkle

The small periwinkle, first named by Carl Linnaeus in 1758, is one of only a minority of marine seashells that like to live on the highest part of the beach where it hides away inside narrow rocky crevices and cracks. Indeed, it is so expert at wedging itself in these spaces, that it must usually be extracted with a pair of tweezers and a great deal of care. The small periwinkle possesses a strong will to live and can tolerate high temperatures, dehydration and long periods without feeding. One rather cruel experiment even determined that small periwinkles can withstand being placed in water at 46°C for periods of up to two hours without ill effect. The pay-off for being so hardy is that this little animal can live in areas that are hostile to other grazers and so has few competitors within its habitat. In fact, the odds are that if you find a live sea shell wedged into a crevice above or around the high tide mark, then it will be a small periwinkle. It occurs on rocky coastlines around the British Isles.

Description: W = 0.6cm; H = 0.5cm. Small; five–six solid whorls; pointed spire; prominent growth lines; colour = brown. Etymology: *Melarhaphe* = uncertain; rhaphe = 'ridge/seam'; *neritoides* = like *Nerita*.

53 – *Skeneopsis planorbis* (Fabricius)

Described in 1780 by the Danish naturalist Otto Fabricius (1744-1822) who found many specimens in Greenland, a place where he spent nearly six years living with an Inuit tribe in order to collect natural history specimens. The result was Fabricius' monumental work *Fauna Groenlandica*, a tome which introduced the scientific world to many new Arctic species. The small, flat-coiled form of this minute sea shell is reminiscent of the small fossilised ammonites that may be found in famous geological sites across Britain. It is rarely difficult to find specimens of *Skeneopsis planorbis* which likes to lurk among short seaweeds on the lower part of the shore, and which often becomes abundant during the summer months. It is so small that it may sometime be found suspended from weed, or even the surface of the water, on fine mucous threads. It is notably clumsy to watch and has to drag its shell sideways when walking. It may be found on all British coasts, sometimes abundantly.

Description: H = 0.075cm; W = 0.15cm. Minute; flat-coiled; four whorls; deep umbilicus; colour = red-brown. Etymology: *Skeneopsis* = resembling *Skenea*; *planorbis* = discoid.

54 – *Eatonina fulgida* (Adams)

Described by the little known Pembrokeshire zoologist John Adams (1740-1798) who came to science late in life and much of whose work was published after his death in 1798. Adams had a passion for microscopic shells and was a major contributor to George Montagu's landmark work on *Testacea Britannica* which contains the first mention of many small gastropods. Adams must have had access to a top quality microscope to identify *Eatonina fulgida* because even decades after his death, conchologists were amazed at the diminutive size of this animal which, at just 1mm tall, is one of the smallest seashells in the world. What *E. fulgida* lacks in size it makes up for in abundance for (with the aid of a sieve) it may be found in great numbers among eelgrass, especially during summer months. Writing several decades after Adams' death, William Clark observed that when 'on the march the eyes are always under the shell, as are usually the muzzle and the foot, the ends of the tentacles only being visible'. It is mostly restricted to the south and west where it lives in rock pools among weed or on eelgrass (*Zostera*).

Description: H = 0.1cm; W = 0.05cm. Minute; shell globular, smooth; four whorls, deep suture; colour = cream-yellow with two red-brown bands on last whorl. Etymology: *Eatonina* = possibly after Amos Eaton; *fulgida* = gem-like.

Rissoidea

The Superfamily Rissoacea (= 'Risso's shells' after Antonio Risso) are small, and sometimes minute, shells often abundant on the seashore, although their size and ability to hide in sand or seaweed may lead to them being overlooked. The paucity of microscopes meant that smaller shells such as these were for many years ignored, and it was not until 1784 that they were taken seriously in George Walker's *Testacea Minuta Rariora*. The majority of British species were not described properly until the Nineteenth Century, beginning with George Montagu's *Testacea Britannica* in 1803, but new species were still being discovered on British seashores a hundred years later, long after most other British molluscs had been described.

Identifying Rissoidea shells is not easy and ideally requires access to a good microscope, although a strong hand lens will do in some circumstances. The identification notes and illustrations given below are rudimentary – those that need detailed notes should see the *Journal of Molluscan Studies* (1978, Supplement 6).

55 – *Barleeia unifasciata* (Montagu)

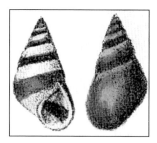

Although this species was described by George Montagu in 1803, the genus was named many years later by William Clark in honour of George Barlee (1794-1861), a former solicitor from Suffolk who, aged 45, was converted to conchology following the death of his young son. The grieving Barlee was apt to take long melancholic walks along Paignton beach, close to where he lived in Devon. One day, he observed a mother and daughter walking ahead of him who spent much of their time bobbing up and down, picking shells from the shore. He offered to help them, and subsequently assisted them many times. Finding shells lifted his depression to such a degree that he retired early and devoted the rest of his life to travelling Britain in search of seashells. Barlee was described as a 'zealous and indefatigable conchologist' by his friend John Jeffreys, whom he accompanied on many collecting expeditions, while James Marshall commented that a person viewing Barlee's collection 'will either be filled with despair or be urged to greater emulation'. Alas, Barlee was to die only a matter of months before Jeffreys published the first volume of his iconic textbook *British Conchology* in 1862, to which Barlee had contributed so much. *Barleeia unifasciata* is an attractive and distinctive shell, which may be found on all but the most northerly of Britain's rocky coasts where it lives on red seaweeds, especially *Chondrus*. It is a fine tribute to this great, but modest, conchologist.

Description: H = 0.3cm. Small, solid and smooth; five slightly tumid whorls; shallow suture; colour = variable but often cream colour with broad red-brown spiral stripe. Etymology: *Barleeia* = after George Barlee; *unifasciata* = single-banded.

56 – *Alvania abyssicola* (Forbes)

First dredged from Loch Fyne in 1845 by the naturalist Edward Forbes (1815-1854), it was not long before other conchologists were hauling specimens from around the Scottish coast. As a minute, deep water dwelling species with a preference for mud, *Alvania abyssicola* is rather uncommon and specimens are difficult to obtain without access to a dredge. As a point of interest, it was largely through Edward Forbes that the use of the dredge became an established scientific discipline. Adapted oyster dredges had been used by naturalists since the 1770s, but it was Forbes who helped standardise the dredge into a rectangular shape around 40cm or so in breath and who promoted its use to conchologists. He was so enthused that at a meeting in 1839, he sang a song which begins: 'Hurrah for the dredge, with its iron edge/And its mystical triangle/And its hided net with meshes set/Odd fishes to entangle!' Modern reports of *Alvania abyssicola* are rather few and far between and never littoral. It lives on muddy seabed at depth around the coast of Scotland.

Description: H = 0.2cm; W = 0.1cm. Solid; five–six tumid whorls which possess strong ribs (approx 12 on bodywhorl) crossed by finer spiral striae; the base of the bodywhorl has no ribs and strong spiral striations; no umbilicus; labial varix; colour = cream. Etymology: *Alvania* = snow white; *abyssicola* = deep-water.

57 – *Alvania beanii* (Thorpe)

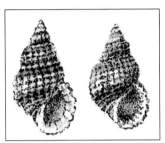

Described as a 'pretty little shell' by its discoverer Charles Thorpe (a pseudonym for the conchologist Sylvanus Hanley; 1819-1899) after a specimen was sent to him from the east coast of England by William Bean. (He was known to fellow conchologists as 'Old Bean' but was better known in his home town of Scarborough as a local politician and fanatical collector of seashells and fossils.) Bean's shell matched some specimens that Hanley had just collected from the Isle of Wight and so Hanley named the shell after his friend, but soon afterwards the species was split into several varieties some of which were contentious. Issues remain around the various varieties, especially *Alvania beanii var. clathrus*, which has fewer striations on its penultimate whorl and is named after a wicker-basket because of the intricacy of its lattice-like ornamentation. In the 1860s, John Jeffreys warned conchologists that they must 'exercise their own discretion as to admitting it' as a variety and that is pretty much the same situation now. *A. beanii* is a predominantly offshore species that occurs around Britain, although specimens may occasionally be found among stones and seaweeds on the lowest spring tides. Empty shells are not uncommonly found onshore but, being minute, they must be searched for very carefully.

Description: H = 0.3cm; W = 0.2cm. Small and solid; contains a reticulate pattern of ribs and spiral striae; distinguished from other *Alvania* by possession of six–seven striae on the penultimate whorl; colour = light yellow-brown. Etymology: *beanii* = after William Bean.

58 – *Alvania cancellata* (da Costa)

'It is the size of a caraway seed,' wrote Emanuel da Costa of this species in 1778. Although certainly minute in its dimensions, this ornamented, slightly plump-looking shell may be locally very common and is said to dominate the famous Shell Beach on the island of Herm, near to Guernsey. During his stay on Herm in the 1840s, the conchologist Sylvanus Hanley was perplexed by this species for, although he found thousands of dead shells, he did not see a single live one. In the end he decided that there must be a colony of them living offshore whose empty shells would be swept onto the beach by favourable currents. It is restricted to southern and western coasts and may be found on the lowest part of the shore on and under rocks and among seaweed.

Description: H = 0.4cm; W = 0.3cm. Shell conic-oval, opaque, somewhat glossy; six–seven rounded whorls; 13-16 spiral striations crossed by strong ribs in lower whorls to form a reticulate pattern; colour = yellow-white, sometimes with with two brown bands. Etymology: *cancellata* = latticed.

59 – *Alvania carinata* (da Costa)

In 1778, Emanuel da Costa sensibly decided to name this species after the keels which encircle its whorls and which make this shell so distinctive. Fresh specimens have an engaging semi-transparent quality to them which allows its ridges and striations to be seen from inside the aperture. In general, *A. carinata* prefers the warmer waters of the Gulf Stream and is generally to be found on the southern and western fringes of Britain on the lower shore among seaweed, under stones and in gravel.

Description: H = 0.5cm; W = 0.3cm. Oval-conic, turreted outline and twisted base; five–six whorls the last forming a third of the overall height; fine ribs and striations intersect to form a lattice pattern; colour = alabaster. Etymology: *carinata* = keeled.

60 – *Alvania cimicoides* (Forbes)

For many years, specimens of *Alvania cimicoides* had been mistaken for *Alvania beanii* which it resembles. The naturalist Edward Forbes was the first to recognise the difference between the two with *Alvania cimicoides* being a much broader and somewhat more elegant shell. It is a minute and generally sublittoral species, whose empty shells may sometimes be found among seaweed, under stones and in gravel on the shores of northern and western Britain.

Description: H = 0.3cm; W = 0.1cm. Solid, opaque and glossy; six–seven whorls, the last forming three-fifths of overall height; decorated with fine ridges and striations which intersect to form tubercles on the lower whorls; yellow-white with a reddish brown tinge. Etymology: *cimicoides* = resembles *cimex*.

61 – *Alvania jeffreysi* (Waller)

Discovered in 1864 by the Irish barrister and amateur dredger Edward Waller (1803-1873) who would often accompany John Jeffreys on his collecting trips, and after whom he named this minute shell. *Alvania jeffreysi* is an exceedingly rare species that has only three British records (of which I am aware) all of which are very old and from deep water: two being from Scotland and one from off Land's End, Cornwall. Its full range is little understood, and this is one species that is most unlikely to be encountered by amateur conchologists walking along the beach (or even professional ones working with a dredge).

Description: H = 0.3cm; W = 0.1cm. Solid, tall and narrow; five–six whorls with a distinct reticulate (waffle-like) pattern formed from the intersection of numerous strong ribs and four concentric ridges with several additional ridges on base of bodywhorl; colour = white. Etymology: *jeffreysi* = after John Gwyn Jeffreys.

62 – *Alvania lactea* (Michaud)

Named in 1830 by the French conchologist André Louis Gaspard Michaud (1795-1880), Victorian conchologists acknowledged this as being one of the rarest British shells and went to some lengths to get hold of specimens. It was unknown in British waters until the 1840s, when Sylvanus Hanley risked his life by wading out into chest deep water in strong currents off the coast of Jersey in order to search under some large stones. He was rewarded with four live specimens of *Alvania lactea*, two of which he subsequently lost after being startled by nearby gunfire. He did not know whether the shot 'was to celebrate his discovery, or to punish his excess jubilation' but on looking for the source, found that the guns of a nearby fort were trained on him. Luckily, the weapons were firing blanks and Hanley 'escaped with life and with my *Alvania lactea*.' By 1900, it was known that certain parts of the Channel Islands could produce many specimens leading the conchologist James Thomas Marshall (1842-1922) to remark that 'it cannot now be called our rarest Rissoea by any means'. Aside from Jersey, where it is generally found under stones very low on the beach or offshore (sometimes in small colonies) it is rare.

Description: W = 0.6cm; H = 0.3cm. Solid; five–six convex whorls, last forms 75% of total height; 20 ribs on body whorl and 10 on penultimate whorl; 15 striae on bodywhorl, nine on penultimate whorl; colour = white. Etymology: *lactea* = milk-white.

63 – *Alvania punctura* (Montagu)

The annals of conchology have had little to say about this delicate shell, which was originally described by George Montagu in 1803, and whose surface is beautifully decorated by a regular lattice-like pattern. It is from this regular ornamentation that the species derives its species name (*punctura:* 'pricked') which refers to the regular rectangular depressions. It has been noted that larvae from these shells are a favourite food of fish and especially herring, in whose stomachs they have been found in some abundance. It occurs on all British coasts very low on the shore among rocks and *Laminaria* seaweed.

Description: H = 0.25cm; W = 0.1cm. Solid; six convex whorls; ornament numerous fine spiral striae and fine ribs forming reticulated pattern; colour = off-white with reddish tinges. Etymology: *punctura* = pricked.

64 – *Alvania semistriata* (**Montagu**)

This is another of George Montagu's minute species from his 1803 *Testacea Britannica*. This attractive shell is said to congregate in 'family groupings' beneath muddy stones with the living animal being described by William Clark as like 'a cat-fish with three tails'. A not uncommon shell which may be found around Britain, although it is suspected to be more common in the south than north. It is found on the lowest part of the shore under stones, in silt and among seaweeds.

Description: H = 0.25cm; W = 0.13cm. Solid; six rounded whorls; slight suture; fine spiral striae; colour = pale yellow with two parallel rows of red-brown marks on body whorl. Etymology: *semistriata* = half-striated.

65 – *Cingula cingillus* (**Montagu**)

This pretty shell prefers life on the beach and is rarely found offshore. Since being described by George Montagu in 1803, *Cingula cingillus* has gone under a number of species names but was finally anchored to *cingillus* in the 1860s by John Jeffreys who used the opportunity to explain the Victorian convention when naming a species: 'Custom wills that, in science as well as literature, names and words in general use should be preferred to those which are obsolete, although the latter may have the claim of priority; nor will the feeble cry of justice to the memory of the author be listened to while the loud and imperious demand of public convenience is ringing in our ears'. Nowadays, the naming of a species is subject to a very strict code which, among other things, gives priority to the oldest scientific name to have been used. Many popular animal and plant species have fallen foul of this code including, most famously, the dinosaur *Brontosaurus* which had to revert to its original, older, name of *Apatosaurus*. *C. cingillus* may be found on beaches around the British Isles under stones where it is often gregarious.

Description: H = 0.5cm; W = 0.2cm. Small, solid, conical; six–seven flattened whorls, a dozen or more spiral ridges on the bodywhorl; distinct suture; colour = cream with red-brown spiral banding. Etymology: *Cingula* & *cingillus* = both mean 'small girdle'.

66 – *Manzonia crassa* (**Kanmacher**)

The genus *Manzonia* was named in 1870 after the Italian palaeontologist Angelo Manzoni (1842-1895), but this species was named in 1798 by the British zoologist Frederick Kanmacher, who worked closely with the optician George Adams. These two gentlemen used their scientific knowledge of optics to construct microscopes through which they observed much wildlife, including seashells. *Manzonia crassa* is an intricate and delicate shell, whose thick twisting ridges, fine striations and glossy lustre are beautiful when observed under the microscope. Few remarks have been made about this species, save for William Clark who, on observing a living specimen, remarked that it was 'a very simple animal'. It is common low down on the shore under stones and among dense seaweed on many British coasts and its empty shells may often be found in sediment.

Description: H = 0.3cm; W = 0.15cm. Small, robust and obliquely twisted; sutures deep; 9-12 curved ribs that stop short of base; numerous fine striations; blunt spire; keel on body whorl; colour = white. Etymology: *Manzonia* = after Angelo Manzoni; *crassa* = thickened.

67 – *Manzonia zetlandica* (Montagu)

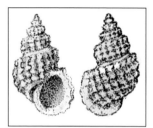

A rather average-looking shell that was first recovered in the Shetland Islands around 1815 and afterwards passed to George Montagu, a gifted naturalist who had laid the foundations for Nineteenth Century conchology. This was one of the last shells that the aging Montagu would describe, for within a few months he had died, ending what was one of the most productive careers in British zoology. *Manzonia zetlandica* is an offshore species which can live in a variety of soft sediments, from mud to gravel and while never abundant, it may be locally common. As with most Rissoacea, it is small and delicate but empty shells may be washed onto the beach by strong currents, although such specimens are invariably rather worn. It is found around most of the British Isles with the possible exception of the eastern end of the English Channel. It lives among seaweeds and stones.

Description: H = 0.3cm; W = 0.1cm. Small, robust and turreted; six–seven whorls; 13-16 ribs underlain by a strong keel; ribs and strong striations intersect to form a reticulate pattern; colour = white-yellow. Etymology: *zetlandica* = from Shetland.

68 – *Onoba aculeus* (Gould)

Named in 1841 by the British ornithologist John Gould (1804-1881), the man whose identification of Charles Darwin's famous Galapagos finches was to help spark the latter's thoughts about evolution through natural selection. *Onoba aculeus* is a plain, simple shell that is easily confused with worn or poorly ribbed specimens of *O. semicostata*, which it greatly resembles. The two shells share the same broad habitat preference for seaweed but *O. aculeus* is generally only known from Scotland where it lives on the lower shore, sometimes in mildly brackish water conditions. Its small size means that a strong hand lens or microscope is needed to obtain a secure identification.

ID: H = 0.3cm; W = 0.1cm. Resembles *Onoba semicostata* but with no ribs on lower whorls and an enlarged protoconch. Etymology: *Onoba* = after a Roman city in Spain; *aculeus* = a needle.

69 – *Onoba semicostata* (**Montagu**)

This is another small species that was first recognised by George Montagu from several British specimens sent to him by co-workers. It is a compact and tidy shell, whose species name (*semicostata* = partially-ribbed) accurately describes the incomplete ribs that run entirely around it. *Onoba semicostata* is a relatively common find that is best obtained by cutting clumps of seaweed (especially coralline ones) from rock pools low down on the sea shore and then gently breaking the fronds apart to reveal the seashells and other animals that live there. In the interests of sustainability, do not over-collect from one single rock pool. It is found all around Britain and may be very common in some areas.

Description: H = 0.4cm; W = 0.2cm. Solid, minute, tall; characterised by numerous fine spiral striae on shell and shortened ribs that do not extend full height of whorl; deep sutures; last whorl occupies two-thirds of overall height; white but some specimens have two red-brown bands on body whorl. Etymology: *semicostata* = partially-ribbed.

70 – *Pusillina inconspicua* (**Alder**)

Named in 1844 for being 'not remarkable' (*inconspicua*) by Joshua Alder (1792-1867) who started life as a Newcastle grocer, but who quit this trade to pursue his interest in molluscs, and especially sea slugs, of which he was pioneering student. *Pusillina inconspicua* has managed to cause a few problems over the years because its shell shape and ornamentation are so variable. Few people could agree where the physical boundaries to this species' shell shape and ornamentation lay and it was not until the late Nineteenth Century that it was realised that several separate species were being described under the same name. Many of what were once thought to be subspecies of *P. inconspicua* are now true species in their own right. This shell may be found around all of Britain and its empty shells may be reasonably common on the lower shore, although the animal itself is somewhat rarer and seems to prefer life in the shallow water under stones and among seaweed. Some textbooks list this under its old name of *Rissoa inconspicua*.

Description: H = 0.2cm; W = 0.12cm. Resembles *Rissoa parva* (see below) but with more convex whorls, finer, more numerous ribs and no markings at the aperture; colour = white with red-brown patterning. Etymology: *Pusillina* = tiny; *inconspicua* = unremarkable.

71 – *Pusillina sarsi* (**Lovén**)

Named after Michael Sars (1805-1869 an early Nineteenth Century Norwegian priest whose talent for natural history saw him quit the church for a career in academia. Sars was a pioneer in the study of the distribution of animals and also in developing techniques to dredge deep sea animals. *Pusillina sarsi* was originally described as a variety of *P. inconspicua*, but was split off as a separate species during late Victorian times. It is a relatively uninteresting shell that has prominent ribs but little other ornamentation, and may be found living amongst eelgrass (*Zostera*) and seaweeds on the lower part of all British coasts. Worn specimens may sometimes be confused with *Rissoa parva* but the latter is more slender and has a greater number of ribs.

Description: H = 0.3cm; W = 0.1cm. Solid, slender and glossy; six–seven rounded whorls; generally smooth with occasional ribs on lower whorls; colour = yellowish-white with reddish-brown tint. Etymology: *sarsi* = after Michael Sars.

72 – *Rissoa guerinii* (Récluz)

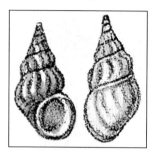

This species was named after Félix Édouard Guérin (1799-1874), an early Nineteenth Century French pharmacist who is credited with introducing silk worms to Europe. The shell was described simultaneously in France and England, and for decades the two nationalities preferred their own names (the English one being *Rissoa costulata*) until the marginally older Franco name of *guerinii* was given preference. This is one of the larger *Rissoa* species and it may be tentatively identified using the naked eye (although a hand lens is preferable). It is found only on western and southern coasts where it lives among stones and seaweed on the lower shore. It may be common in some areas.

Description: H = 0.6cm; W = 0.3cm. Large (for a *Rissoa*), oblong, conic and spindle-shaped; eight whorls; strong ribs except on top; three whorls and last bit of bodywhorl; numerous fine spiral striations; colour = cream to brown, ribs are usually white. Etymology: *Rissoa* = after Antonio Risso; *guerinii* = after Félix Édouard Guérin.

73 – *Rissoa lilacina* (Récluz)

Generally restricted to the western side of Britain and only locally common, *Rissoa lilacina* is not as commonly encountered as many other species within this genus. The striations occur only between the ribs which means that worn specimens can easily be confused with other ribbed rissoides including *R. parva* and *Pusillina sarsi*.

Description: H = 0.5cm; W = 0.25cm. Solid, conic; seven whorls the last forming three-fifths of the height; lower whorls possess prominent ribs and striae; colour = white tinged with yellow, brown, violet and purple. Etymology: *lilacina* = lilac.

74 – *Rissoa membranacea* (Adams)

This is one of those shells that takes refuge among colonies of eelgrass (*Zostera*) and thus best searched for at low tide using a sieve. It is a distinctive shell and rather large for a *Rissoa*. It may be tolerably common in local areas and also within shell-sand samples.

Description: H = 0.75cm; W = 0.3cm. Large (for a *Rissoa*), solid and elongate; seven slightly convex whorls; bodywhorl is third of overall height; 15-18 ribs on penultimate whorl; aperture broad with flared outer lip and tooth-like fold at the base of pillar; colour = cream with red-brown patterning. Etymology: *membranacea* = membrane-like.

75 – *Rissoa parva* (da Costa)

First described by Emanuel da Costa in 1778 from specimens taken from the south-west of England (or possibly Guernsey). He describes it as being 'about the size of a common ant'. This simple species is one of our commonest seashells, found in hundreds and thousands among seaweeds or as empty shells in sediment samples on all British coasts. Many conchologists tire of seeing dozens upon dozens of empty *Rissoa parva* specimens in sieved seashore sediment samples where, after several hours of picking, their presence starts to become an irritation. It is highly variable but occurs chiefly in two distinct forms: one with thick ribs around the lower whorls, the other smooth (this is the variety *interupta* which is sometimes described as a species in its own right). The defining characteristic for both forms is a pair of brown streaks (described as comma-like by some) that is found on the outer lip, although this may be missing in some worn specimens. Illustration shows *Rissoa parva* (left) and *Rissoa parva* var. *interupta* (right)

Description: H = 0.35cm; W = 0.25cm. A minute but solid shell that is highly variable and may occur in smooth and ribbed forms; it may be identified by a comma-shaped brown streak that occurs on the apical part of the outer lip although this may be absent in worn specimens; the ribbed variety typically has eight ribs on the bodywhorl which start at the suture but do not reach the base; colour = yellow-white with occasional brown streaking. Etymology: *parva* = small.

76 – *Setia pulcherrima* (Jeffreys)

This minute shell was first found in Guernsey by George Barlee during the 1840s and was afterwards sent by him to his friend John Jeffreys, who formally described it. British specimens of *Setia pulcherrima* are known only from the Channel Islands and offer us an object lesson as to why equipment should always be thoroughly cleaned before and after use. A few years after first describing it, John Jeffreys was excited to discover three *S. pulcherrima* specimens after sieving seaweeds in Exmouth. Jeffreys believed he had secured the first UK mainland record for this animal but his friend Mr Barlee soon disavowed him of the notion. It turned out that the sieves Jeffreys had used in Exmouth had been lent by Barlee and were previously used in Guernsey, but neither man had cleaned them properly since. Thus, the *S. pulcherrima* specimens from Exmouth were most probably contaminant specimens that had stuck to the sieve following its use in the Channel Islands. Despite not being found on the mainland, *Setia pulcherrima* is common in the Channel Islands where it lives on the lower shore on seaweeds and eelgrass (*Zostera*).

Description: H = 0.2cm; W = 1.2cm. Minute, delicate, conical and glossy; four rounded whorls; deep suture; almost smooth; colour = opaque often with parallel bands of brown streaks or spots on lower whorls. Etymology: *Setia* = possibly after an Italian province; *pulcherrima* = most beautiful.

77 – *Ceratia proxima* (Forbes and Hanley)

It was the great conchology duo of Edward Forbes and Sylvanus Hanley, authors of *A History of British Mollusca*, who first described this shell in 1850 after finding specimens in Ireland. The *proxima* (= 'nearest to') of the species name refers to this shell's similarity to *Hyala vitrea*, with which it may be easily confused. However, *Ceratia proxima* is more restricted in its distribution, is much rarer than *H. vitrea* and, according to its describer, 'the practiced eye of a conchologist will distinguish each individual by its more compact style of gyration' (i.e. it is more slender than *H. vitrea*). It lives offshore on sandy or muddy ground and is restricted to the western and south-western coasts of Britain.

Description: H = 0.3cm. Subcylindrical, solid; like *Hyala vitrea* but encircled with numerous spiral striae; colour = snow white. Etymology: *Ceratia* = little horns; *proxima* = nearest to.

78 – *Hyala vitrea* (Montagu)

George Montagu first described this shell in 1803 and, for a while, believed that it was not one, but three separate species. It is widespread around Britain but lives offshore in mud and sand, sometimes in quite deep water. Many conchologists found specimens surprisingly hard to obtain, even using a dredge, but it is common in deeper waters and it has recently been reported from new areas along the continental North Sea coastline which suggests that its British range may be expanding.

Description: H = 0.3cm; W = 0.12cm. Elongate, thin and lustrous; six slightly rounded whorls; deep sutures; growth lines visible; colour = white or yellow. H: SL to OS; muddy substrates. D: CI: Gu. UK: all coasts. Etymology: *Hyala* = glassy; *vitrea* = glassy.

79 – *Caecum clarkii* (Carpenter)

Named in 1858 by Philip Pearsall Carpenter (1819-1877), a clergyman and amateur conchologist who lived in Warrington, Cheshire, before emigrating to Canada. Carpenter named this species in honour of the conchologist William Clark, who was one of the earliest people to capture sea animals alive and then study them in an aquarium. It is minute and apparently very rare with the only definite British records I am aware of coming from Guernsey, where a small number of specimens were discovered in the 1980s. There are also apparently reports of it being found in south-western England. In his original 1858 description, Philip Carpenter hedges his bets as to whether *Caecum clarkii* is just a variable form of another species, *C. vitreum*. 'As the plugs in each form are more variable than usual, *C. clarkii* is not constituted until more is known,' he wrote and there have since been questions about its validity. It is an offshore species that prefers soft sediment such as sand and mud.

Description: H = 0.2cm. Short, tusk-shaped with a coarse granular surface. Shell is thin with no ornamentation; colour = dirty white or pale yellow. Etymology: *Caecum* = blinded; *clarkii* = after William Clark.

80 – *Caecum glabrum* (**Montagu**)

A minute species described by George Montagu in 1803. The British *Caecum* may be small, but they are noticeably active creatures, so much so that there is a recorded instance of a Victorian naturalist racing specimens of the smaller *Caecum glabrum* against the larger ones of *C. imperforatum*. Explains William Clark: 'I thought *Caecum imperforatum* to be quite active, but it is far surpassed by this animal. I put one of each in a watch-glass of sea water, and with a camel's hair brush gave them a fair start, but the little one beat its competitor hollow and accomplished a distance of two inches in 55 seconds; thus affording proof that, even in the Mollusca, nature compensates for the small volume of the minute beings in giving them greater energy, vivacity and quickness.' It dwells offshore in mud and sand around all of Britain.

Description: H = 0.2cm; W = 0.03cm. Short, tusk-shaped, thin and transparent; smooth or frosted surface; colour = white. Etymology: *glabrum* = smooth.

81 – *Caecum imperforatum* (**Kanmacher**)

First described by the British zoologist Frederick Kanmacher, whose love of the microscope caused him to take an interest in minute shells. The various species of *Caecum*, including this one, have been compared to many things including elephants' tusks, drainpipes and even old cigarette ends. This species was, however, thought to resemble the human windpipe and for many years went under the specific name of *trachea*. The tubular shell is in fact the animal's bodywhorl (i.e. the final whorl) which, on entering adulthood, becomes separated from the rest of the shell (the protoconch) with the resultant hole being sealed with a plug of calcite. *Caecum imperforatum* is restricted to the west and south-west of Britain where it lives offshore in sand and mud.

Description: H = 0.3cm; W = 0.07cm. Tusk-shaped, thin; differs from *Caecum glabrum* by the possession of numerous ring-like concentric ribs; colour = yellow to reddish-brown. Etymology: *imperforatum* = not perforated.

82 – *Tornus subcarinatus* (**Montagu**)

Most conchologists, including its discoverer George Montagu, acknowledge that, while being absolutely minute, this shell is aesthetically pleasing to the eye. Its beauty is derived chiefly from its regular, rounded shape and intricate ornamentation, neither of which can be appreciated without the aid of a decent microscope. The *subcarinatus* of its name literally translates as 'somewhat keeled' and it is this feature that is immediately obvious on the shell, which is smooth on top but has a body whorl that is adorned with several strong spiral ridges crossed by smaller striations. The effect can be quite mesmeric and it is always a delight to find individual specimens. *Tornus subcarinatus* is restricted to southern and western regions where it may be found among oarweed (*Laminaria*) on the lowest rocky shores. Live specimens are rather rare but empty shells are not uncommon

Description: H = 0.1cm; W = 0.25cm. Solid and circular; three–four whorls the last of which makes up most of the shell; complex ornamentation of strong spiral ridges crossed by striations; large umbilicus. Colour = snow white sometimes with an orange cast. Etymology: *Tornus* = a turner's wheel; *subcarinatus* = slightly keeled.

Mud Snails

The mud snails (most of which are in Family Hydrobiidae = 'water dwellers') are not included in some seashore books as many are not fully marine but instead prefer brackish water. However, these small shells are a regular occurrence on some beaches and, as their name suggests, they love nothing more than muddy locations such as estuaries, harbours and sheltered coves. They may be abundant and, while small, are relatively easy to identify using a hand lens or microscope.

83 – *Hydrobia ulvae* (Pennant); Laver Spire Shell

The laver spire shell was described by Thomas Pennant in 1777 based on some specimens that were discovered in Flintshire living on sea lettuce (*Ulva* spp.). *Hydrobia ulvae* is a lover of mud and lower salinity water and thus may be found in vast abundance on tidal estuaries, mud flats, coastal marshes, etc., all around Britain. It is a major source of food for various seabirds and large fish, such as mullet, and as such, forms an important component of estuarine ecosystems. Finding specimens should not present a problem, although obtaining them alive sometimes requires getting very muddy. Some people have observed that this animal will sometimes trap air inside its shell and float upside down for short periods of time, a habit that is thought to be used when they wish to relocate to another area without the hassle of walking.

Description: H = 0.6cm; W = 0.3cm. Shell solid, smooth, glossy and conic; six–seven mildly rounded whorls; pointed apex. Etymology: *ulvae* = sea lettuce.

84 – *Hydrobia neglecta* (Muus)

Science was a long time in recognising this species which greatly resembles *Hydrobia ulvae*, and which shares the same broad habitat. However, since its discovery in 1963 by the Danish zoologist Bent Jørgen Muus (1926-), *H. neglecta* has revealed itself to be quite different from other British species in this genus. It is, for example, not as tolerant of cold conditions as *H. ulvae* and during the severe winter of 1985, populations were preferentially killed by the freezing conditions. Like most *Hydrobia*, it is tolerant of brackish water and may be commonly discovered in estuaries and salt marshes and is known from right around Britain where suitable conditions exist.

Description: H = 0.4cm; W = 0.15cm. Distinguished from other *Hydrobia* chiefly by blackened pigmentation on the tentacles but also by being more slender with a blunter apex. Etymology: *Hydrobia* = water-dweller; *neglecta* = overlooked.

85 – *Ventrosia ventrosa* (**Montagu**)

It was George Montagu who, in 1803, distinguished this species from its cousin *Hydrobia ulvae* which, to the naked eye, it resembles. It is closely related to the *Hydrobia* and shares the same broad habitat preferences and distribution, although it generally will not tolerate fully marine conditions. It is an extremely hardy animal that may survive for some days without food and which has been observed to survive ambient temperatures as low as –8°C. In some localities, *Ventrosia ventrosa* can reach extraordinary densities of up to sixteen individuals per square centimetre. It is speculated that the ability of this species to trap air in its shell and float might be a method of escaping overcrowding and find new areas.

Description: H = 0.5cm; W = 0.25cm. Shell solid and conic but much more rounded and irregular than *Hydrobia ulvae*; apex rounded. Etymology: *Ventrosia* & *ventrosa* = both mean 'swollen'.

86 – *Potamopyrgus antipodarum* (**Gray**); **Jenkin's Spire Shell; New Zealand Mud Snail**

This small snail was originally a native of New Zealand, but it is now firmly established on many parts of the British coast, especially in estuaries and other brackish water areas. It is believed to have travelled to southern England within barrels of drinking water that were stored aboard boats. It was certainly living in the Thames by 1859 but may have arrived up to twenty years earlier. Once established, it spread at a rapid pace and was known from many parts of England, Ireland and Wales by 1900 and Scotland shortly afterwards. It may now be found around much of Britain and Europe where it can survive in brackish and freshwater conditions in a variety of habitats from rivers to tidal ponds.

Description: H = 0.6cm; W = 0.3cm (occasionally more). Elongate; robust; glossy; five–six slightly rounded whorls; deep suture; usually smooth but keeled varieties occur; umbilicus closed; colour = light to dark brown. Etymology: *Potamopyrgus* = a river tower; *antipodarum* = from the antipodes.

87 – *Truncatella subcylindrica* (**Linnaeus**)

This shell featured in Carl Linnaeus' 1758 edition of *Systema Naturae*, which is somewhat unusual as smaller species such as this were often described later in the Eighteenth Century. It is rather truncated in shape and has a very limited distribution, being known only from a few places along the Dorset coast. It is one of only a handful of molluscs that prefer to live in the 'splash zone' – a harsh area at the very top of the beach which receives salt water in the form of sea spray. Here, *T. subcylindrica* hides itself in mud, under stones or among seaweed and from which, being only a couple of millimetres in height, must generally be obtained using a sieve. Reports of *T. subcylindrica* are rare and it is speculated that its geographical range might have decreased during the last century, perhaps due to a loss of suitable habitat, although its apparent scarcity might be due to a lack of conchologists searching for it.

Description: H = 0.5cm; W = 0.2cm. A distinctive shell; solid, cylindrical with irregular outline; four–five rounded whorls; middle whorls may be wider than the apex and body whorl; blunt apex; narrow aperture. Etymology: *Truncatella* = small truncated; *subcylindrica* = almost cylindrical.

88 – *Paludinella litorina* (delle Chiaje)

First discovered in Italy in 1828 by the medic turned zoologist Stefano Delle Chiaje (1794-1860). For such a small shell, *Paludinella litorina* is remarkably compact and robust which perhaps reflects its ability to survive the harsh conditions in the 'splash zone' right at the top of the beach. Although undoubtedly hardy, *P. litorina* is somewhat dull, being uniformly pale in colour and almost entirely smooth. For many years, conchologists were unsure about the evolutionary affinities of *P. litorina* and it has resided in a variety of genera including *Rissoa* and *Assiminea*. It is comparatively rare within Britain and is generally restricted to southern and south-western coastlines, where it wedges itself into muddy crevices and under stones.

Description: H = 0.2cm; W = 0.15cm. Minute, globose and glossy; four whorls, the last being 75% of overall height; deep suture; small umbilicus; colour = semitransparent. May be confused with juvenile *Littorina saxatilis*. Etymology: *Paludinella* = a small marsh; *litorina* = seashore dweller.

Slipper Limpets and Cowries

Within this broad group of four superfamilies (Strombacea; Calyptraeacea; Cypraeacea; Lamellariacea) are shells whose shape and glossy nature are perhaps more reminiscent of warmer southern waters than Britain's chilly seas. Many of these species hold a symmetry and colour patterning that renders them attractive to commercial collectors. The splayed pelican's foot (*Aporrhais pespelecani*) has long been a favourite of souvenir shops, while the cowries have a natural attraction to conchologists and schoolchildren alike. A recent addition to this select group is the slipper limpet (*Crepidula fornicata*) which hitched a lift to our shores with imported American oysters.

89 – *Aporrhais pespelecani* (Linnaeus); Pelican's Foot

First described by Carl Linnaeus in 1758. Those that have seen this shell will immediately understand why both its common and Latin name refer to it as being a pelican's foot. That said, in the Eighteenth Century it was known by the far less attractive sounding name of 'blobber-lipped Edinburgh whelk'. The attractive shape, ornamentation and glossy colour of this shell has endeared it to naturalists throughout the ages, including Aristotle who once commented on the ragged nature of its outer lip. This shell is popular with seaside tourists and commercial conchologists and has the benefit of being widely distributed about Britain, although it is encountered more rarely in the south than the north. The magnificent splaying of the outer lip which so distinguishes this species is only fully developed in adult shells. It is a sluggish animal that lives partially buried in muddy sediment in shallow to moderate depths of water, but whose empty shells may be found washed up on sandy shores. There is a related species, *Aporrhais serresianus*, which is found in deeper water off Scotland and western Ireland. Illustration shows *Aporrhais pespelecani* (left) and *Aporrhais serresianus* (right)]

Description: H = 4.6cm; W = 3.1cm. Immediately identifiable because of its flared, fingered outer lip (which is present only in the adult shell). Etymology: *Aporrhais* = probably means 'I break'; *pespelecani* = pelican's foot.

90 – *Calyptraea chinensis* **(Linnaeus); Chinaman's Hat**

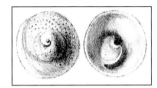

The Latin name *chinensis* means 'originated from China' and has caused some vexation because the shell was neither first discovered in China and nor is it native to that region (although similar species do exist in the Pacific). The original describer, Carl Linnaeus, was referring to the shell's low conical shape which gave it the resemblance to the straw hats worn by native Chinese workers. It has also been known as the 'cup and saucer shell' which I assume refers to its circular shape and distinctive inner shelf. Many conchologists have mistakenly taken living specimens of this limpet-like animal home after collecting empty bivalves which it may cling to inside, only to be discovered several hours later when the specimens are unpacked and examined. Fortunately, it is a phenomenally hardy animal which can live for extended periods of time out of water, giving the conchologist time to return it to the sea, if they so wish. It is restricted to southern and western regions where it may be found on the lower shore attached to rocks and old shells. It may be locally common.

Description: W = 1.5cm; H = 0.6cm. Distinctive; shell conical with circular base; thin, semi-transparent, dull and almost smooth; inside is an inner shelf; colour = off white. Etymology: *Calyptraea* = a woman's cap; *chinensis* = Chinese.

91 – *Crepidula fornicata* **(Linnaeus); American Slipper Limpet**

The slipper limpet, which was first described by Carl Linnaeus, is one of a handful of alien molluscs that have entered British waters from foreign shores and have subsequently gone on to thrive here. In this case, the place of origin was the USA from whence oyster spats were brought into Britain following the collapse of native stocks due to disease. With the oysters came *Crepidula fornicata* which was first recorded on this side of the Atlantic in 1872 in Liverpool Bay, but it has since spread to many other parts of the coast, and is especially common in the south and east of England. The slipper limpet is not an unattractive shell and it may be found on the lower shore attached to rocks, shells, seaweed or other solid object. It often occurs in stacks of several individuals which decrease in size. The complicated love life of this shell means that as the individuals work their way down the stack, so they change sex from male to female. Their spread has been rapid in some areas. In Jersey, for example, the first recorded occurrence of a slipper limpet is in the 1950s, when it was very rare, but by the early 1980s it had become one of the commonest large shells on the beach. Its geographical range is thought to be increasing, especially along the south coast of England.

Description: W = 5cm; H = 2.1cm. Oval with reduced spire; distinguished by its large aperture which has a shelf (septum), extending half its length; colour = variable, cream, yellow or pinkish with patches red or brown. Etymology: *Crepidula* = small slipper; *fornicata* = arched.

92 – *Capulus ungaricus* (Linnaeus); Fool's Cap; Hungarian Cap

Another Linnaean discovery whose designated specific name, *ungaricus* (meaning Hungarian), caused some Nineteenth Century conchologists to bristle at an apparent misspelling. Some would add an 'H' to make it *Hungaricus*, but the strict laws governing the naming of species mean that the original spelling must be used, regardless of error. Originally known from the Devonshire coast (where it was called the Torbay bonnet) it has since been found around the whole of Britain where it lives offshore attached to rocks, stones and shells. It is notably common in scallop and mussel beds where it attaches itself to large bivalves and lives a semi-parasitic lifestyle.

Description: H = 1.5cm; W = 2.5cm. Solid and horn shaped in top profile; apex highly recurved; surface covered in fine growth lines and ridges; colour = brown. Etymology: *Capulus* = a container; *ungaricus* = Hungarian.

93 – *Trichotropis borealis* (Broderip and Sowerby)

First described in 1829 by William John Broderip (1789-1859) a lawyer who was also a passionate conchologist and well-connected member of the early Nineteenth Century natural history community. Broderip worked closely with the natural history dealer George Sowerby (the elder; 1788-1854) whose purchase of a vast collection of shells (the Tankerville Collection) in 1825, served to introduce him into the conchological community. *Trichotropis borealis* is a delicate and appealing shell whose adult form presents dozens of stiff hair-like projections along its lower whorls. It is a cold-water species that lives offshore, often in quite deep waters, around the coast of Scotland. Their thin shell and fragile ornamentation mean that perfect specimens are a relative rarity. In late Victorian times, collectors would pay handsomely for a good example and so shells were imported from Arctic waters, where it is more commonly found, and passed off as being British. It is very rare and British records are few and far between, with there being only a handful of recent reports, mostly from northern Scotland. It lives on rocky ground but is not known from the seashore.

Description: H = 1cm; W = 0.6cm. Fresh specimens may be immediately distinguished by the periostracum which forms into hairy spines along the spiral keels; five–six whorls each with around three strong keels giving the appearance of being twisted; wise aperture with flaring outer lip; colour = off-white or pink. Etymology: *Trichotropis* = hairy; *borealis* = northern.

94 – *Simnia patula* (Pennant)

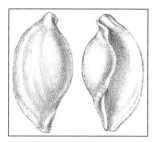

Described in 1777 by Thomas Pennant from a specimen acquired in Weymouth. It is difficult to mistake this beautiful and somewhat fragile shell with any other native British species. It has a wonderfully elongated curved shape and a cowrie-like glossy lustre which made it quite a prize by conchologists. However, it is a rarely-encountered animal that lives offshore in the south and west of Britain where it feeds exclusively on sea fans and the soft corals *Alcyonium* and *Tubularia*. Its empty shell is so fragile that it rarely makes it onto the seashore intact. Most specimens are obtained using a dredge.

Description: H = 2.5cm; W = 1.2cm; shell is spindle-shaped and semi-transparent; many minute, wavy spiral striations; in life the mantle may cover the shell; colour = yellowish-white. Etymology: *Simnia* = meaning not known; *patula* = open.

95 – *Erato voluta* (Montagu)

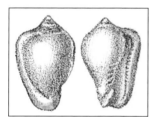

With a shape and glossy lustre that resembles some of the tropical cowries, this small shell is highly attractive both in life and when empty. It is another small species first described by George Montagu in 1803 from a British specimen. Like all cowries, the mantle of the animal extends beyond the aperture and can envelop the shell where it deposits the thin layers of enamel that give its surface a glossy lustre. In life, the mantle is vividly-coloured with purple-brown spots and studded with yellowish tubercles (raised lumps). It occurs round Britain where it lives offshore in association with ascidians, on which it feeds. It is rarely seen onshore alive, although the robust shell may survive the rigors of wave and current action to be cast onto the beach.

Description: H = 1cm; W = 0.6cm; shell is solid, harp-shaped and has a glossy lustre; smooth surface; five–six whorls; colour = milky-white. Etymology: *Erato* = a lyrical muse; *voluta* = rolled.

96 – *Trivia arctica* (Pulteney); Arctic Cowrie

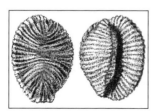

First found on the Dorset coast in 1799 by the local medic and amateur naturalist Richard Pulteney (1730-1801), whose work was extensively utilised by George Montagu in his 1803 survey of British shells. Many people are fascinated to learn that Britain has its own species of cowrie which, while not as spectacular as some tropical forms, are in their own way highly attractive, especially when alive. William Clark kept specimens in an aquarium and observed their wonderfully coloured mantle which envelopes the whole shell, ensuring that it remains clean and glossy. The animal is a prodigious producer of slime and at low tide, they may be seen hanging from rock overhangs by a thin thread of mucus. Empty shells may sometimes be found on the beach, but they are best sought by looking on the lowest of spring tides among stones and in shaded, muddy gullies close to the ascidians on which it feeds. It can be found around all of Britain but may be more common in northern regions.

Description: H = 1cm; W = 0.8cm. Identical to *Trivia monacha* (see below) but lacks the spots. Etymology: *arctica* = Arctic.

97 – *Trivia monacha* (da Costa); Spotted Cowrie

When writing in general terms about British cowries – which were historically known locally as 'sea lice' or, in the Orkneys, 'John-a-Groats buckies' – the father of taxonomy, Carl Linnaeus, remarked in 1758 that 'English shells are only white, and without spots'. In 1778, Emanuel da Costa proved Linnaeus wrong when he described *Trivia monacha* as having three distinct spots. The spotted cowrie was the first British cowrie to be afforded a scientific name and the only discernable difference between this species and *Trivia arctica* are three dark spots that may be found on the very top of the shell. For many decades this difference was considered to be an irrelevance and caused most conchologists to lump both species together under the name *Trivia europaea*. It was not until the 1930s that they were segregated again. Both species have the same broad habitat and feed on ascidians, but the Arctic Cowrie (*T. arctica*) has a preference for colder waters and is generally more common in northern regions than the spotted cowrie. Although attractive to the eye, the collection of these animals should be kept to the absolute minimum.

Description: H = 1.1cm; W = 0.9cm. A small, solid shell that adopts the classic cowrie shape; distinguished by its highly ridged shell, white-reddish colour and three dark spots; the animal's mantle is also colourful. Etymology: *Trivia* = commonly occurring; *monacha* = solitary or a nun.

98 – *Lamellaria latens* (Müller)

Although related to the cowries, the shell in *Lamellaria* species is internal and thus entirely hidden from view beneath the animal's brown, warty mantle. In life, this is not a very attractive animal and resembles a flattened, somewhat lumpy garden slug. The shell is more attractive, being translucent and flattened with a huge sweeping aperture. It is, however, perilously thin and thus rarely encountered as an empty shell which means that most specimens are obtained from the living animal. Nineteenth Century naturalists had no problem with killing molluscs for their shells. Nowadays, this ought to be a last resort. It may be found on all British coasts on, or around, stones in association with the ascidians on which it feeds.

Description: H = 1cm. The animal has an internal shell, is brown, oval and slug-like. Shell is much broader than it is tall with a wide aperture; thin, glossy and white. Etymology: *Lamellaria* = lamelliform; *latens* = hidden.

99 – *Lamellaria perspicua* (Linnaeus)

Much of what has been said about *Lamellaria latens* applies here also. The species name *perspicua*, which was provided by Carl Linnaeus, refers to the transparent nature of this shell which resembles that of *Lamellaria latens* but with a smaller aperture and raised spire. The *Lamellaria* were initially considered to be opisthobranchs (sea slugs) but they are actually members of the cowrie family whose mantle has fused over the shell to form a permanent covering. Like our other species of native cowrie, they are carnivorous and feed upon ascidians. Its habitat and distribution are identical to *Lamellaria latens*.

Description: H = 2cm. Animal very similar to *Lamellaria latens* but larger; shell thin, semi-transparent, highly rounded. Etymology: *perspicua* = translucent.

100 – *Velutina plicatilis* (Müller)

The original description of this shell, made in 1776 by Otto Friedrich Müller, was highly inadequate ('Utterly inadequate!' complained Edward Forbes) and for some decades, British conchologists rebelled against it by rejecting its designated name of *plicatilis* for the *flexilis* assigned to it in 1803 by the English naturalist George Montagu. John Jeffreys described the living animal as 'seemingly fond of floating and of getting out of the water if confined in a vessel' while Edward Forbes noted that it could swim if necessary. Although found in much the same habitat as *Velutina velutina*, it is a cold water animal and generally restricted to the offshore regions of the Scottish coast, where it lives offshore on stony ground. It is uncommon and not known from the seashore.

Description: H = 1.4cm; W = 1.1cm. Shell thin and often covered by periostracum; three flattened whorls, the last of which occupying almost the entire height; aperture very elongate and rounded; colour = transparent. Etymology: *Velutina* = velvety; *plicatilis* = pliable.

101 – *Velutina velutina* (Müller); Velvet Shell

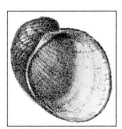

There is little mistaking this animal which is another of Otto Müller's Danish discoveries from 1776. The shell is thin and tightly-curled and the final whorl is expanded to such a degree that it forms almost the entire height of the animal. (In side profile it is shaped like a tuba.) The animal may be found offshore around all of Britain, where it lives among rocks and feeds upon ascidians. Although the living animal is not uncommonly seen (especially when SCUBA diving), empty shells are rarely cast up on the shore. It is a cold water species that prefers the chilly subarctic region to the warmer waters of southern Europe and so is perhaps rarer in the south than the north.

Description: H = 2cm; W = 2cm. Shell thin, semi-transparent; body whorl makes up four fifths of shell height; aperture very broad; surface brown and, in life, hairy. Etymology: *velutina* = velvety.

Necklace Shells

The necklace shells (Superfamily Naticacea = 'to swim') are a small family of similar-looking shells whose large size and glossy nature makes them an attractive addition to any collection of seashells. They are generally easy to identify and, although most prefer to live offshore, their empty shells are not uncommon on sandy beaches. Good clues to their presence on a beach are the semi-circular and collar-shaped egg masses which are commonly seen lying on the sand in the spring and summer. These are constructed from a mixture of jelly and sand and are sometimes difficult to spot. It is after this necklace-shaped egg mass that the necklace shells are named. In life, they are voracious predators that move stealthily across the sand in search of the bivalves upon which they feed. Live animals may occasionally be found at low tide but most take the precaution of burying themselves and this must be obtained by raking or digging.

102 – *Amauropsis islandicus* (Gmelin); Icelandic Moonsnail

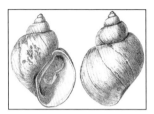

Named by the German botanist Johann Friedrich Gmelin in 1791, this animal is commonly called the Moonsnail because of its rounded, cream-coloured shell. The Latin name afforded to it by Gmelin (*islandica* = Icelandic) was derived from a particularly clear description of this shell made in the travel journal of Eggert Olafsen and Bjarne Povelsen who, in 1772, toured the then little known territory of Iceland. The Icelandic moonsnail is fragile but attractive, and was much sought-after by early Victorian collectors. Unfortunately for them, the animal is a deep-water dweller and specimens could only be gathered using a dredge but even so, the shell was rarely encountered driving up its commercial price. The lack of specimens was resolved in the 1840s, when it was discovered that large fish, such as cod and haddock, were apt to pluck this shell from the seabed and then swallow it whole: thus the stomachs of such fish became a source of Icelandic moonsnails. It may be found along all of Britain's coasts, but it lives offshore, often in very deep water, and although empty shells are known from the beach, they are usually quite worn.

> Description: H = 2.5cm; W = 1.6cm. Longitudinally oval; five–seven rounded whorls; suture is channelled; small umbilicus; colour = white. Etymology: *Amauropsis* = behaving blindly; *islandica* = Icelandic.

103 – *Euspira catena* (da Costa); Common Necklace Shell

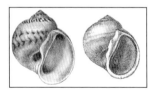

The Eighteenth Century naturalist James Petiver provided this animal with the inconvenient name of 'English-chain-headed-sea-button-shell'. A few decades later, Emanuel da Costa also used the term 'chain' when choosing a scientific name. He did so because the intricate patterning on the shell 'appears like a very pretty chain-work'. The common necklace shell is one of the few large gastropods to be found on wide sandy beaches where it preys upon small and shallow burrowing bivalves. William Clark remarked that 'it is scarcely possible to contemplate a more beautiful and interesting object, with its shell rising as a globular pyramid from its immense circular disk, elegantly marked with fine dark lines on a clear-drab background'. Many agree with him and to this day, finding specimens on the seashore remains a delightful experience. It occurs around Britain on the lower part of sandy shores where it burrows in sand. Empty shells are often utilised by hermit crabs and may be found washed higher up the beach. There is a related, but rare, circum-Arctic species called *Euspira pallida* which is known from several offshore records around Scotland and SW Ireland. Illustration shows *Euspira catena* (left) and *Euspira pallida* with operculum (right).

> Description: H = 3.5cm; W = 3.5cm. Large, globular, smooth and solid; seven whorls, the last of which occupies half the overall height; broad aperture; deep umbilicus; colour = cream with a row of red-brown streaks on the top of the whorls. Etymology: *Euspira* = well-coiled; *catena* = a chain.

104 – *Polinices fuscus* (de Blainville); Dark Necklace Shell

Described in 1825 by the French zoologist (and former painter) Henri-Marie de Blainville (1777-1850), a worker at the Muséum National d'Histoire Naturelle in Paris, whose quick temper frequently landed him in trouble with his co-workers. The dark necklace shell is an offshore, sand-loving species whose distribution is restricted to western coasts but even there, its occurrence is somewhat sporadic. To judge by its absence from the lists of many of the great conchologists, it is rare and unlikely to be found on the seashore.

Description: H = 2.5cm. Six whorls; body whorl not as globular as in other species of *Polinices*; spire compressed; deep umbilicus; aperture D-shaped. Colour = sandy brown with no pattern. Etymology: *Polinices* = possibly after a Greek mythological figure; *fuscus* = dark.

105 – *Polinices montagui* (Forbes)

At just over than a centimetre in height, *Polinices montagui* is our smallest necklace shell and, as a cold water species, is more commonly found in the north of Britain than the south. Named by Edward Forbes in 1838, it is carnivorous and makes a living by using its wide, muscular foot to push its way through soft sediment in search of bivalves. When prey is encountered, the foot expands to envelop the bivalve so that the necklace shell can use a combination of chemicals and physical drilling to make a hole in the bivalve near the point where the two valves are attached. Once this is accomplished, the necklace shell severs the bivalve's adductor muscle so that the shell opens, exposing the animal inside. While wandering the beach, one will find many small bivalves lying open, butterfly-like, on the surface. On closer examination, many will have a minute hole near the umbones. This is the calling card of a necklace shell. It is restricted to the western and northern parts of Britain and lives offshore on sand or gravel.

Description: H = 1.25cm; W = 1.2cm. Solid, globular; five–six rounded whorls, the last occupying around 60% of overall height; deep sutures which are channelled; inner lip out-turned; deep umbilicus; colour = fawn with red-brown interior and white outer lip. Etymology: *montagui* = after George Montagu.

106 – *Polinices pulchellus* (Risso); Alder's Necklace Shell

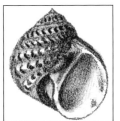

Although easily confused with the common necklace shell (*Euspira catena*), this species is generally smaller, has an outer lip which joins with the last whorl at right angles, and has spiral markings along the length of its shell. It was named by the French pharmacist Joseph Antoine Risso in 1826 and generally lives some distance offshore and, although common and widely distributed, it will be rarely encountered on the beach.

Description: H = 1.75cm; W = 1.7cm. Solid, globular; six rounded whorls; spire prominent; deep umbilicus which is partially obscured by columella; broad inner lip; colour = cream with up to five rows of red-brown streaks. Etymology: *pulchellus* = small and pretty.

Tritons

It may be surprising to learn that one of the largest and most robust shells to occur in British coastal waters is a triton shell (Superfamily Tonnacea) of the same type that may be found in the sub-tropical and tropical oceans of the world. As the descriptions below detail, it took some while before the entire conchological community came to terms with the idea that such animals are native to our coasts; many were in denial until quite recently. It must be said that these spectacular shells are very rare seen in British waters and generally hide in deep water making it unlikely that the average collector will get their hands on a specimen but the story behind their discovery is fascinating.

107 – *Charonia lampas* (Linnaeus); The Knobbed Triton

This extraordinary shell, first described by Carl Linnaeus in 1758, is our largest and most spectacular gastropod. Although well-known from the Mediterranean Sea, three living specimens *Charonia lampas* were dredged off Guernsey between 1825 and 1847 by fishermen and ended up in the hands of local conchologist Frederick Corbin Lukis (1788-1871) who managed to keep one of them alive for two weeks in a bucket. In 1858, Lukis's son (also named Frederick) told John Jeffreys about the Guernsey triton specimens who, in turn, told the wider conchological community. Jeffreys had no doubt that *C. lampas* was a native British species, but a majority of his colleagues were sceptical of Lukis' claim and suggested that the shells had been dumped near Guernsey by a French trawler coming north from Spain. 'Those who believe this to be a British species have much more faith than I can lay claim to,' said William Clark in 1859. This incredulous stance appeared to be confirmed when no new specimens were forthcoming other than a battered shell recovered from the Isle of Wight in 1914, which was again blamed on French fishermen. By the 1970s, even some Channel Island naturalists were beginning to doubt their own triton records when, in the space of a few years, several new specimens were dredged off Guernsey, Cornwall and to the south of Ireland. This time the scientific community took more notice and *C. lampas* enjoyed the pleasure of being a confirmed part of the British fauna. Occasional specimens continue to be found, the most recent being dredged in March 2005 by a fisherman working to the east of Guernsey. He commented that he had been fishing for scallops for 43 years but in this time, had only seen three *C. lampas* specimens. There is now little doubt that this is a native deep water species in the south-west and Channel Island regions. Naturally, the amateur conchologist is very unlikely to find this species but if you do, then please inform your local museum! It lives in moderate water depths where it feeds on sea urchins, starfish and other medium-sized benthonic fauna.

Description: L= 22cm. A solid shell whose size and bright colouration makes it unmistakable. Etymology: *Charonia* = the mythical boatman Charon; *lampas* = a lamp.

108 – *Cymatium cutaceum* **(Linnaeus)**

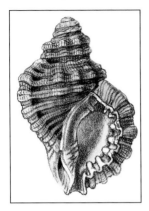

Like the knobbed triton (*Charonia lampas*), the inclusion of this smaller (but no less spectacular) species as a native British mollusc was, for a time, controversial. Although described in 1758 by Carl Linnaeus, its earliest British record is in 1826 when William Turton recounts that 'several specimens of the *Tritonia cutacea* [*Cymatium cutaceum*] were last winter cast on shore at Padstow, Cornwall.' By 1834, Turton had added Guernsey to this list, and it was here in 1857 and 1885 that living specimens were dredged by Frederick Collings Lukis, George Barlee and James Marshall, respectively. The recovery of the 1857 specimens, which were alive, caused William Clark to admit grudgingly that they must be native British species, although he did suggest that they might have hitchhiked their way to the Channel Islands by clinging to the hull of a boat! (Clark was later mocked for this idea.) Specimens have been found on shore (most notably by a tourist to Alderney in 1902) but a live *C. cutaceum* has not been seen since 1932 when a single dead specimen was dredged from deep water off Guernsey. It is currently suspected to be locally extinct although a lack of scientific dredging in the region may be a cause of its apparent absence.

Description: H = 6.5cm; W = 4.3cm; a very solid shell; five whorls; two thick spiral striations on spire; several thick striations on body whorl; wide aperture with semi-circular outer lip. Etymology: *Cymatium* = a small wave; *cutaceum* = a cuticle.

Wentletraps and Tower Shells

Of the many spectacularly conical species within these two family superfamilies (Triphoracea and Epitoniacea), it is the wentletraps (whose name means 'spiral staircase' in German) that have attracted the most attention. There was a period in the mid-Seventeenth Century when there was such a desire for these shells that collectors were literally paying a fortune for individual specimens. In 1751, Carl Linnaeus recalled seeing wentletraps being sold for 200 gold pieces each and the creature remained desirable right through the Nineteenth Century when a good specimen could fetch several pounds, although, by the First World War, such shells could be bought for a couple of shillings. (It should be noted that it was not the humble European wentletrap species that were fetching these prices, but the larger, more exotic tropical ones, though the effect made all wentletraps valuable to one degree or another.)

109 – *Cheirodonta pallescens* **(Jeffreys)**

First found in Guernsey by John Jeffreys in 1867, *Cheirodonta pallescens* is actually a southern European species whose range just includes the extreme south and south-west of Britain. Its tower shape, sinistral (left-handed) coiling and rows of tubercles means that it is commonly confused with *Marshallora adversa* and *Monophorus perversus* (of which it was initially considered to be a variety). Fortunately, *C. pallescens* may be distinguished from these other species by looking closely at the final whorl which will have five distinct rows of tubercles. Although small, this is an attractive species which lives on sand and mud on the lower shore. It is rarely seen in British waters.

Description: H = 0.9cm; W = 0.3cm. Very similar to *Marshallora adversa* (see below) with the main difference being the presence of five rows of tubercles on the last whorl. Shell solid, conic; about 10 whorls, not rounded; strong ribs and striae intersect to form a reticulate pattern; colour = whitish, tinged with yellowish brown. Etymology: *Cheirodonta* = hand-toothed; *pallescens* = paler.

110 – *Marshallora adversa* (Montagu)

This shell was first described in 1803 by George Montagu, although the genus in which it current resides, *Marshallora*, was only erected in 1985 and named after the living New Zealand conchologist Bruce Marshall. *Marshallora adversa* is certainly an attractive shell and its left-handed coiling sets it apart from most other gastropods, which coil to the right. Edward Forbes and Sylvanus Hanley record no difficulty in finding empty shells, many of which were badly worn, but searched in vain for a live specimen. It is widely distributed about the British Isles, being absent only from the North Sea and eastern English Channel. It may be found low on rocky shores, under stones, in sponges or seaweed.

Description: H = 0.7cm; W = 0.2cm. Needle-shaped, solid and sinistrally coiled; 15 whorls; spiral ridges and ribs intersect to form tuberculate rows with three rows on last whorl; colour = yellow-brown. Etymology: *Marshallora* = after Bruce Marshall; *adversa* = reversed.

111 – *Metaxia metaxa* (delle Chiaje)

First identified from the Mediterranean Sea in 1828, and named after the Italian physician Luigi Metaxa (1778-1842), this is the rarest British triphorid shell. As a warm-water dweller, it has only rarely been encountered on the extreme southern and western fringes of Britain, although one Victorian report does place it in the Shetland Islands. It is an elegant shell which is slim and elongate with well-defined, rounded whorls and distinct sutures. As such, it is quite distinct from the other British species in this family. An offshore dweller that lives among rocks on or among sponges (on which it feeds), it has no British records (of which I am aware) since 1893 and is extremely rare.

Description: H = 0.6cm; W = 0.2cm. Elongate, cylindrical; 12 to 14 whorls; strongly ornamented body with small, regular rows of tubercles formed by intersecting ridges and ribs. Etymology: *Metaxia* & *metaxa* = both after Luigi Metaxa.

112 – *Monophorus perversus* (Linnaeus)

The species name *perversus* provided by Carl Linnaeus, refers to the position of the aperture which (like *Cheirodonta pallescens*, *Marshallora adversa* and *Metaxia metaxa*) is on the left-hand side rather than the right. It is easily confused with *Marshallora adversa*, and some recent conchologists have assumed that all records of *Monophorus perversus* are misidentifications and so exclude it from the list of British species. Others take the opposing view and believe that it may be found all around our coasts. It is certainly common in the warmer waters of the Mediterranean, where it lives low on sandy shores, but it remains a doubtful British species.

Description: H = 0.9cm; W = 0.3cm; elongate, narrow shell; 16-20 whorls; ornamentation consists of fine rows of small tubercles produced by intersecting ribs and ridges. Etymology: *Monophorus* = single carrier shell; *perversus* = wrong way round.

113 – *Epitonium clathratulum* (Kanmacher in Adams); Small Wentletrap

'This creature is very free in showing its peculiarities,' remarked William Clark who became fascinated with a large purple vein behind the animal's neck. For most of the rest of us, it is not the animal that fascinates, but its distinctive and intricate shell which, with its regular outline and thick ribbing, is perhaps more reminiscent of molluscs from warmer seas. *Epitonium clathratulum* was first described by Frederick Kanmacher in 1798, and is the smallest and rarest of the British wentletraps. It will usually only be encountered by those who dredge offshore sediments for their specimens. This does not mean that it is any less spectacular than its larger cousins, but it does mean that a microscope or hand lens is needed to appreciate the intricate ribbing. It occurs offshore around all Britain where it lives on muddy seabeds.

Description: H = 1.5cm; W = 0.5cm. Small, solid, thin; 12-13 whorls; strong, sharp longitudinal ribs, 18 on bodywhorl; colour = white and semi-transparent. Etymology: *Epitonium* = stretched; *clathratulum* = finely latticed.

114 – *Epitonium clathrus* (Linnaeus); Common Wentletrap

Our commonest wentletrap is also something of a seaside icon and, although rarely encountered by tourists, it does tend to feature as an extra on picture postcards and other souvenirs. It was first described by Carl Linnaeus and prefers to live offshore but will move into shallower water and even onto the beach during its spring spawning season. It is best searched for among patches of eelgrass (*Zostera*) at low water on large tides during the spring and summer months. The common wentletrap seems to have a particular following in Belgium and Holland, where a mass stranding of dead shells and the recovery of an unusually large specimen were deemed newsworthy events, suggesting that the historical mania which once surrounded this animal is not quite dead (see introduction above). It is found around Britain where it burrows into muddy sand.

Description: H = 4cm; W = 1.3cm. Tall, pointed and solid; 15-16 whorls; strong longitudinal ribs, nine on bodywhorl; colour = cream with bands of purple streaks. Etymology: *clathrus* = latticed.

115 – *Epitonium turtonis* (Turton); Turton's Wentletrap

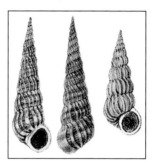

Although marginally larger than the common wentletrap (*Epitonium clathrus*), and arguably more elegant, *Epitonium turtonis* is much rarer. As such, it was highly sought after by Victorian collectors which meant that a decent specimen could set a dealer back several shillings or more. It is found around Britain but by nature, is an offshore dweller and its empty shells are very rarely to be found washed up on the beach. Its Latin name of *turtonis* does not refer to the great conchologist William Turton who first described it, as many expect, but to one of his daughters who pointed out to her father than this was a different species to *E. clathrus*. There is a related species, *Epitonium trevelyanum*, which is known from a handful of offshore records around Britain. Illustration shows *Epitonium turtonis* (left); *Epitonium trevelyanum* (right).

Description: H = 4.5cm; W = 1.25cm. Similar to *Epitonium clathrus* but larger with more ribs (12 on bodywhorl); colour = yellow-brown with purple banding. Etymology: *turtonis* = after William Turton's daughter.

116 – *Janthina janthina* (Linnaeus); Violet Sea Snail

The violet sea snail is an open ocean animal that floats just under the surface of the sea by creating a raft of bubbles out of mucus. They are drifters and as such, are subject to the vagaries of wind and current which may carry them many hundreds of kilometres. The violet sea snail feeds on cnidarians such as the small hydroid *Vellela* (sometimes called the by-the-wind-sailor) and the infamous Portuguese man-of-war (*Physalia* spp.). It will spend its entire life away from the land, but prolonged south-westerly winds may drive specimens away from the mid-Atlantic and onto British shores. It is most commonly found as an empty shell washed up on the beach, but live specimens are not unheard of and will sometimes be stranded with their prey. **(Warning – do not touch a Portuguese Man-of-War, even if it appears to be dead.)** It is most commonly found on the Atlantic exposed coasts and almost never in the North Sea or eastern English Channel. Three other similar but much rarer species have been reported from Britain.

Description: H = 4cm; W = 2.8cm. Shell shape resembles a land snail; floats on a raft of foam-like bubbles; upper surface of whorls light-coloured with violet or purple beneath. Etymology: *Janthina* & *janthina* = both meaning 'violet'.

117 – *Aclis ascaris* **(Turton)**

'It is impossible to mistake this minute and very elegant species,' wrote its discoverer William Turton in 1819, who then chose to name it after a tapeworm (*ascaris*). This shell is considered to be somewhat rare, although this may be a function of its small size, offshore habitat and restricted distribution to the northern and western coasts of Britain. It lives in sand and mud and is an unlikely find on the seashore, even when dead.

Description: H = 0.25cm; W = 0.06cm. Minute, tall, pointed; eight–nine whorls; deep suture; strong spiral striations (five on bodywhorl); umbilical chink; colour = white. Etymology: *Aclis* = a small javelin; *ascaris* = a tapeworm.

118 – *Aclis gulsonae* **(Clark)**

It was 1850 when William Clark named this minute shell, which is one of Britain's smallest molluscs, after Anne Cook Gulson (1809-1871), a woman from Leicestershire whose two teenage daughters lived and attended school in Exmouth, Devon. On her visits to Exmouth, Mrs Gulson developed an interest in seaweeds and was soon befriended by Clark, a conchologist who hoped to 'encourage her inclination to natural history'. Afterwards, Mrs Gulson was often to be seen in a boat with her two daughters, dredging the seabed, but she was frequently away from the coast because of her husband's work and it appears that although she made many interesting discoveries, including a new species of seaweed, she did not publish anything under her own name. This minute shell, which is only found offshore in sand and mud along the southern and western coasts, is a testimony to her otherwise unsung efforts.

Description: H = 0.16cm; W = 0.06cm. Cylindrical, thin, slender, transparent; six–seven whorls; smooth; wide aperture; colour = white. Etymology: *gulsonae* = after Anne Cook Gulson.

119 – *Aclis minor* **(Brown)**

Captain Thomas Brown (1785-1862) was responsible for naming this species after finding a specimen in Perthshire in 1827. Brown was the author of several conchological guides, but his efforts were not always appreciated. John Jeffreys wrote of his work 'The task of scrutinising this author's numerous ill-defined and often questionable species, and the mental torture caused by hammering at the horrible names he invented, are enough to give any one not having nerves of catgut a most excruciating headache.' Perhaps this species is a case in point, for although Brown named it *minor*, it is actually the largest of the *Aclis* species but still ranks as one Britain's smallest shells and one of the rarest. In Victorian times, precious specimens were swapped backwards and forwards by conchologists anxious to see the shell for themselves. Even today, it is rarely reported and usually only as a part of scientific surveys. For the amateur conchologist, the best hope of finding a specimen probably relies upon either dredging for material offshore and then carefully sieving and searching the sediment for empty specimens. It is absent from the North Sea and eastern English

Channel. A related species, *Aclis walleri*, is known only from Plymouth and Orkney where it lives in deep water. Illustration shows *Aclis minor* (left); *Aclis walleri* (right).

Description: H = 0.6cm; W = 0.25cm. Resembles *Aclis ascaris* but is larger with more rounded whorls; 12 whorls; ornamentation variable but usually strong spiral striations; deep umbilicus; colour = white. Etymology: *minor* = smaller.

120 – *Graphis albida* (Kanmacher)

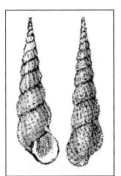

Named by the microscope pioneer Frederick Kanmacher, *Graphis albida* is another minute shell that, according to one conchologist, enjoys making its home amongst 'mud that has an offensive odour'. It has been noted for its tenacity and was once observed by William Clark to make repeated escape attempts from an aquarium: 'However often brushed down,' he noted, 'it starts again with unabated vigour.' It occurs on all British coasts in sand and mud on the lower shore and, although reasonably common, must be searched for with some care due to its small size.

Description: H = 0.4cm. Small, narrow and needle-like; 9-10 whorls; numerous ribs and spiral striations which intersect to form a fine reticulate pattern; no umbilicus; colour = white. Etymology: *Graphis* = a brush; *albida* = white.

Obelisk Shells

Obelisk Shells (Superfamily Eulimacea) are small (often minute) and needle-shaped with a smooth or glossy surface. They may occasionally be found on the lower shore, but are more commonly encountered in offshore waters. Because they are small and superficially similar, Eulimacea can only really be identified through access to a good dissecting microscope and a specialist guide, such as *Molluscs: Prosobranch and Pyramidellid Gastropods* (Graham, A., Linnean Society of London, 1988).

121 – *Crinophtheiros collinsi* (Sykes)

The first specimens of this species were dredged in deep water off Guernsey around 1901 by James Thomas Marshall, who believed it to be a variety of *Vitreolina philippi*. A couple of years later, some further specimens were hauled from the same locality by James Charles Collins (1870-1903) who, being unable to identify them, handed them to the Dorset conchologist Ernest Ruthven Sykes (1867-1954). Sykes declared the shells to be a new species, but before they could be described Collins, who was aged just 33, died. Sykes named the shell after its discoverer, whom he describes as 'a painstaking dredger of the Channel Islands'. It was afterwards found to live in sand and mud in deep water along much of the western coast of Britain but it is very rare and I am not aware of any recent reports.

Description: H = 0.4cm; W = 0.1cm. Resembles *Vitreolina philippi* but is straighter; approximately 10 whorls with an angled protoconch; colour = white with bluish tinge. Etymology: *Crinophtheiros* = possibly meaning thin hair; *collinsi* = after James Collins.

122 – *Eulima bilineata* (Alder)

A small, smooth and pointed shell that was first described by Joshua Alder in 1848 but which has received little attention from conchologists since. It is quite common and is relatively easy to distinguish, even with the naked eye, although a hand lens is needed to make a secure identification. John Jeffreys notes that his live specimens did not like being immersed in sea water and would immediately crawl out of the Petri dish in which he had placed them. This is odd as *Eulima bilineata* is predominantly a sublittoral species. It is found around Britain in muddy sand and is rarely encountered alive on the shore, although empty shells may be a reasonably common.

Description: H = 0.75cm; W = 0.2cm. Tall, narrow and pointed; 10-11 flat whorls; colour = off white with two adjacent reddish yellow lines encircling the lower half of the upper whorls. Etymology: *Eulima* = highly polished; *bilineata* = two lined.

123 – *Eulima glabra* (da Costa)

The London-based British conchologist Emanuel da Costa described this species in 1778 after being sent three specimens from Exmouth, Devon, which, he informs us, were 'found in the stomach of a common *Stella marina* [starfish]'. Da Costa's description is vague, and early conchologists found it easy to confuse *Eulima glabra* with *Eulima bilineata*, although the two species are quite distinct. Aside from being much larger, *E. glabra* also has many more brown spiral bands on its body whorl. It is an offshore species living in sand or mud around much of Britain (except the North Sea) and it is, in general, rarely encountered except by those conchologists who choose to dredge for their specimens.

Description: H = 1.25cm; W = 0.25cm. Tall, pointed and glossy; 12-13 whorls; aperture narrow, occupying one-third the total height; off white with a reddish-yellow spiral band on upper whorls and three (occasionally more) on the bodywhorl. Etymology: *glabra* = smooth.

124 – *Melanella alba* (da Costa)

Although not especially small, this is a tricky species to find as it lives in the company of the sea cucumber *Neopentadactyla mixta* with which it forms a parasitic relationship. Furthermore, *Neopentadactyla mixta* itself is not all that common as it likes to bury itself offshore, in coarse sand and gravel and in fast flowing currents. Its discoverer, Emanuel da Costa, knew nothing of this association and based his 1778 description on some empty shells he had received from southern England. The sea cucumber and *Melanella alba* are found around Britain but most specimens are obtained as empty shells.

Description: H = 1.8cm; W = 0.5cm. Club-shaped, opaque and glossy; 15 to 18 whorls, the last of which forms a third of overall height; colour = cream or white. Etymology: *Melanella* = a small *Melania*; *alba* = white.

125 – *Melanella frielei* (Jordan)

Named by H. K. Jordan (1838-1923) after the little-known Norwegian naturalist Herman Friele (1838-1921), who lived in Bergen and was possibly related to the coffee merchant family of that name whose company still operates from that city. The manner in which this shell leans to the right is reminiscent of a wonky church steeple. *Melanella frielei* may be found in western and northern coasts. It is not rare but obtaining specimens will be troublesome for the beach-based conchologist, as the animal generally lives at depths of fifteen metres or more. SCUBA diving or dredging is an option but most will simply have to rely on a good storm or strong currents bringing specimens into the littoral zone. It has been observed to float just above the sediment surface, possibly by filling its upper whorls with air.

Description: H = 1.1cm; W = 0.12cm. Spindle-shaped, semi-transparent and lustrous; 15 to 16 whorls, flattened and ornamented with numerous fine striae; colour = white. Etymology: *frielei* = after Herman Friele.

126 – *Melanella lubrica* (Monterosato)

Named in 1890 by the Marquis of Monterosato (Tommaso de Maria; 1841-1927), an Italian gentleman conchologist who based himself in Palermo. *Melanella lubrica* is a Mediterranean species that reaches the south-western tip of England. As such, it is a rarely encountered British species, specimens of which are currently fetching several pounds apiece at shell auctions. This is a deep-water dweller (usually below 40 metres) that is thought to be parasitic and to live in association with sea cucumbers.

Description: H = 0.45cm. Sharply conical, glossy, solid with a pointed apex; 10 to 12 whorls, flat sided, shallow suture; body whorl is approximately a quarter of height; cream colour with mottled brown patches; sometimes with white apex. Etymology: *lubrica* = slippery.

127 – *Polygireulima polita* (Linnaeus)

Described in 1758 by Carl Linnaeus. In 1867, John Jeffreys wrote of this species: 'It would be a beautiful object for the aquarium, with its pencilled tentacles, golden markings and its bright eyes peering through the porcelain shell.' He is right. This is indeed an attractive animal and, at nearly 2cm in height, it is large enough to be appreciated with the naked eye. It is an offshore dweller in muddy sand around all of Britain, but it does not live as deep as most of the other Eulimacea species and is tolerably common, especially in the south of Britain where specimens will occasionally be cast up onto the beach.

Description: H = 1.8cm; W = 0.5cm. Large, smooth, solid and pointed; aperture ovate or oval; 13-14 flat whorls; colour = white. Etymology: *Polygireulima* = many whorled *Eulima*; *polita* = polished.

128 – *Vitreolina curva* (Monterosato)

This shell was described in 1874 from specimens obtained by the Marquis of Monterosato off the Italian coast. It is a deep sea animal (rarely seen above 40 metres) that was assumed to be restricted to southern Europe until specimens were recovered from Cornwall and the Scilly and Channel Islands. It lives in muddy sand and is exceedingly rare with few modern British reports.

Description: H = 0.4cm. Solid, conical, glossy with a distinctive sinistral curve in the last three–four whorls; seven–eight flattened whorls the last of which occupies about a third of the height; suture shallow; colour variable but generally cream background with reddish-brown mottling. Etymology: *Vitreolina* = glassy; *curva* = curved.

129 – *Vitreolina philippi* (Rayneval and Ponzi)

Named after the German zoologist Rodolfo Philippi (1808-1904) who, as a permanent resident of Santiago, Chile, made a minor contribution to European conchology but who is celebrated for his fine illustrated monographs. In contrast to most of the British Eulimacea species, *Vitreolina philippi* is both reasonably common and littoral in its habit. It is an ectoparasite that likes to live with various species of heart urchin (burrowing echinoderms which are sometimes referred to as sea potatoes) and so may best be obtained by digging on the lower part of sandy shores. (Although I have seen it written that the best way of obtaining live specimens is to collect a tub full of sediment, cover it with sea water and then leave it alone for an hour, by which time any living animals will have worked their way to the surface.) It occurs around most of Britain (except the southern North Sea and eastern English Channel) where it lives in sand and mud in association with burrowing echinoids. Empty shells should be sought by sieving sand on the lowest part of the beach. Alas, worn specimens do not retain the glossy translucent quality of live ones and tend to be quite dull and opaque.

Description: H = 0.8cm; W = 0.2cm. Minute, slender, thin, semi-transparent and glossy; 10-15 flattened whorls; shallow suture; no ornamentation; colour = clear white. Etymology: *philippi* = after Rodolfo Armando Philippi.

Chapter Four

Neogastropods

THE NEOGASTROPODS ('new gastropods') are believed to have evolved around 70 million years ago, during the last days of the dinosaurs. They are distinguished from the other orders of gastropod by the possession of only one gill, one auricle and one kidney (a feature shared with the Mesogastropods) and also a siphon (an extensible tube which is formed from a fold of the mantle and is used to draw water into the mantle cavity). This group is generally considered to be the most advanced of the prosobranch molluscs and includes many large, robust and easily recognisable shells such as the whelks.

Whelks

The whelks (Superfamily Muricacea ('rough' or 'prickly') are a large family of robust shells that are well-adapted to our cool seas. The commercially fished common whelk (*Buccinum undatum*) is probably the most famous species, but there are many smaller species, such as the dog whelk (*Nucella lapillus*), which are more colourful and easier to find. Most whelks are large and may be identified with relative ease using general guides to the seashore.

130 – *Nucella lapillus* (Linnaeus); Dog Whelk

The Victorian conchologist William Bean of Scarborough had a fondness for the dog whelk which may be both obvious and abundant on our sea shore. 'Old Bean', as this venerable and aged conchologist was often called, recalled how he had once sent his granddaughter down to Scarborough Pier on an errand, but the girl took her time and was scolded by her grandfather. The young girl burst into tears and, on raising her apron to wipe her eyes, dropped several seashells onto the ground. One of them was a very rare left-hand (sinistral) coiling dog whelk. The granddaughter was immediately forgiven. Some fishermen dislike the dog whelk because it feeds upon shell-fish including commercial species such as mussels, but in historical times it was much prized as a source of a pigment that could be used to dye clothing purple. Finding dog whelk specimens (alive or empty shells) should present no problem whatsoever as they occur around Britain on most rocky shores and are sometimes abundant. They are highly variable both in colour and patterning. Some older specimens may even be covered in barnacles and other encrusting organisms.

Description: H = 4cm; W = 2.5cm; shell very solid; broadly conical with short spire; ornamentation consists of many striations which vary from fine to prominent; larger specimens may be encrusted with barnacles; colour = very variable including white, yellow, brown and banded varieties. Etymology: *Nucella* = possibly meaning small kernel; *lapillus* = a pebble.

131 – *Ocenebra erinacea* (Linnaeus); European Sting Winkle

Named by Carl Linnaeus after a hedgehog (*erinaceus*), the Sting Winkle was once known as the 'urchin shell' because of its spiky outline. It has been loathed by fishermen because of its ability to drill a small hole into the shells of oysters, through which it would place its proboscis and then kill and digest the animal inside. The destruction wreaked on the old-fashioned oyster beds by sting winkles was considerable, but the recent propagation of oysters in plastic or metal sacks has lessened the effect of their predation. The sting winkle is rugged, handsome, if slightly dull-coloured, and interesting to look at. It is generally only found in southern and western areas of Britain, but it is reasonably common and may be found alive on the lowest part of the beach, usually among rocks or seaweed. Some historical records describe it as being abundant, but this is not my general experience and may infer that the decline of offshore oyster beds (see common oyster; *Ostrea edulis*) may also have lowered the overall numbers of sting winkles.

Description: H = 6cm; W = 3cm. A very robust and angular shell; 8 to 10 whorls; strong spiral striations and angular ribs; aperture oval; colour: yellowish-white to brown. Etymology: *Ocenebra* = possibly meaning dwarfed; *erinacea* = hedgehog.

132 – *Ocinebrina aciculata* (Lamarck)

This species is more commonly found in southern Europe and is something of a British rarity. It has been found rarely in the Scilly Islands and more commonly in Channel Islands but is probably also native to parts of Cornwall and Devon. Live shells were once commonly found at very low tide on the Channel Island of Herm but from the 1840s onward, over-collecting by visiting conchologists managed to reduce its numbers considerably. Larger populations in southern Europe have been affected by the use of tributyltin (TBT), an anti-fouling paint used on boats during the 1970s and 1980s, which disrupted its ability to reproduce. The live animal is quite distinctive, being bright scarlet in colour, and is generally to be found on rocky coasts, among or under stones.

Description: H = 1.5cm; W = 0.6cm; solid shell with strong ornamentation; seven whorls; strong ribs crossed by spiral striations; aperture narrow and slit-like. Etymology: *Ocinebrina* = small *Ocenebra*; *aciculata* = finely pointed.

133 – *Urosalpinx cinerea* (Say); American Oyster Drill

First described in 1822 by the pioneering American zoologist and Quaker apothecary Thomas Say (1787-1834), the American oyster drill is a relatively recent import from the USA. It is a predator of oysters and was first noticed in Britain in the 1920s, when specimens were found living along the Essex coast in areas associated with commercial oyster beds. The decline of the native oyster population in the Nineteenth Century (see *Ostrea edulis*) led to the importation of disease-resistant American oysters and it is believed that *Urosalpinx cinerea* was accidentally imported with them. Following its initial identification in 1927, *U. cinerea* spread its way along the coast to Kent and looked to be an established part of the marine fauna but then, after World War II, it became rare and disappeared from some areas altogether. It is only thought to survive in small populations in the oyster grounds off Whitstable, Kent, and in some Essex estuaries (e.g. Blackwater and Crouch). The cause of this decline is uncertain, but *U. cinerea* is known to be especially sensitive to tributyltin (see notes on the species above) which was used until a UK ban in 1987. *U. cinerea* is currently rare in Britain and largely restricted to the Kent coast, although isolated reports have been made from other parts of the southern and south-eastern coasts as well as the Channel Islands.

Description: H = 3cm; W = 1.7cm. Resembles *Ocenebra erinacea* but is less ornamented with rounded ribs and no varices; seven whorls; multiple strong ribs intersected by numerous spiral ridges; canal is open; colour = white with brown banding. Etymology: *Urosalpinx* = possibly meaning burning/stinging trumpet; *cinerea* = ash-coloured.

134 – *Trophon muricatus* (Montagu)

Since its description by George Montagu in 1803, few conchologists have been interested enough in this small shell to say much about it. It is, however, an attractive species, especially under the microscope when its robust but intricate ornamentation may be properly viewed. It is an offshore species but its empty shell is remarkably hardy and may be found on the beach, although it is difficult to spot with the naked eye.

Description: H = 1.3cm; W = 0.6cm; shell solid; many longitudinal ribs and pronounced striations; six–eight whorls; long siphonal canal terminating in deep notch; colour yellowish-white to pink. Etymology: *Trophon* = after Trophonius, a mythical god; *muricatus* = prickly.

135 – *Trophon truncatus* (Ström)

First described by the Norwegian clergyman and zoologist Hans Ström (1726-1797), from specimens obtained along the Scandinavian coastline, *Trophon truncatus* is an Arctic species whose southerly range includes western and north-eastern Britain. Although found on the lower shore in the northern-most part of its range, most British specimens have been obtained offshore from mud and sand. It is relatively rare.

Description: H = 1.5cm; W = 0.7cm. Robust, conical; seven whorls, deep sutures; strong ribs on lower whorls (approximately 20 on last whorl); broad aperture, open siphonal canal; colour = yellow-brown. Etymology: *truncatus* = truncated.

136 – *Beringius turtoni* (Bean)

This 'is one of the rarest and most beautiful of British shells,' wrote Edward Forbes of this species in 1853. It was a comparatively late addition to the British fauna, being discovered in 1834 by William Bean of Scarborough, who dredged it from deep water off the Dogger Bank and afterwards named it in honour of his fellow conchologist William Turton (who died shortly afterwards). John Jeffreys remarks of Bean that he did much to promote the cause of natural history in the north of England and that he was 'true in all his dealings – not a common virtue in these times'. This shell was known to Yorkshire fishermen who called it 'long-neck' but it is comparatively rare and is found only in deep water off the Yorkshire and Scottish coasts, where it lives on rocky coasts and therefore unlikely to come into the hands of the casual beachcomber.

Description: H = 13cm; W = 6cm. Large, solid, tall; seven–eight rounded whorls; deep suture; numerous distinct spiral striations crossed by oblique growth lines; wide aperture with flared outer lip; colour = white, periostracum green/yellow. Etymology: *Beringius* = after Vitus Bering; *turtoni* = after William Turton.

137 – *Buccinum humphreysianum* (Bennett)

This rare, and somewhat elegant shell, was first found living off Bearhaven, Cork, in the 1820s by the naturalist and author John D. Humphreys (1775-1864) after whom it was named by Edward Bennett (1797-1836) in 1824. This locality turned out to be at the very southern limit of this species' geographical range, and in the coming decades it was only found in a handful of other localities, all of them off the Scottish coast. As a deep water dweller, *Buccinum humphreysianum* is seldom seen these days. The last British records of which I am aware are over a century old, although there are probably more recent ones which have escaped my notice. The conchologist James Marshall once came across some shells exhibited as *B. humphreysianum* at a Conchological Society meeting in London which were alleged to have been found in the shallow seas around Jersey. Given its deep water preference, Marshall remarked that the shells either 'could not have been *B. humphreysianum* or they could not have come from Jersey.' It is a deep water animal that lives on sand and gravel, and whose shells are most unlikely to be found on the seashore. The illustration has a more complex colouration than most specimens.

Description: 4.5cm; W = 2.5cm. Smaller, swollen, fragile; eight very rounded whorls with numerous fine spiral striations; suture deep; aperture broad with thin outer lip; colour = white. Etymology: *Buccinum* = a shell-trumpet; *undatum* = after John Humphreys.

138 – *Buccinum undatum* **(Linnaeus); Common Whelk**

The common whelk is familiar to most seaside visitors as the salty, succulent animal that is sold by the carton from seafood stalls on piers and along the beachfront. As such, it is one of the rare molluscs whose soft parts are more often seen by the public than its hard shell. Nonetheless, the empty shell of the common whelk is far from rare and specimens may be readily obtained with little effort along most of Britain's coastline, where it lives on variety of substrates including rock and sand. The common whelk is a commercially fished species that has been eaten for centuries by a majority of Britain's seaside communities. The animals are caught using baited pots which entice dozens of individuals into them at a time. This practice is centuries old and has been very lucrative. In 1504, for example, a feast to celebrate the appointment of an Archbishop of Canterbury saw 8,000 whelks consumed at a cost of some 40 shillings. By the 1860s, the whelk industry at Whitstable was worth over £12,000 a year to the town and was second only to its oyster fisheries. Because of its importance, the whelk is known by many different names. In Scotland it is called the 'buckie'; in the Isle of Man it is a 'mutlag' and in the Channel Islands, a 'v'lique'. The empty shells are frequently gathered by tourists as souvenirs, but those that remain on the beach are often used as homes by larger hermit crabs such as *Pagurus bernhardus*. The animal itself lives offshore and is often prey for large fish species such as cod. Its sponge-like egg cases may be frequently found cast up on the strandline during springtime. These were at one time called 'sea-wash balls' because sailors would use them to clean their hands in the absence of any soap.

Description: H = 10cm; W = 6cm; a robust and distinctive shell; six–seven whorls the last of which may occupy two-thirds of the height; ornamentation consists of deep ribs and fine striations; aperture is wide and oval in shape. Etymology: *Buccinum* = a shell-trumpet; *undatum* = wavy.

139 – *Chauvetia brunnea* **(Donovan)**

Named in 1804 by the Irish conchologist Edward Donovan (1768-1837) in his multivolume *Natural History of British Shells*, (a work that was immediately eclipsed by the publication of George Montagu's monumental *Testacea Britannica*). Donovan is one of many historical naturalists who started life wealthy, but whose passion for specimens drained their resources to such a degree that they ended up in poverty. In contrast to the large and well-distributed common whelk (*Buccinum undatum*), this species is small and quite restricted in its distribution. It somewhat resembles a miniature version of the common whelk and was for some time known as 'the smallest whelk' to conchologists. It is a southern European species which, up until the 1840s, had not been discovered alive on our coast, leading to the idea that the then known specimens had been dumped from trawlers returning from southern waters. It is, however, unquestionably a British species, but it is restricted to western and southern coasts and is only common in the Channel Islands where it lives low on rocky shores. The shell is often dark brown in life but on death it will take on a much redder hue.

Description: H = 0.5cm; W = 0.25cm; a small elongate shell; strong ribs with many fine striations; six–seven whorls; colour = brown. Etymology: *Chauvetia* = after G. Chauvet; *brunnea* = brown.

140 – *Colus gracilis* (da Costa)

A large, slender and handsome shell first described by Emanuel da Costa in 1778. It is found around Britain but is more common in the north, where it used to be known as the 'borer' by fishermen – perhaps because its regular spiral ornamentation resembles the thread on a screw. It is inedible, but in historical times it was common for fishermen to slip a few specimens in with their edible whelks to bulk out their catch. Like all whelks, it is a scavenger and generally lives some distance offshore on sand and mud, but its robust shell may occasionally be found on the beach.

Description: H = 7.5cm; W = 3.5cm; a slender shell with straight-sided profile; many fine spiral striations; nine whorls; colour = white. Etymology: *Colus* = a distaff; *gracilis* = slender.

141 – *Colus islandicus* (Mohr); Icelandic Whelk

The Icelandic whelk is a very large sea shell and quite spectacular, but it is also rare in our waters and is generally restricted to deeper waters in the northern parts of Britain, although it has been found in southern areas too. Large specimens have long been sought after by conchologists and were eagerly swapped or purchased by collectors. The Icelandic whelk is a cold water species that has been discovered at depths of 3,000 metres. It is speculated that warmer sea temperatures (perhaps as consequence of climate change) might be driving it to the north, away from our shores altogether.

Description: H = 13.8cm; W = 5cm. Large, spindle-shaped but delicate for its size; seven–nine rounded whorls, the last of which has an elongate 'tail' which, together with the body whorl, occupies a third of the overall height; suture deep; colour = white or pinkish-white. Etymology: *islandicus* = Icelandic.

142 – *Hinia incrassata* (Ström); Thick-Lipped Dog Whelk

The Seventeenth Century naturalist James Petiver, called this shell the 'small Gibraltar ruggle' but it is better known as one of the dog whelks which also include the distantly-related species *Nucella lapillus* (dog whelk). The thick-lipped dog whelk is easily confused with the netted dog whelk (*Hinia reticulata*) but it is smaller, with generally more inflated whorls. It is abundant on all our sandy shores among eelgrass (*Zostera*) and close to stones. It is very robust but check any empty specimens for hermit crabs which frequently utilise these shells.

Description: H = 1.3cm; W = 0.8cm; resembles *Hinia reticulata* but is small and thicker with an aperture that is rounded with a smaller number of pointed teeth on inner lip; eight–nine whorls; colour = pale-buff. Etymology: *Hinia* = possibly after an Egyptian measurement unit; *incrassata* = thickened.

143 – *Hinia pygmaea* (Lamarck); Small Dog Whelk

Named by the French evolutionary scientist Jean-Baptiste Lamarck (1744-1829), the small dog whelk is in fact marginally larger than the thick-lipped dog whelk (*Hinia incrassata*) with better defined ridges and a wider, more rounded aperture. It is not generally a littoral species, but it may be found in shallow water on western and southern coasts and is noted as being common or even abundant in some areas. It is the most attractive of the dog whelks.

Description: H = 1.4cm; W = 0.8cm. Resembles Hinia incrassata but is more slender; many ribs (15-20 on bodywhorl) intersected by spiral striations; each whorl has a varix; colour varies as with *Hinia incrassata* but lacks brown blotch on its base. Etymology: *pygmaea* = dwarfed.

144 – *Hinia reticulata* (Linnaeus); Netted Dog Whelk

Described by Carl Linnaeus, large numbers of netted dog whelks may often be found crowded around dead crabs, fish or other sources of meat. When underwater, the animal is not at all shy and will plough its way through soft sediment, leaving an obvious trail behind it. But on the retreat of the tide, it will bury itself in the sand at an angle, creating a small hillock on the beach. They are found on sandy shores around Britain and are often seen inside crab and lobster pots which they enter in order to raid the bait.

Description: H = 3.5cm; W = 2cm; a solid, rotund shell; thick longitudinal ribs intersected by many fine spiral striations giving the shell its distinctive net-like appearance; 10 whorls; the aperture is small with 8 to 12 teeth on the outer lip; colour = buff. Etymology: *reticulata* = reticulated.

145 – *Neptunea antiqua* (Linnaeus, 1758); Red Whelk

Most red whelk specimens are about the same size as a common whelk (*Buccinum undatum*), but over the decades a number of so-called 'monstrous forms' have come to light, including some that reach 20cm in height. Although not eaten today, the red whelk was highly prized among London's Victorian working classes who called it 'almond'. The liver was particularly sought and is said to have been 'more fat and tender than a lobster'. Red whelks shells are common in coastal fossil deposits and in some areas, shells found on the beach may be fossil specimens that have washed out of the cliffs. It lives offshore on a variety of rocky and sandy substrates around Britain but tends to be rarer in the south. Empty shells may be washed up onto the beach, but the best specimens are obtained using a dredge or by begging a favour from a friendly whelk fisherman.

Description: H = 8.5 but can reach 20cm; W = 5cm; broadly resembles *Buccinum undatum* but is more slender, has a narrower aperture and is without the thick ribbing; seven–eight whorls; many fine spiral striations; yellowish or reddish-white. Etymology: *Neptunea* = after Neptune; *antiqua* = ancient.

Turret Shells

The turret shells (Superfamily Conacea = 'conical') are generally small, robust and highly ornamented. They mostly live offshore, but their empty shells may sometimes be found washed up on the beach. The family is worldwide and very diverse; British species tend to be restricted to the warmer waters of the western and southern coasts. A good many of the species below were first described by George Montagu in his 1803 book *Testacea Britannica*, a work which is responsible for naming many small British shells, and were based on specimens he obtained from various parts of England and Wales.

146 – *Comarmondia gracilis* (**Montagu**)

Small, elegant and somewhat whelk-like its appearance, *Comarmondia gracilis* is a warmer water species whose range clips the southern parts of Britain (although individual specimens are known from further north). It lives offshore on sand and gravel, often in the company of the auger shell (*Turritella communis*) but its empty shell may occasionally be found on the beach.

Description: H = 2.5cm; W = 1cm. Distinctive, elongate, solid; 10-11 rounded whorls; deep suture; many strong ribs (14-16 on bodywhorl) intersected by numerous spiral striations; outer lip has a fissure where it joins body; colour = red-brown with white banding. Etymology: *Comarmondia* = meaning unknown; *gracilis* = slender.

147 – *Haedropleura septangularis* (**Montagu**)

Another of George Montagu's 1803 discoveries, this is a relatively rare British shell whose range is restricted to the southern and western coasts where it lives in sand and gravel. It is listed as a littoral species, but most conchologists seem to have obtained their specimens using a dredge. Empty shells found onshore tend to be battered and worn.

Description: H = 1.5cm; W = 0.5cm; a small, thick shell; eight–nine whorls; prominent ribs; aperture narrow; colour = chestnut or red-brown with paler ribs. Etymology: *Haedropleura* = possibly meaning water ribs; *septangularis* = heptagonal.

148 – *Mangelia attenuata* (Montagu)

The genus *Mangelia* is named after the Italian naturalist Guiseppe Mangili (1767-1829) who, amongst other things, was renowned for his work with venomous snakes. This genus contains a multiplicity of similar-looking species, many of which have been little studied or commented on by conchologists. This shell, for example, is described as being beautiful by several shell collectors (which it is) but they have little else to add, although William Clark did note that 'the male organ is a pea-green colour'. It has been found around Britain, but is more common in the west. It lives offshore in sand or muddy sand, but empty shells do get washed onto the beach.

Description: H = 1.9cm; W = 0.6cm. Slender, solid; nine whorls; 9-10 longitudinal ribs; aperture about half the height; canal elongated; colour = orange-brown with red-brown banding. Etymology: *Mangelia* = after Guiseppe Mangili; *attenuata* = attenuated.

149 – *Mangelia brachystoma* (Philippi)

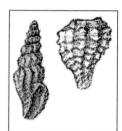

Named by Rudolph Philippi (see *Gibbula pennanti*), its Latin name of 'short mouth' (*brachystomum*) is a reference to its thin, elongate aperture. This shell is found offshore around Britain on sand and under stones. It is uncommon but darker specimens, which may be red-brown in colour, are prominent in shell sand samples. Paler specimens may sometimes have an orange band on the outermost part of its whorls. Illustration shows *Mangelia brachystoma* with detail of body-whorl.

Description: H = 0.75cm; W = 0.25cm. Small, solid; eight–nine rounded whorls; seven–nine strong longitudinal ridges; many spiral striations (15 on bodywhorl); colour = brown. H: SL to OS; muddy and sandy substrates and under stones. Etymology: *brachystoma* = short mouthed.

150 – *Mangelia coarctata* (Forbes)

First described by Joshua Alder in 1840, the living animal was shortly afterwards described by the Victorian conchologist William Clark, as being 'azure, shot with brilliant snow-white streams'. The shell is visually similar to *Mangelia brachystoma* but is generally larger, regular and more slender. It is widely distributed on the lower shore among sand and mud, but is perhaps more frequent in western regions.

Description: H = 1.2cm; W = 0.5cm. Small, solid, turreted; eight–nine whorls; seven–eight ribs on lower whorls; no striations; colour = yellow with dark brown banding. Etymology: *coarctata* = uncertain possibly concerns boxes.

151 – *Mangelia nebula* (**Montagu**)

Described by George Montagu in 1803, the shell is very variable in shape and colour which soon led to it being afforded three different subspecies, two of which were dwarf forms with the third being larger and more elongate. The Victorians were fond of creating such subspecies (or varieties), but modern science generally frowns upon such excessive 'splitting' and few such 'varieties', as they are called, have survived through to the modern day. Live specimens of this shell may be obtained in southern and western regions by digging in sand on the lowest part of the shore. Empty shells are not uncommon.

Description: H = 2cm; W = 0.5cm. A narrow, pointed shell; 9 to 11 whorls; thick ribs and fine spiral striations; aperture narrow and curved; colour = yellowish-white. Etymology: *nebula* = vapour.

152 – *Mangelia powisiana* (**Dautzenberg**)

Named in 1887 by the Belgian conchologist Philippe Dautzenberg, (1849-1935), *Mangelia powisiana* is a relatively common, but fairly unremarkable shell, that burrows in soft sand on the lowest part of the shore in the south-west of England. It has at times, been regarded as a variety of *Mangelia nebula* but it is more slender with a narrower aperture and less pronounced ribs and striations.

Description: H = 1.5cm; W = 0.5cm. Solid, tall, narrow, pointed; 9-10 flat whorls with around 10 ribs (costae) on middle whorls; numerous distinct spiral striations and a broader furrow below the sutures; aperture long and narrow; colour = brown with darker spiral banding. Etymology: *powisiana* = after Powis.

153 – *Mangelia rugulosa* (**Philippi**)

First described by the German conchologist Rudolph Philippi, this small species is a warm-water form that is exceedingly rare in Britain and is known only from Cornwall and the Channel Islands, where it was found offshore in sand. It has only a handful of British records, all of which are over a century old and so may be extinct in this part of the Atlantic.

Description: H – 0.6cm; W = 0.3cm. Resembles *Mangelia coarctata* but may be distinguished by its boarder base, shorter spire, thickened ribs and uneven striations on the body whorl; colour = yellowish-white occasionally with brown banding. Etymology: *rugulosa* = wrinkled.

154 – *Mangelia smithii* (Forbes)

Formerly known as *Pleurotoma striolata*, this shell has recently reverted to the name afforded to it by Edward Forbes in 1840 which honoured his friend and dredging partner James Smith. *Mangelia smithii* is another relatively rare shell from southern Europe that may sometimes be found on sand and mud in southern and western regions. It is elegant with a noticeably narrow, elongate and crenulated aperture and a deep reticulated pattern on its whorls.

Description: H = 1.5cm; W = 0.5cm. Solid, tall, narrow, pointed; eight slightly rounded whorls; very strong wavy ribs (around eight or nine per whorl) crossed by very fine striations; suture deep; aperture elongate and narrow; colour = pale brown or yellow. Etymology: *smithii* = James Smith.

155 – *Oenopota rufa* (Montagu)

A cold water species found on the Arctic coasts of Greenland and Scandinavia, and also widespread and common around the entire British coast. Like most of the Turridae species, *Oenopota rufa* buries in soft sediment but it may be found around Britain by digging and sieving on the lowest part of the beach. The Latin name (*rufa*) afforded to it by George Montagu, refers to the red colour of its shell which is striking in life but which fades considerably after death.

Description: H = 1.2cm; W = 0.5cm. Small, solid; prominent ribs; seven whorls; colour = purplish-brown with paler ribs. Etymology: *Oenopota* = meaning unknown; *rufa* = red-coloured.

156 – *Oenopota turricula* (Montagu)

'There is no British shell with which this pretty species can be confused,' wrote Edward Forbes in 1853. This is preferentially northern in distribution, but specimens have sometimes been found in the English Channel, albeit very rarely. It is robust and attractive with the shell colour varying from milky-white to a dark yellow and has been popular with shell collectors and conchologists through the ages.

Description: H = 1.6cm; W = 0.6cm. Robust, turreted; seven–eight flat whorls; deep suture; strong ribs intersected by fine spiral striations; colour = white tinged with rose. Etymology: *turricula* = turreted.

157 – *Raphitoma boothii* (**Brown**)

Named in 1839 by William Brown after Henry Gore Booth, an aristocratic naturalist who worked at the Andersonian Museum in Glasgow during the 1830s. This is a robust, highly ornamented and somewhat spiky sea shell that is reasonably common on a variety of substrates, including sand, rocks and gravel. It was first dredged off the Isle of Arran by the naturalist James Smith in 1838, and then formally described by his cousin William Brown. It has since been found across the northern, western and southern coasts of Britain but it appears to be rare or absent in much of the North Sea.

Description: H = 1.5cm; W = 0.6cm. Strong curved ribs crossed by deep striations; oval aperture with a flared outer lip; colour = white or cream with faint red and purple patches. Etymology: *Raphitoma* = meaning unknown; *boothii* = after Henry Booth.

158 – *Raphitoma echinata* (**Brocchi**)

First discovered in the Mediterranean and described by the Italian geologist Giovanni Brocchi, little has been written about this species over the years, although John Jeffreys does note that his specimens vary greatly in size. Its distribution and occurrence is similar to *Raphitoma boothii*, which restricts it to western and southern coasts where it has a preference for coarse sediment such as gravel or shell-sand in shallow offshore waters.

Description: H = 1.2cm; W = 0.5cm. Shell conic, slender, glossy and semi-transparent; 9 to 10 highly convex whorls the last whorl of which is elongated into a siphon; there are strong ribs and striations which intersect to produce a strong lattice effect that may be prickly to the touch; outer lip crenulated; colour yellow with mottle-brown streaks. Etymology: *echinata* = prickly.

159 – *Raphitoma linearis* (**Montagu**)

A somewhat sluggish and retiring species that may be found hiding inside old bivalves or under rocks on the lowest part of the beach. It was first named by George Montagu and is the smallest of the *Raphitoma* species. It is widely distributed about the British coast on the lower shore under or among large stones.

Description: H = 0.8cm; W = 0.4cm. Solid, narrow and small; eight–nine whorls; many strong ribs (12 on bodywhorl); fine spiral striations (12 on bodywhorl); colour = yellow-white with red-brown patterning. Etymology: *linearis* = linear.

160 – *Raphitoma purpurea* (Montagu)

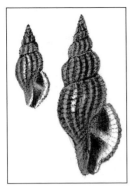

The largest of the *Raphitoma* species is also somewhat scarce in its occurrence and is more common in southern Britain than the north. It is a very striking shell whose surface is covered in a deeply incised reticulate pattern of ribs and striations with a wonderfully broad and crenulated outer lip. Larger specimens are readily identifiable using the naked eye and may be found by careful searching on the lower shore among muddy stones, or by sieving sediment in or around areas of eelgrass (*Zostera*) and oarweed (*Laminaria*).

Description: H = 2.5cm; W = 1cm. Shell solid and slim; strong ribs and striations intersect to give a reticulate ('netted') pattern; 12 whorls; aperture semi-circular with outer lip notched by spiral striations; colour = purple-brown, red-brown and chocolate.

Etymology: *purpurea* = purple.

Chapter Five

Heterostrophans

$\mathcal{T}$HE HETEROSTROPHAN (possibly meaning 'different headband') gastropods may be recognised by their protoconch (the top-most whorls which represent the youngest stage of the animal), which coil in the opposite direction to the adult whorls underneath. This order was, and remains, problematic. For many years they were believed to be part of the opisthobranchs (Chapter Six) or perhaps an evolutionary link between the opistho-branchs and other shelled gastropoda orders, such as the neogastropods. The evolutionary relationship between the individual heterostrophan species has not been resolved, but doubt-less forthcoming genetic studies will have more to say on the matter. Most British heterostrophan molluscs are minute which, combined with their propensity to live offshore, means that they are commonly overlooked. Most species are parasitic and may be found in association with specific types of marine worm, bivalve mollusc or echinoderm. Over a hundred species are known from Western Europe, but making a firm identification is diffi-cult and relies on subtle ornamental features. The use of a strong hand lens or microscope is essential, as is a specialist guide to the British species such as may be found in *Journal of Molluscan Studies* (Supplement 16; 1986) or *Molluscs: Prosobranch and Pyramidellid Gastropods* (Graham, A., Linnean Society of London, 1988).

Rissoellacea and Omalogyracea

The superfamilies Rissoellacea ('small *Rissoa*') and Omalogyracea ('flattened circle') are a large group of very minute, thin-shelled molluscs that may be found amongst seaweed in rock pools. Due to their small size, many species went largely unrecognised until the 1840s and 1950s when advances in microscope technology permitted conchologists to describe them in detail. Spotting these shells with the naked eye is very difficult and so most must be washed from sediment or seaweed into a fine sieve and then identified using a microscope.

161 – *Rissoella diaphana* (Alder)

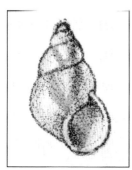

First described by Joshua Alder in 1848, it takes a sharp eye to find this delicate and diminutive shell on the seashore. *Rissoella diaphana* likes to hide itself in rock pools among seaweed, but can be teased out by placing a clump of weed into a small dish of seawater. After a while, the small shells will crawl out into the open to see what is happening. If several specimens emerge, then they will gravitate towards each other to form a cluster. Its Latin name means 'transparent' (*diaphana*) and is a reflection of the thin translucent nature of the shell. Despite being hard to find, it can be abundant on some sheltered rocky shores in the west and south of Britain.

Description: H = 0.2cm; W = 0.15cm. Minute, conical and solid; four–five rounded whorls; suture deep; aperture circular; colour = semi-transparent or white. Etymology: *Rissoella* = a small *Rissoa; diaphana* = transparent.

162 – *Rissoella globularis* (Forbes and Hanley)

This species managed to gain the attention of four of the most prolific Victorian conchologists. It was discovered in 1851 on the seashore at Skye by George Barlee who, as usual when confronted with unusual specimens, sent them to his friend John Gwyn Jeffreys. This gentleman, who would later pen the authoritative *British Conchology*, submitted a written description to Edward Forbes and Sylvanus Hanley who were at the time putting the finishing touches to their multi-volume *History of the British Mollusca*. Jeffreys' description made it into the appendices of the last volume in 1852, but although Jeffreys was the official describer, it is usually Forbes and Hanley who are credited with the honour. This animal lives on the Scottish coast, where it hides on the lower shore in rock pools among seaweeds and loose detritus, and it is sometimes described as being common. Its small size means that it is most often discovered using a hand lens or, better still, a microscope.

Description: H = 0.2cm; W = 0.15cm. Minute, fragile, globular; three–four very rounded whorls the last two of which occupy 80% of total height; deep sutures; surface smooth; prominent umbilicus; colour = semi-transparent. Etymology: *globularis* = globular.

163 – *Rissoella opalina* (Jeffreys)

Despite being a beach species that is commonly found in western and southern regions, its small size and ability to hide in weed led to it being overlooked by the naturalist community until 1848, when John Jeffreys described it. Victorian conchologists noticed that its distribution could be patchy but that it was usually abundant near to fish factories where discarded offal was discharged directly into the sea. Nowadays, the fish factories are mostly gone but *Rissoella opalina* remains quite localised in its occurrence and will be abundant on some shore and almost absent on others.

Description: H = 0.25cm; W = 0.17cm. Thin, globular and short; three–four highly rounded whorls, the last being 75% of height; deep suture; colour = horn to light yellow. Etymology: *opalina* = opal-like.

164 – *Cima minima* (Jeffreys)

At just 1mm in height, this is one of Britain's smallest shells. In fact, it is so small that for decades it must have passed through the sieves of many conchologists before finally being noticed by John Jeffreys in 1858. Naturally, finding this species is a difficulty in itself, especially as it often hides itself within the holdfasts of oarweed (*Laminaria*), but identifying it may be even more tricky and will require a decent microscope. Specimens are often dwarfed by the tests of foraminifera which, as single-celled organisms, are themselves amongst the smallest beach animals. *Cima minima* is found on most British coasts, with the exception of the North Sea and eastern English Channel.

Description: H = 0.1cm. Shell forms an oblong cone, very thin and lustrous; four–five convex whorls; longitudinal wavy striations. Colour = white. Etymology: *Cima* = summit; *minima* = smallest.

165 – *Ammonicerina rota* (Forbes and Hanley)

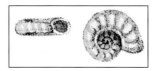

This attractive shell is tightly coiled, like an ammonite, but measures just 0.6mm across its broadest axis and is Britain's smallest species of mollusc. It cannot be seen without the aid of a microscope and can only be picked from sediment using a fine gauge paintbrush. Specimens are best kept by lightly sticking them to a cardboard slide using a water-based glue. One conchologist wrote of his first encounter with *Ammonicera rota*: 'You are shown what appears to be a minute speck of dust. Examine it under a microscope and the wheel of Aurora's chariot, with its refulgent spokes, must have been a piece of ordinary workmanship compared with this. Its compactly convoluted shape, fine curved ribs and encircling rings of gold, call forth an admiration which, if expressed with regard to human feeling, might be termed doting. It unquestionably bears the stamp and figure of power divine.' It is absent from the North Sea and eastern English Channel, but may be found on the lower part of rocky coasts in the sediment that accumulates under stones.

Description: H = 0.03cm; W = 0.06cm. Extremely minute; resembles a fossil ammonite; flat with ribs radiating from the sutures; three whorls with three spiral keels; colour = red-brown. Etymology: *Ammonicera* = possibly meaning the horn of Ammon; *rota* = a wheel.

166 – *Omalogyra atomus* (Philippi)

Only marginally larger than *Ammonicera rota*, this absolutely minute species possesses a transparent shell that fascinated John Jeffreys. He observed that even after the animal had withdrawn 'it seemed to reconnoitre me through the shell, with its dark eyes, like a porter from within a window in the hall'. Its Latin name (*atomus* = an atom) refers to its small size, and although often abundant on the lower half of the beach, where it lives in rock pools among seaweed, it is often overlooked by conchologists. It is absent from the North Sea and eastern English Channel.

Description: H = 0.03cm; W = 0.08cm. Extremely minute; flat, circular; three flat whorls; wide umbilicus; colour = red-brown. Etymology: *Omalogyra* = a flat circle; *atomus* = an atom.

Pyramid Shells

The pyramid shells (Superfamily Pyramidellacea = 'pyramidal') are a very diverse superfamily with an estimated 6,000 species worldwide in around a hundred genera. Most are small (less than 1cm long) and parasitic, living with echinoderms, worms, larger molluscs and other fauna. Their size, preference for offshore waters and parasitic nature, mean that they are usually only encountered by dedicated conchologists. For many years, the pyramid shells were a much ignored group and in 1853, Edward Forbes wrote that 'few cabinets could boast more than three or four species'. By the 1860s, the situation was very different as the desire for new and interesting shells drove members of the conchological community to spend hours raking the seabed with dredges in search of minute shells. The descriptions provided in this book are rudimentary. To obtain a secure identification use a good hand lens or microscope and an expert guide such as is found in *The Journal of Molluscan Studies* (Supplement 16; 1986) or *Molluscs: Prosobranch and Pyramidellid Gastropods* (Graham, A., Linnean Society of London, 1988).

167 – *Brachystomia carrozzai* (Aartsen)

Named by Jacobus van Aartsen (1936-) after the living Italian shell collector Ferdinando Carrozza, this species was first identified in the 1840s, but for taxonomic reasons, it was renamed in 1987. There is little to remark about it other than the observation that, when cooked, the body of the animal turns from a creamy-white colour to a bright orange. Like many of the pyramid shells, this species lives very low down on the shore around or under stones and prefers the warmer Atlantic coastlines along the western and southern parts of Britain.

Description: H = 0.3cm; W = 0.1cm. Resembles *Barchystelmia scalaris* but is smaller, less rounded and with a smaller, less rounded aperture. Shell is conical, slender, minute and lustrous; three–five rounded whorls, the last occupying three-fifths of the entire height. Etymology: *Brachystomia* = short mouthed; *carrozzai* = after Ferdinando Carrozza.

168 – *Brachystomia eulimoides* (Hanley)

This is a widespread and reasonably common shell, but it escaped notice until 1844 when Sylvanus Hanley first described it. This is perhaps because *Brachystomia eulimoides* is parasitic and is most usually found living on the ears of large bivalves, especially the great scallop (*Pectin maximus*) and queen scallop (*Aequipectin opercularis*) where it feeds upon loose detritus. *Brachystomia eulimoides* is found on all coasts and may be seen very low on the shore, but is more common in shallow water. A good way of sourcing empty shells can be to search amongst the debris discarded into harbours by trawlers.

Description: H = 0.5cm; W = 0.25cm. Small, solid and glossy; five–six whorls; numerous very fine spiral striations and growth lines; colour = white. Etymology: *eulimoides* = like *Eulima*.

169 – *Brachystomia lukisii* (Jeffreys)

Dr Frederick Collings Lukis, after whom this shell was named, was a Guernsey-based surgeon who, together with his father Frederick Corbin Lukis, was able to turn his hand to just about any branch of science. Being based in the southern-most part of the British Isles, the Lukis family was a valuable asset to English conchologists, many of whom would beg for specimens from their vast shell collection. In particular, Frederick Collings Lukis and John Jeffreys were very close and as well as swapping dozens of letters, they also collected together in Guernsey and Herm. Dr Lukis died young in 1863, leading Jeffreys to write that 'his gifted mind, various acquirements, generous nature and great amiability fascinated all who had good fortune to know him. He was a true naturalist.' Lukis' reward was to have this minute, ivory-white shell, named after him by John Jeffreys. It is common in the western and southern parts of the British Isles where it lives on the lower shore, often in association with the tube worm *Pomatoceros*.

Description: H = 0.25cm; W = 0.1cm. Shell conic, slender and glossy; five–six whorls; apex is blunt; no visible striations; colour = cream. Etymology: *lukisi* = after Frederick Collings Lukis.

170 – *Brachystomia scalaris* (MacGillivray)

It was the Scottish ornithologist William MacGillivray (1796-1852) that first described this shell in 1843. MacGillivray was a keen naturalist and was often hired by others to do collecting work. These included the conchologist Edward Forbes, and it was perhaps through him that MacGillivray came to find and describe this species which is one of only two molluscs credited to him. *Brachystomia scalaris* is a very delicate, somewhat dull-looking shell that dwelt for many years under the name *Odostomia rissoides* before reverting to its older, more valid name. It is one of the more common and widely distributed of the pyramid shells and is often found on the lowest part of the beach in association with bivalves and especially mussels (e.g. *Mytilus edulis*).

Description: H = 0.6cm; W = 0.2cm. Small, turreted and tapering; five–seven rounded whorls; deep sutures; umbilical chick and tooth; colour = white or pink. Etymology: *scalaris* = stepped.

171 – *Chrysallida decussata* (Montagu)

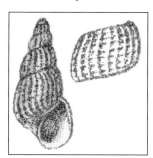

In 1803, George Montagu gave this shell a name that means 'cut crosswise' (*decussata*) which refers to its beautiful lattice-work pattern that is a pleasure to observe under the microscope. There are several similar-looking species, a fact which has caused more than one conchologist to get themselves into a muddle. Captain Thomas Brown, the curator of the Manchester Museum, was one. The mistakes he made over pyramid shells in his various conchological manuals took his fellow conchologists decades to sort out. This minute shell can be found on western and southern coasts where it lives offshore on sand and mud. It can only be seen using a microscope. Illustration shows detail of ornamentation on the last whorl.

Description: H = 0.12cm; W = 0.06cm. Minute, oblong; four rounded whorls; moderate suture; many ribs (25 on bodywhorl) intersected with fine spiral striations; colour = white. Etymology: *Chrysallida* = golden; *decussata* = 'cut crosswise'.

172 – *Chrysallida indistincta* (**Montagu**)

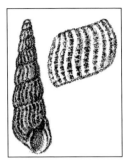

A generally uncommon species, whose original description by George Montagu in 1803 is so vague that the current definition is often said to be 'more traditional than positive' when compared with it. *Chrysallida indistincta* is sometimes found in rock pools on the lowest part of the shore, but it is more common in shallow water on Britain's southern and western coasts. The venerable conchologist William Clark remarked that his specimens' came mostly from 'a peculiar district of shelly mud between the laminarian and coralline zones in ten fathoms of water'. Illustration shows detail of ornamentation on the last whorl.

Description: H = 0.4cm; W = 0.1cm. Small, slender; seven–eight whorls; many depressed ribs (six–eight on bodywhorl); colour = white. Etymology: *indistincta* = obscure.

173 – *Chrysallida interstincta* (**Adams**)

This common shell was also one of the first to attract the attention of scientists. It was studied by the Welsh naturalist John Adams at the end of the Eighteenth Century, which was some years in advance of most other British pyramid shells, a majority of which were not described until a couple of decades later. Although quite distinctive as a species, the closeness in spelling between it and *Chrysallida indistincta* has caused problems and led one conchologist to remark that 'the two names are inconveniently similar'. It may be found on all British coasts on the lower part of rocky shores, under stones, in old shells and in the base of seaweeds. There is a related species, *Chrysallida terebellum*, which is known from a handful of specimens in the Channel Islands and is not covered in this book. Illustration shows detail of ornamentation on the last whorl.

Description: H = 0.4cm; W = 0.1cm. Small, robust, turreted; many flexuous ribs (up to 30 on bodywhorl); spiral striations near base of whorls; colour = white. Etymology: *interstincta* = divided.

174 – *Eulimella laevis* (**Brown**)

For many years, this small shell was more commonly known under the species name *acicula* (given by Rudolph Philippi in 1836), allegedly because it resembled 'a small pin for a head-dress, used by Italian women in ancient and modern times'. However, recently it was discovered that an older name had been given to it by Thomas Brown in 1827 which, under international taxonomic rules, means it supersedes Philippi's name. Although known from most parts, except the North Sea and eastern English Channel, it is relatively sparse in its distribution, being known from and preferring muddy sediment in deeper offshore waters.

Description: H = 0.4cm; W = 0.125cm. Tall, thin, slender and glossy; eight–nine flattened whorls; distinct suture; very fine spiral striation; colour = white. Etymology: *Eulimella* = a little *Eulima*; *laevis* = smooth.

175 – *Eulimella ventricosa* (Forbes)

Originally considered to be a variety of *Odostomia acicula* (but now *Eulimella laevis*, see above), this species is much less robust and has better defined whorls. It is, however, just as rare as *Eulimella laevis* and lives offshore chiefly in western regions. It has traditionally been sought using a naturalist's dredge.

Description: H = 0.4cm; W = 0.125cm. Slender, conical and delicate; 9-11 rounded whorls; deep suture; colour = white. Etymology: *ventricosa* = swollen.

176 – *Folinella excavata* (Philippi)

First discovered in Sicily by Rudolph Philippi in 1836 and relatively common in the Mediterranean, *Folinella excavata* is very rare in the British Isles. It is most likely to be found in south-western England and is so seldom seen that the first three British conchologists to discover it declared it to be a new species and named it, respectively, *Cingula sculpta*, *Rissoa harveyi* and *Parthenia turrita*. Only in the 1850s was it realised that these British species were identical to the one discovered by Philippi in Sicily. *F. excavata* generally lives offshore below about five metres in depth, although there are reports of *F. excavata* being found in rock pools, usually among coralline weeds. All the British specimens are of empty shells, except for two live animal dredged from Guernsey and Jersey in the 1870s.

Description: H = 0.3cm; W = 0.15cm. Minute, pyramidal, robust, turreted; six whorls five–six whorls; many strong, inclined ribs (25 on bodywhorl) intersected by two strong spiral striations, forming a reticulate pattern; colour white. Etymology: *Folinella* = meaning unknown; *excavata* = excavata.

177 – *Jordaniella nivosa* (Montagu)

In 1853, the conchologist Joshua Alder was so irritated by the paucity of George Montagu's 1803 description of this minute shell, he declared: 'Montagu has forfeited his claim to priority'. Alder thus gave the shell a new name of his own choosing – *Odostomia cylindrica*. However, in an age of gentlemanly science, such a move was not only discourteous but also against the strict rule which holds that the oldest name is the most valid. It was left to John Jeffreys to reinstate Montagu's original name a decade or so later. In 1843, William MacGillivray mistakenly thought that this was a new species and so named it *Odostomia annae* after his daughter Anne. Such nepotism was a noted habit of MacGillivray who, in his book on Scottish seashells, mentioned his various children so many times that George Johnson finished his review of the work with the comment 'God bless them all!'. *Jordaniella nivosa* is found low on rocky shores, among *Laminaria*, on the west and south-west of Britain.

Description: H = 0.15cm; W = 0.08cm. Minute, thin and blunt; four–five rounded whorls; deep suture; distinct growth lines and very fine spiral striations; colour = white. Etymology: *Jordaniella* = after H.K. Jordan; *nivosa* = snow-like.

178 – *Jordaniella truncatula* (Jeffreys)

It is surprising that although large for a pyramid shell (4mm), this species should only have been discovered as late as 1850, although it is conceivable that it hitherto may have been mistaken for a monstrous (i.e. larger) version of *Jordaniella nivosa*, which it resembles. It is yet another pyramid shell that is restricted to the southern and western provinces of the British Isles, where it may live at some considerable depth. Even within its range *J. truncatula* is somewhat localised in its distribution and was apparently once very common off Plymouth, where several collectors found specimens among the refuse discarded by commercial trawling boats. There are no recent records of this species of which I am aware.

Description: H = 0.4cm; W = 0.15cm. Tall, narrow, solid; five–six whorls, uneven with upper whorls sometimes wider than ones below; deep suture; numerous fine ribs and fine spiral striations; tooth on the pillar; colour = red-white. Etymology: *truncatula* = truncated.

179 – *Liostomia clavula* (Lovén)

Named by the Swedish zoologist Sven Ludvig Lovén, (1809-1895), *Liostomia clavula* was so rare that the few known British specimens were in constant demand by naturalists who would beg or borrow them from one another. More specimens have come to light since but even so, this is arguably our scarcest pyramid shell and although it has been found as far north as the Hebrides, most specimens have been taken from Devon and Cornwall where it lives offshore in sand and mud.

Description: H = 0.2cm; W = 0.1cm. Minute, thin, turreted and glossy; four–five rounded whorls; deep suture; fine growth lines; small umbilicus; colour = white. Etymology: *Liostomia* = smooth mouthed; *clavula* = a small club.

180 – *Megastomia conoidea* (Brocchi)

'The animal is vivacious,' wrote William Clark of living specimens, noting that they would display their eyes prominently when on the move. This species is one of those pyramid shells that is parasitic upon echinoderms, in this instance the sand star (*Astropecten irregularis*) which lives on soft sediment offshore. Originally described from a fossilised specimen found in the Apennine mountains of Italy by Giovanni Brocchi in 1814, it has since been discovered across the Mediterranean and along the Atlantic coast as far as Scandinavia. Not uncommon in sand and mud on western coasts but it tends to live in deeper offshore waters.

Description: H = 0.6cm; W = 0.1cm. Small, squat and solid; five–six slightly rounded whorls; distinct suture; fine growth lines; distinguished by several ridges on the inside of the inner lip; colour = white. Etymology: *Megastomia* = large mouthed; *conoidea* = conical.

181 – *Megastomia conspicua* (Alder)

Officially described as 'remarkable' (*conspicua*) by Joshua Alder, this shell was at one time thought to be the largest and rarest of the British pyramid shells and, as such, wrote John Jeffreys, 'it deserves its specific name'. In fact, there are several pyramid shell species that are either of a similar or greater size (e.g. *Odostomia turrita*), or which are more scarce (e.g. *Liostomia clavula*). Originally just known from the Isle of Man and Herm, this species has since been found from many locations along the western coast of the British Isles, but it seems to be quite local in its distribution. As an offshore species, *Megastomia conspicua* is generally only obtained using a dredge, although some empty specimens have been found washed onto the shore.

Description: H = 0.8cm; W = 0.3cm. Large (for a Pyramid Shell) and solid; six–seven slightly rounded whorls; deep suture; colour = white or cream. Etymology: *conspicua* = remarkable.

182 – *Noemiamea dolioliformis* (Jeffreys)

This small shell was first discovered in shell-sand deposits taken from Scarborough in the early 1840s by John Jeffreys and, for decades afterwards, was believed to be one of the rarest British molluscs. Isolated examples were known from many parts of the British Isles, but live specimens were a rarity. William Clark recovered one from Exmouth and noted that it was not a very lively animal. The key to its rarity was only discovered a few years ago, when it was established that *Noemiamea dolioliformis* only lives in association with the tube-forming worm *Sabellaria* (sometimes called the ross worm). Knowledge of this exclusive association, which is rare in pyramid shells, has allowed scientists and conchologists to find further specimens by targeting their collecting on *Sabellaria* worms. It is found on all coasts on the lower part of sandy shores.

Description: H = 0.3cm; W = 0.11cm. Small, thin and glossy; three whorls, the last occupying about half of the total height; around 20 spiral striations on body whorl and 10 on penultimate whorl; large aperture; deep umbilicus; colour = buff. Etymology: *Noemiamea* = like *Noemia*; *dolioliformis* = a small *Dolium*.

183 – *Odostomia acuta* (Jeffreys)

John Gwyn Jeffreys named this species 1848 after being sent specimens from several different localities including Devon, Ireland and Scotland. The somewhat pointed nature of the spire on this species provides the origin for its species name (*acuta* = sharp). It is a little known and little remarked upon animal that would appear to prefer the warmer western coasts of the British Isles, where it lives offshore in sand and mud and is localised in its occurrence.

Description: H = 0.4cm; W = 0.18cm. Tall, conical and solid; five–six flattish whorls; fine spiral striations; moderate suture; oval aperture; distinct umbilicus; colour = white/off white. Etymology: *Odostomia* = tooth mouthed; *acuta* = sharp.

184 – *Odostomia plicata* (Montagu)

This is another pyramid shell that was first named by George Montagu in 1803. It is a reasonably common species around much of Britain, but in the past it has been confused with *Odostomia turrita*. The two may be distinguished by *Odostomia plicata*'s longer spire, different shaped mouth and its lack of a keel. It is commonly, but not exclusively, found alive in the company of the tube-worm *Pomatoceros* which encrusts rocks and old shells. Diligent searching among rocks on the lowest part of rocky beaches will normally be rewarded with a few specimens. It is absent from the southern North Sea and the eastern English Channel.

Description: H = 0.25cm; W = 0.11cm. Shell conical, thin, transparent, smooth and lustrous; five–six rounded whorls the last of which is nearly half the overall height; colour = white or pale yellow. Etymology: *plicata* = folded.

185 – *Odostomia turrita* Hanley

The first specimen of this species was discovered in 1844 by Sylvanus Hanley on the famous Shell Beach of Herm Island. He describes the specimen as being 'worn, broken-mouthed and a little distorted' but was nonetheless convinced that it was entirely different to any other pyramid shell he had ever seen. Hanley duly named it *Odostomia turrita*, but a few years later he lost his nerve and declared his broken shell to have been a variety of *Odostomia unidentata*. Fortunately, some of Hanley's learned conchological friends had more faith, and within a decade, *Odostomia turrita* had been resurrected as a separate species and has been recognised as such ever since. It may be found low on the shore among stones and seaweeds, but is absent from the eastern English Channel.

Description: H = 1.2cm; W = 0.6cm. Shell solid, transparent and glossy; five–six whorls the last two of which are of approximately equal breadth; deep suture; colour = pale yellow. Etymology: *turrita* = turreted.

186 – *Odostomia unidentata* (Montagu)

At half a centimetre in height, this is one of the larger pyramid shells and hence, was also one of the first to be noticed by conchologists (in this case George Montagu in 1803). It is common around the British Isles and may be found alive and dead on the lower part of the beach where, like *Odostomia plicata*, it often lives in association with the encrusting tube-worm *Pomatoceros*. The shell shape can be quite variable and for a while, *Odostomia unidentata* was used as something of a 'dustbin species' (a slang scientific term) to which any similar-looking shell that could not otherwise be indentified would be assigned. The *unidentata* of its species name refers to a small tooth-like projection on the aperture pillar, but this may be worn away or obscured by debris in battered specimens. It may be found on all coasts on the lower shore with *Pomatoceros* on stones and inside old oyster and scallop shells.

Description: H = 0.5cm; W = 0.25cm. Similar to *Odostomia acuta* but broader with smaller umbilicus; 6 whorls; fine spiral striations; deep suture; aperture squarish with tooth; colour = cream. Etymology: *unidentata* = single-toothed.

187 – *Ondina diaphana* (Jeffreys)

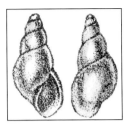

This is a much neglected and little remarked upon species, the first specimens of which were dredged from Exmouth, Devon, by William Clark and then sent them to John Jeffreys for identification. In 1848 Jeffreys recognised this as a new species, but he had little to say about it, except that some of his colleagues had confused it with *Ondina obliqua*. More recent research has established an association between this shell and with *Phascolion strombi*, a sipunculid worm which itself likes to live inside the abandoned shells of large gastropods. Live shells will only rarely be encountered onshore, although empty specimens may be cast up and sought using a fine sieve. It is absent from the North Sea and eastern English Channel.

Description: H = 0.25; W = 0.11cm. Shell spindle-shaped, thin and lustrous; four whorls, rapidly enlarging, the last forming two-thirds of overall height; colour = white or pale yellow. Etymology: *Ondina* = possibly a Germanic water sprite; *diaphana* = transparent.

188 – *Ondina divisa* (Adams)

Named in 1797 by John Adams on specimens he obtained from the Pembrokeshire coast, this is one of the few pyramid shells that may be identified using the naked eye. Certainly, it has been said that *Ondina divisa* 'cannot well be confounded with any other of our native species'. This is quite a claim for a shell that is, at most, 3mm in height. The boast springs from the deep spiral striations that are etched into the shell surface and which earned the animal its (now invalid) Nineteenth Century name of *insculpta* (meaning 'engraved'). *O. divisa* is widespread around the British coast, but is unlikely to be found alive on the shore although empty shells are commonly cast up.

Description: H = 0.3cm; W = 0.15cm. Small, glossy and cylindrical; four rounded whorls; deep spiral striations (around 18 on bodywhorl); aperture elongate; small umbilicus; colour = buff. Etymology: *divisa* = divided.

189 – *Ondina obliqua* (Alder)

Ondina obliqua is a rare pyramid shell that has managed to elude a majority of British conchologists. It lives offshore and seems to prefer slightly deeper waters on the northern and western coasts of Britain. Most specimens, even the dead ones, seem to have been taken by dredging in waters of 15 metres or more. It is therefore unlikely to be found by most casual conchologists whose hunting ground tends to be the seashore. So called 'monstrous specimens' (i.e. larger than usual) have been found from time to time, although in this instance, monstrous means a shell height of nearly a centimetre rather than five millimetres.

Description: H = 0.5cm; W = 0.2cm. Thin, rounded; four–five rounded whorls; deep suture; fine spiral striations and growth lines; aperture large and elongate; distinct umbilicus; colour = buff. Etymology: *obliqua* = oblique.

190 – *Ondina warreni* (Thompson)

First described from Dublin Bay in 1845, where it was recovered by the Irish naturalist Amelia Elizabeth Mary Warren whose brother Robert, an ornithologist, was a correspondent to William Thompson of Belfast. It was Thompson who eventually received the shell and named it after its discoverer. This species was once thought to be a smaller variety of *Ondina obliqua* which it resembles. (*Ondina warreni* is smaller with distinct striations on the base and an umbilicus.) It is relatively rare and following its discovery, there was a period of several years when no specimens were recovered at all. Fortunately, it was discovered to be common off Burrow Island, Devon, allowing the nation's conchologists to get their hands on specimens for their collections. Like *Ondina obliqua*, this is a species that has usually been obtained by taking sediment samples from offshore locations (usually by dredging) although there are reports of dead specimens being recovered from shell sand deposits in south-western England.

Description: H = 0.4cm; W = 0.2cm. Tall, conical, turreted; four whorls; deep suture; spiral striations fine and sparse on upper whorls (around six per whorl) but more numerous and distinct on base (around 18); aperture long and thin; distinct umbilicus; colour = white. Etymology: *warreni* = after Amelia Mary Warren.

191 – *Partulida pellucida* (Dillwyn)

The describer of *Partulida pellucida* was Lewis Weston Dillwyn (1778-1855), a Welsh pottery merchant whose fascination with natural history was reflected in the artistic designs on his porcelain plates and cups. Dillwyn discovered specimens of this species near to Swansea in 1817 and, although a passionate collector of shells, this is one his few solid contributions to conchology. There can be no mistaking *Partulida pellucida* which, when viewed with a hand lens, has a strong pattern of ribs and striations that set it apart from all other pyramid shells. Some conchologists used to call this the 'Celtic shell' because specimens were known only from Wales, Scotland and Ireland but it has since been recovered from around the entire British coast. It is another of those pyramid shells that may often be found on the lower shore living in association with tube-forming worms, especially *Pomatoceros* and *Sabellaria*, and although it is not common, it may neither be described as rarely occurring either.

Description: H = 0.3cm; W = 0.1cm. Conical, solid, blunt; four slightly rounded whorls; distinct sutures; upper whorls with strong ribs (around 30 on body whorl); base encircled with six–eight spiral striations; tooth on columella; distinct umbilicus; colour = opaque. Etymology: *Partulida* = after the goddess Partula; *pellucida* = transparent.

192 – *Tragula fenestrata* (Forbes)

This beautifully ornamented shell was discovered by Edward Forbes, who dredged it from the entrance at Dartmouth Harbour and who announced and named the new species *Odostomia fenestrata* at a meeting of the British Association in 1846. However, before a species name can become valid, it has to appear in print and, for some reason, all mention of Forbes's new species was omitted from the British Association's journal. Such mistakes leave the way open for a rival conchologist to step in and take the credit by publishing a description of the same species themselves using their own name. Fortunately, John Jeffreys spotted the omission and was swift to include *Odostomia fenestrata* in a publication of his own, crediting the name and the discovery to his friend Forbes. Such gentlemanly behaviour does not always exist in science.

One only has to think of the 1870s 'bone war' between the American palaeontologists Othniel Marsh and Edward Cope, which saw both men fighting to be the first to the same species of dinosaur. *Tragula fenestrata* is something of a rarity and is known only from the extreme south-west of England and the Channel Islands, where it lives offshore in muddy ground: the discovery of specimen is a noteworthy event.

Description: H = 0.3cm; W = 0.1cm. Elongate, small, turreted, solid; eight–nine slightly rounded whorls; deep sutures; strong ribs (about 20 on bodywhorl) intersected close to suture by two–three spiral striations; tubercles form at intersection; no umbilicus; colour = white. Etymology: *Tragula* = a javelin; *fenestrata* = a window.

193 – *Turbonilla lactea* (Linnaeus)

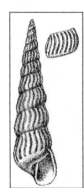

A distinctive and common species, whose empty shells (often worn and battered) regularly turn up on the seashore all around Britain. Like so many pyramid shells, it associates itself with polychaete worms, in this case *Audouinia* and *Amphitrite*, and live specimens may be found with careful searching among stones and rocks. The first description of this species was given by Carl Linnaeus in 1758 in his *System Naturae*, the book which sets out basic rules for the modern classification and naming of species. However, Linnaeus' description is a bit ambiguous and led some later conchologists to argue that his name should be abandoned in favour of a newer title, *Chemnitzia elegantissimus*. Even then, such a move was controversial and led to John Jeffreys (who was ever the Victorian voice of reason) to plead the case for Linnaeus: 'Let us not be too indolent, nor too selfish. Posterity has its claim and I write (as everyone does on a subject of natural history) not just for this generation but for all those to succeed it.' Even so, Linnaeus' *lactea* (meaning milky white) did not become widely used until the 1980s, when it was recognised that his older name had priority. It may be found on the lower shore among stones and associated with the polychaetes *Audouinia* and *Amphitrite*, and is sometimes found with *Turbonilla pusilla*.

Description: H = 0.8cm; W = 0.25cm. Very elongate, slender, solid; 10-13 flattened whorls; distinct sutures; characterised by many sinuous ribs (around 20 on bodywhorl); base smooth; colour = white. Etymology: *Turbonilla* = a little *Turbo*; *lactea* = milky.

194 – *Turbonilla pumila* (Seguenza)

A rather glossy, rounded shell, whose minute size caused it to be missed by even the most active Victorian conchologists until its discovery in 1876 by the Sicilian zoologist Giuseppe Seguenza (1833-1889). Its first British reports came at the turn of the Twentieth Century and it has since been found in the Channel Islands and along the southern and western coasts of England, Wales and Scotland. It lives offshore in sand and mud and would appear to be generally quite rare.

Description: H = 0.3cm. Shell solid, glossy, and semi-transparent; 8 to 9 flattened whorls; shell characterised by a deep suture and by a distinctive pattern of deep, straight and regularly spaced ribs that adjunct with the suture at a slight angle; colour clear white. Etymology: *pumila* = dwarfed.

195 – *Turbonilla pusilla* (Philippi)

First described by Rudolph Philippi in 1844, this is another attractive species which may sometimes be found living with *Turbonilla lactea*, which it resembles. It is uncommon, but not rare, in south-west England and Wales where it lives low on the shore among stones, often with the polychaetes *Audouinia* and *Amphitrite*. Its name means 'minute' but it is in fact one of the larger pyramid shells and it is visible to the sharp-eyed conchologist on the seashore. Those who have observed the living animal, remark that it does not so much carry its shell when moving but drags it, a bit like a petulant child pulling a schoolbag along a pavement. There are several other very rare *Turbonilla* species known from British waters that have not been included in this book.

Description: H = 0.7cm; W = 0.21cm. Similar to *Turbonilla pumila* but more conical, more solid and with curved ribs. Etymology: *pusilla* = very minute.

196 – *Ebala nitidissima* (Montagu)

Although first described by George Montagu from English specimens, *Ebala nitidissima* was rarely encountered alive, and for a time it was believed that this shell's geographical range stopped just south of Britain. However, live animals have since been found around much of the British coast, with the exception of the southern North Sea and the eastern Channel, where the colder winter temperature probably prevent populations establishing themselves. The shell is notably slender and glossy, although empty shells have often had their surface worn to a white granular finish. It lives offshore in sandy mud.

Description: H = 0.25cm; W = 0.05cm. Needle-shaped, thin with seven concave whorls; surface ornamented with fine spiral striations; colour = yellow-brown when fresh; white when dead. Etymology: *Ebala* = a dart; *nitidissima* = very glossy.

Chapter Six

Opisthobranchs

T HE TERM OPISTHOBRANCH (meaning 'behind gill' referring to their having a gill behind the heart) was coined in 1931 by the German zoologist Johannes Thiele (1860-1935). The opisthobranchs are a large subclass which generally contain those gastropods whose shell is greatly diminished or entirely absent. This includes the colourful and much admired sea slugs (nudibranchs = 'naked gills'; see chapter seventeen), the enigmatic sea butterflies (gymnosomata = 'naked body') and several other orders of naked (i.e. shell-less) mollusc. As with most other areas of gastropod classification, the exact scope and definition of the opisthobranchs is the subject of debate and will be prone to revision in the coming years.

There are hundreds of British opisthobranch species, many of which are known from only one or two reports; for this and other reasons, only those species which have a tangible shell (although few can actually withdraw into it) are included here. For those that need further information on British opisthobranchs (and especially the nudibranchs) should see *British Opisthobranch Molluscs* (Thompson, T. and Brown, G., Linnean Society of London, 1976).

Headshield Slugs

The headshield slugs (*Order Cephalispidea*) are generally considered to be the most primitive of the opisthobranchs and are thought to be transitional between the prosobranchs (gastropods with shells) and the shell-less orders of opisthobranch, such as the nudibranchs (sea slugs), although genetic studies will probably disprove this. Most cephalispideans possess a shell of some kind, even if it is reduced or internal. They typically have a broad, well-developed headshield and a muscular foot which is often used to push them through soft sediment. Many species are carnivorous and prey on small worms, single-celled organisms or other opisthobranchs. Most have highly developed sensory organs to help them find and tackle their prey.

197 – *Acteon tornatilis* (Linnaeus)

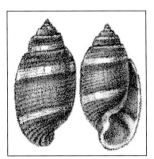

Known as 'barrels' to historical conchologists, this distinctive shell was first described by Carl Linnaeus in 1758. It is a sea slug-like animal that has a great deal of difficulty withdrawing into its shell and has been reported to emit a milky fluid when disturbed. This animal burrows in soft sand all around Britain, but those living on the seashore are generally smaller than the offshore specimens whose shells may reach 2.5 centimetres in height. Notably robust and colourful, this shell is a favourite amongst collectors and it is widely distributed about the British Isles. It is a voracious predator of other molluscs.

Description: H = 2.5cm; W = 0.9cm. A solid shell with up to eight whorls; distinguished by its glossy lustre and one to three white bands that run about the large body whorl. Colour = pink. Etymology: *Acteon* = a mythological name; *tornatilis* = turned on a lathe.

198 – *Scaphander lignarius* (Linnaeus)

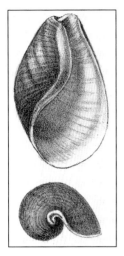

A large, active mollusc that was described by Carl Linnaeus in 1758 and which has astounded scientists with its displays of gluttony on the sea shore. 'It does not despise any animal,' wrote one naturalist, 'from the minute foraminifera to the sea mouse [*Aphordita aculeata*; a large, bristly worm].' The dissection of individual animals reveals that they have fed upon tusk shells, marine worms and many different species of small bivalve. One study revealed that several specimens had fed exclusively on one type of bivalve, *Mactra subtruncata*, leading to the comment that *Scaphander lignarius* 'is wiser than our biped gourmands and keeps to one dish'. The prey is swallowed whole with any hard parts, such as a shell, being ground to a paste and excreted later. John Jeffreys recounts a fishermen telling him that when captured in a crab pot, *Scaphander lignarius* would bite off its outer lip in a bid to escape through the netting. It is rarely seen on shore, and the fragile shell does not survive prolonged transportation. It is found on all coasts (although rare in the east) in muddy sand on the lower shore.

Description: H = 5.8cm; W = 3.7cm. The shell is thick and pear-shaped with many fine spiral striations; aperture wide with a flared outer lip; colour = orange or chestnut. Etymology: *Scaphander* = a boatman; *lignarius* = wood-like.

199 – *Cylichna cylindracea* (Pennant)

A small, somewhat sluggish animal which was first described by Thomas Pennant in his volume of British shell in 1777 *Cylichna cylindracea* lives in muddy sand on the lowest part of the beach and may be found by careful sorting sediment using a fine mesh sieve. There are a number of similar-looking species and it can difficult to make a positive identification using the live animal which is so large that it often obscures the shell. Empty shells are, however, relatively easy to identify using a hand lens or microscope. It is a predator that snuffles its way slowly through sediment in search of minute animals such as worms. It is said to emit a saffron-coloured liquid when alarmed.

Description: H = 1.5cm; W = 0.5cm. A cylindrical, polished shell which consists almost entirely of one whorl; aperture is wide and the lip greatly flared; many very fine spiral striations; colour = brownish-yellow. Etymology: *Cylichna* = pointed; *cylindracea* = cylindrical.

200 – *Philine aperta* (**Linnaeus**)

Another species that is first mentioned by Carl Linnaeus' in 1758. It is common, widely distributed, lives on the sea shore and was popular with conchologists in years gone by, several of whom went to great lengths to dissect out its minute rib-like teeth. The animal is large and white which makes it easy to spot against darker, more muddier sediments along the sea shore. It was once believed to have a worldwide distribution with reports coming from Australia, South Africa and other such distant coastlines. However, recent studies suggest that it is not quite so widespread and is restricted to the Atlantic and Mediterranean coasts of Europe and Africa. One naturalist noted that as it moves through sand, *Philine aperta* leaves a burrow that looks similar to that of a mole.

Description: H = 7cm; W = 3.5cm. A large shell comparative to the animal's body; squarish oval in outline; aperture extends across 80% of circumference; colour = white sometimes with three clear streaks. Etymology: *aperta* = open.

201 – *Philine catena* (**Montagu**)

First described in 1803 by George Montagu, *Philine catena* is currently localised in its distribution, possibly because it is very sensitive to man-made pollution, a factor which may have caused it to disappear from some sections of coastline, especially in the Mediterranean. In its absence, other less environmentally sensitive opisthobranch molluscs have exploited *Philine catena*'s niche as a seashore predator. It is found on all British coasts low down on rocky seashores where it may be found in rock pools.

Description: H = 0.4cm; W = 0.3cm. The shell is thin, oval and with an aperture that occupies around 75% of the circumference; glossy texture with numerous spiral striations; colour = milky-white. Etymology: *catena* = chain-like.

202 – *Philine pruinosa* (**Clark**)

The living animal of this species was first encountered by William Clark who dredged a specimen from Exmouth, Devon, in 1827. It is the smallest of the British *Philine* species, but this did not stop Clark from being able to observe that 'it flaps the sides of its foot upwards and downwards, as if beating at the sea, especially when first removed from the sea'. *Philine pruinosa* lives all around Britain, but at just a couple of millimetres in height and dwelling offshore, it will take some dedication to find specimens.

Description: H = 0.2cm. Shell internal, minute and fragile; wide aperture with flared lip that is equal to or just longer than the spire; ornamented with rows of minute dots or lines; colour = translucent or white. Etymology: *pruinosa* = frosty.

203 – *Philine punctata* (Adams)

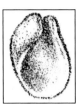

The Devonshire naturalist William Clark held a fondness for members of the *Philine* genus, which he would retrieve by dredging and then, by lifting their fragile bodies with a paintbrush, place them into watch glass to see how they would behave. When he encountered this species at Exmouth, he decided that it was most probably the same as the animal described earlier as *Bulla punctata* by the Hampshire conchologist Arthur Adams (1820-1878). However, in doing so, Clark faced the wrath of Edward Forbes who complained that 'Adams has rudely delineated, under the name *Bulla punctata*, a shell, which bears no more resemblance to the present species [i.e. *Philine punctata*] than to any other sculptured member of the genus'. Despite this, Adams remains credited with this species, although it is Clark's detailed description that defines the animal and its shell. It may be found on all rocky coasts but it is rarely seen onshore.

Description: H = 0.25cm; W = 0.18cm; shell is small, oval and delicate; glossy and semi-transparent with minute randomly scattered 'dots'; colour = milky-white. Etymology: *punctata* = pricked.

204 – *Philine scabra* (Müller)

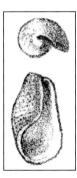

This species was first discovered on the Danish coast by Otto Friedrich Müller, who described it in 1784. Like *Philine catena*, this is a highly pollution sensitive species, whose distribution was, in the past, very wide across Europe but which may now be somewhat reduced. Many specimens have been obtained from the stomachs of various large fish species, some of whom seem to gorge themselves on the living animal. The shell is minute, but distinctive and pretty. It is delicate and has been recorded from shell sand deposits, but it is generally rare with most specimens being obtained through dredging or other offshore collecting techniques. It inhabits sand and gravel offshore all around Britain.

Description: H = 2cm. Shell internal, thin, semi-transparent, cylindrical with a wide aperture; ornamented with rows of spiral dots. Etymology: *scabra* = scratched.

205 – *Diaphana minuta* Brown

Described in 1827 by the Scottish conchologist Captain Thomas Brown, this slug-like animal is tricky to find on the seashore where it hides effectively in muddy sand. It is more easily obtained by sieving sediment where the compact nature and minute size (often just 2mm) of the shell, offers it some protection against wear and tear. It is one of those species that seems to have caused many scientists to describe the specimens they have found as a new species. By my count, it has been described under seven different names over the years. It may be found all around Britain on fine sand or mud.

Description: H = 0.5cm; W = 0.3cm; small, fragile shell; cylindrical in shape, broader in middle; colour = white. Etymology: *Diaphana* = transparent; *minuta* = small.

206 – *Haminoea hydatis* (**Linnaeus**)

A species first described by Carl Linnaeus in 1758, this mollusc is more typical of southern Europe and the Mediterranean Sea, but it does turn up in southwest England and the Channel Islands on occasion, where it inhabits silty sand or mud. Specimens are generally rare, but in the 1820s John Jeffreys and William Clark had the pleasure of stumbling across hundreds of these creatures that had become stranded in shallow tidal pools at Dawish Warren, Devon.

Description: H = 2.5cm; W = 2cm. The shell is oval, fragile, semi-transparent and glossy; aperture is elongate with an outer lip that does not curl inwards; colour = bluish-white. Etymology: *Haminoea* = meaning unknown; *hydatis* = water-coloured.

207 – *Haminoea navicula* (**da Costa**)

First described by Emanuel da Costa in 1778, but for much of the following century there was a debate about whether *Haminoea navicula* and *Haminoea hydatis* were the same species. They are actually quite different animals but the confusion resulting from this has made it difficult to plot out the historical geographical occurrence for both animals. It was recently discovered that *Haminoea navicula* has a novel means of self-defence. When it senses that a predator (usually another *Haminoea*) is following its trail along the seabed, *Haminoea navicula* releases a cloud of pheromones (called haminols) that induces panic in its enemy. It is found in the south-west and west on the lowest part of the shore in mud and silty sand and among eelgrass (*Zostera*).

Description: H = 0.7cm. Shell is small and fragile with a wide aperture and broad, flared outer lip that extends above the spire. Animal is brown with flattened cephalic area and broad parapodial lobes. Colour = white. Etymology: *navicula* = little boat.

208 – *Retusa obtusa* (**Montagu**)

A common, but often localised animal that was first described by George Montagu in 1803. It may be found burrowing in muddy sand on the lower shore all around Britain. It can be abundant on some beaches while, just a couple of miles away, may be entirely absent. It seems to be especially common in estuaries, with one scientific study estimating that during the spawning season there may be up to 73,200 eggs per square metre. The empty shell is robust and survives wear and tear quite well. It is cast up on the shore and the stomach of some fish, such as mullet, may be filled with the shells of *Retusa obtusa*.

Description: H = 0.6cm; W = 0.3cm. A small, fragile shell; cylindrical shell which is broad in the middle and tapers towards the base; shell glossy; colour = white. Etymology: *Retusa* = blunt; *obtusa* = blunt.

209 – *Retusa truncatula* (**Bruguiére**)

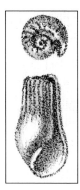

First described in 1792 by the overweight French zoologist Jean-Guillaume Bruguière (1749-1798), this, like some other *Retusa* species, is noted as something of a pioneering animal that is among the first to colonise an area of sea bed that has been destroyed or disrupted by dredging, storm damage or tidal action. Such early colonisation offers many advantages as there is usually a general lack of competitors and predators, a situation that permits prolific breeding until, in time, other species move in to restore the ecological balance once more. This animal is not uncommon on British shores but it can be quite localised in its occurrence.

Description: H = 0.4cm; W = 0.2cm. A small, fragile shell; a conical cylinder which is narrower at the top, constricted in the middle and flared towards the base; it has a glossy surface covered in fine ribs; colour = white. Etymology: *truncatula* = truncated.

210 – *Retusa umbilicata* (**Montagu**)

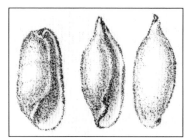

This is less commonly encountered than some of the other British *Retusa* species, perhaps because it does not habitually live on the seashore, although it is found right around Britain. There is a variety, *Retusa umbilicata* var. *mammillata*, which is smaller, more constricted and generally less common than the type species. It is prey to a variety of animals including starfish, whose stomachs have been found to contain their shells. There is a related species, *Rhizorus acuminatus*, which is found offshore around most of Britain. Illustration shows *Retusa umbilicata* (left); *Rhizorus acuminatus* (right).

Description: H = 0.3cm; W = 0.15cm. Minute, fragile; oval in shape; broad in middle tapering to both ends; rounded; non-protruding spire; colour = white/translucent. Etymology: *umbilicata* = with umbilicus.

Chapter Seven

Tusk Shells

I T IS NOT DIFFICULT to understand how the tusk shells (Class Scaphopoda) gained their vernacular name as they strongly resemble the white, curved tusk of an elephant. The tusk shells form a separate class of molluscs known as the Scaphopoda (= 'shovel footed'), which contains around 500 living species. The scaphopods used to be thought of as an evolutionary link between the gastropods and bivalves (Pelycopoda), but modern research places them closer to the latter than the former. Geologically speaking, the tusk shells are the youngest class of mollusc and have a fossil record that stretches back to the mid-Ordovician period (around 450 million years ago). Aside from the shape of their shell, they are characterised by the possession of a powerful muscular foot and a primitive vascular system. All live on the seabed, burrowing in soft sediment where they feed on detritus but most species prefer very deep-water and are not encountered except during scientific expedition.

Readily identifiable even to the uninitiated conchologist, the tusk shells were known to the Romans and have been a source of interest to the general public for many centuries. It is said that in pre-colonial days, tusk shells were used as a currency by the Canadian native tribes, with the size of a shell determining its value. The British naturalist John Keast Lord (1817—1872), who worked for the Hudson Bay Company, remarked that: 'A squaw, slave or canoe is worth these days so many blankets, but it used to be so many strings of tusk shells.' He notes that 25 shells strung together made a 'hi-qua' which, in the 1860s, was worth around £50 (about £3,500 today).

Of the seven known British species, none lives on the seashore, and only two are found in water that is shallow enough to allow the amateur conchologist a chance of finding them. For further information on the British scaphopods, see *Molluscs: Caudofoveata, Solenogastres, Polyplacophora and Scaphopoda* (Jones, A. and Baxter, J., Linnean Society of London, 1987).

211 – *Antalis entalis* (Linnaeus)

As he did with so many other organisms, the father of taxonomy Carl Linnaeus was the first person to describe formally a tusk shell in his *Systema Naturae* of 1758. Linnaeus named *entalis* after the Latin slang for these shells, *enthalium*, which is, as far as I can gather, derived from the Latin for the chemical alum (*entali*; a generic term that covers several compounds). This perhaps refers to the time when scaphopods had a commercial use in the medical and chemical industries. Their shells would be dried out and ground up into a 'testaceous power' which could be used to absorb alkaline chemicals. *Antalis entalis* is generally a northern species that lives offshore on mud, although it has been found in southern waters also. It is most likely to be discovered as an empty shell cast up onto the beach.

Description: H = 3.8cm; W = 0.5cm.Shaped, solid; smooth with an oval posterior orifice; colour = white. Etymology: *Antalis* & *entalis* = both Latin slang terns for these shells.

212 – *Antalis vulgaris* (da Costa); Common Tusk Shell

The Seventeenth Century conchologist Martin Lister first noticed this shell while walking on a beach near Barnstaple, Devon and thus, has the honour of being its first British discoverer. Known locally as 'pipe shells', it was two centuries before the naturalist Emanuel da Costa provided a full description, during which he referred to the live animal as being a 'whimble worm'. Da Costa noted that the animal could commonly be found in the south and west of England, a situation that remains true today. In fact, it is foremost a southern species that lives on sand or mud just offshore down to considerable depths. In some places, dozens of dead shells may be cast up on the beach but these are often very worn. To get good specimens it is necessary to search offshore. I have, for example, encountered live tusk shells while SCUBA diving in areas with a muddy seabed, but in the process of looking for them, I disturbed great quantities of clay and detritus turning the water into an inky soup. The live animal is shy and prefers to be covered by sediment at all times. If placed on top of the seabed, it will quickly haul itself upright and then bury itself vertically in the sand or mud until the narrow end just protrudes.

Description: H = 6cm. Tusk-shaped, solid; longitudinal striations at posterior end; some growth rings; colour = white. Etymology: *vulgaris* = common.

Part Two

Bivalves

THE BIVALVES (Class Pelecypoda = 'axe foot') are a large class of molluscs that possess a shell made from two hinged valves, but which may also be known under the scientific names of Bivalvia and Lamellibranchia. Bivalves are generally large, often symmetrical, and include such familiar groups as the scallops, oysters and mussels. They are exclusively aquatic and occupy a wide variety of habitats, including freshwater, as well as all areas of the marine environment. There are around 30,000 known species worldwide which range from the tropical giant clam (which may reach 230 kg in weight) to minute species no bigger than an ant. Britain is home to around 220 species of bivalve which range from a couple of millimetres in length (e.g. *Lasaea adansoni*) to 30cm or more (*Atrina fragilis*). Most live either on the seashore or in shallow water, although some deeper water forms do occur.

Bivalves are generally sessile and either burrow in soft sediment or attach themselves to hard surfaces using byssus threads or organic cement (although some species rest on the seabed and/or can 'swim' or move short distances). Almost all are filter-feeders (some carnivorous species are known) which live on micro-organisms and food detritus, something which makes them susceptible to parasitic organisms. The bivalves have been subject to much study and the British species are generally well-defined, although there is still some debate over their higher taxonomy arrangement. For further information on the British bivalve species, I recommend consulting *British Bivalve Seashells* (Tebble, N., British Museum: Natural History, 1966) which, while slightly out of date, remains a comprehensive work on this subject.

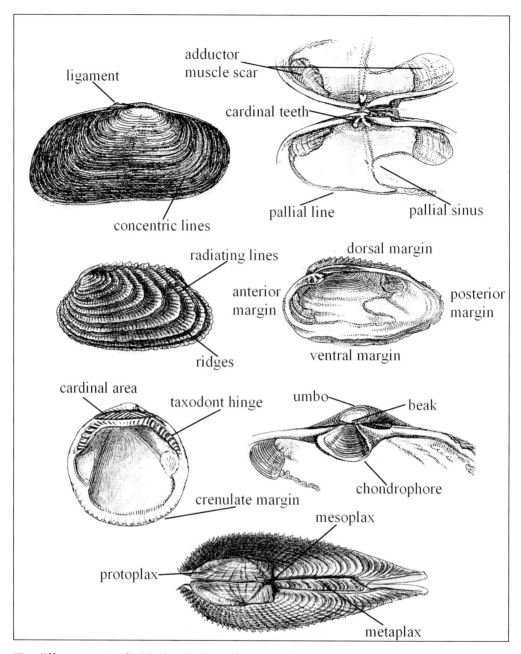

The different parts of a bivalve shell. For further information see Appendix 1.

Chapter Eight

Nut Shells

NUT SHELLS (Order Nuculoida) are a small order of triangular or oval shells which live very low on sandy seashores or are sublittoral. They prefer soft sediment and are often gregarious, but are notoriously difficult to identify, requiring the use of a strong hand-lens or microscope to see fine features such as ornament and individual teeth. Nut shells are common in the British Isles and, although they often live offshore, their empty shells may be found in some numbers on many beaches. The exact number of British nut shell species remains a matter of debate (for further details see *Journal of the Marine Biological Association of the UK*, vol.33, pp.457-72, 1954).

213 – *Nucula hanleyi* (Winckworth)

Named in 1931 by the proactive British conchologist Ronald Winckworth (1884-1950), a man who authored a 'Who's Who' index of conchologists that still resides in London's Natural history Museum. Winckworth specialised in studying groups of shells that others had long ignored. The British nut shells were one such problem group and during the late 1920s and 1930s, Winckworth was able to find four separate species, two of which were either new or had to be afforded new names. This species was originally known as *Nucula turgida*, a name that was invalid, and so Winckworth chose to rename it after the great Victorian conchologist Sylvanus Hanley. *Nucula hanleyi* is an offshore species that lives in coarse sand and gravel but which is known only from southern and western parts of Britain.

Description: L = 1.3cm. Anterior hinge with 15-25 teeth, posterior with 10-12; numerous radiating lines and some concentric lines on shell; periostracum shiny; colour = yellow or grey-brown with radiating darker bands. Etymology: *Nucula* = a small nut; *hanleyi* = after Sylvanus Hanley.

214 – *Nucula nitidosa* Winckworth

Another new species to emerge from Ronald Winckworth's 1930s review. *Nucula nitidosa* may be found on the lower part of all British coasts where it lives in a variety of soft sediment; like most nut shells. A short cut to identifying it, is to count the anterior and posterior teeth, but a good hands lens is needed to do so.

Description: L = 1.1cm. Noticeably more triangular in outline than *N. nucleus* and with a shell surface that is more glossy; sculpture of fine radiating ribs but few concentric lines; 20-30 anterior teeth and 10-14 posteriorly; the margin is crenulate; colour = olive-brown sometimes with radiating purple rays. Etymology: *nitidosa* = glossy.

215 – *Nucula nucleus* (Linnaeus)

Nucula nucleus is the original nut shell as named by Carl Linnaeus in 1758. Its size and similarity to other *Nucula* species has led to much confusion, especially among amateur conchologists, many of whom would routinely refer to any nut shell as *Nucula nucleus*. This shell may be found on the lowest part of the shore in sandy or silty sediment. It occurs right around Britain with empty shells being quite common.

Description: L = 1.25cm. Triangular outline but rounded; 11-14 posterior teeth, 16-25 anterior teeth; numerous fine radiating striations; crenulate margin; periostracum not glossy; colour = green-brown. Etymology: *nucleus* = a small nut.

216 – *Nucula sulcata* (Bronn)

The largest of the British Nut Shells, *Nucula sulcata* is an offshore species that is rarely seen in waters shallower than about 20 metres. It was named in 1831 by the German geologist Heinrich Georg Bronn, (1800-1862) who first found it as a fossil in the Alps and only later realised that the species was still living in modern seas. It is relatively rarely encountered and is chiefly known from the western coast, although some southern and northern reports do occur.

Description: L = 2cm; Equivalve; solid and triangular in outline; sculpture of fine radiating ribs and concentric lines; periostracum matt; lunule heart-shaped; 22-29 anterior teeth and 12-14 posterior teeth. Colour = olive brown with red patches. Etymology: *sulcata* = furrowed.

217 – *Nuculoma tenuis* (Montagu)

First described by George Montagu in 1803, *Nuculoma tenuis* may be distinguished from other species of nut shell by its smooth (as opposed to crenulate) ventral margin. This is a sub-Arctic offshore species that was once deemed to be common in the deepest parts of certain Scottish lochs but with reports south of the Irish Sea and Firth of Forth being rare. It prefers mud and is known from as far north as Greenland and as far west as New England. It is unlikely ever to be found onshore, dead or alive, but it would appear that in the past people have mistaken worn examples of other nut shells for this species.

Description: L =1.3cm. Triangular, thin; margin smooth, not crenulate; 6-10 posterior teeth, 16-18 anterior teeth; numerous fine radiating striae and concentric lines; periostracum glossy; colour = green-brown.

Chapter Nine

Ark Shells and Dog Cockles

ARK SHELLS AND DOG COCKLES (Order Arcoida) are a small order of solid shells which possess a well-developed hinge plate containing small alternating teeth and sockets. Ark shells generally have thick, angular, oblong shaped shells and typically attach themselves to rocks and stones using byssus threads. Dog cockles, of which there is just one British species, are similarly solid but are circular in outline. Both types are rugged, and the two valves may remain locked together for some time after death. They are generally found on the lowest part of the shore or in shallow water (although some non-British species are known from abyssal depths) and are relatively easy to identify. Probably the most recognisable member of this order is the dog cockle (*Glycymeris glycymeris*) which may be found in large numbers on some coasts and which has a fossil record that stretches back millions of years.

218 – *Arca tetragona* (Poli); the Ark Shell

A distinctive animal that likes to wedge itself into tight crevices and holes on the lowest part of the seashore and in offshore waters. This habit meant that the shell was commonly overlooked by the early conchologists who, until the 1840s, believed to it to be one of the rarest British species. Indeed, considering how distinctive it is, it is surprising that it did not get a formal scientific description until 1795 when it came to the attention of the Italian conchologist Giuseppe Poli (1746-1825). (Some speculate that it may be an unnamed small species of *Arca* mentioned by Linnaeus in 1758.) *Arca tetragona* may be found on the lower shore where it is attached by byssus threads, under stones and in crevices. It is not uncommon on most British coasts, although finding and extracting the shells from their hideaway can be quite a task. Etymology: *Arca* = a chest; *tetragona* = tetragonal.

Description: L = 5cm. Solid, box-like; surface finely reticulated; hinge 40-50 teeth; colour = yellow-brown with brown periostracum.

219 – *Bathyarca pectunculoides* (Scacchi)

First described in 1834 from the Mediterranean Sea by the Italian conchologist Archangelo Scacchi (1810-1893), this rare bivalve was known in Britain for many years only from dead shells until, in the 1840s, naturalist Robert MacAndrew recovered a living specimen in 100 metres of water off the Hebrides. This would appear to be one of its shallower habitats as it has been recovered from very deep water indeed. Because of its preference for deeper water and also for northern British waters (although it is known from the Mediterranean Sea), it is very unlikely to be encountered on the seashore. It is, however, quite common as a fossil in some coastal deposits dating back to the last Ice Age. Thus, most conchologists that want specimens of this shell will have to turn to the parallel science of palaeontology.

Description: L = 0.5cm. Solid, oblong, inequivalve; left valve is more rounded than right; hinge straight with many small teeth in the central region bounded on either side by about three larger teeth; surface with distinct radiating and concentric striations; colour = white. Etymology: *Bathyarca* = deep *Arca*; *pectunculoides* = like *Pectunculus*.

220 – *Striarca lactea* (Linnaeus); Hairy Ark Shell

The common name for this animal dates back to 1799, when Richard Pulteney referred to some specimens he had retrieved from Dorset as the hairy ark shell. This was picked up by Edward Donovan in his *Natural History of British Shells* (the first multivolume book of British shells) and, unlike so many other vernacular names afforded by naturalists, it has survived to the modern day. The shell itself is relatively small and may be quite variable in its shape. It is considered a rare shell within Britain and although it has been found in the south and west, it is only common in the Channel Islands where, according to the conchologist James Marshall, the aptly named Shell Beach on Herm is principally formed from empty *Striarca lactea* specimens. It lives in sand and gravel but is relatively rare onshore, although empty shells are robust enough to be found washed onshore.

Description: L = 1.9cm. Hairy periostracum; rhomboidal with straight hinge-line; 35 teeth; colour = yellow-white, periostracum brown. Etymology: *Striarca* = hairy *Arca*; *lactea* = milky.

221 – *Glycymeris glycymeris* (Linnaeus); Dog Cockle

It is difficult to mistake adult specimens of the dog cockle, whose orbicular outline, robust shell and characteristic zig-zag patterning make it quite distinctive. The name 'dog cockle' (originally dog's cockle) is at least three hundred years old but its origins are uncertain, although in Eighteenth Century books it is sometimes called the 'bastard cockle'. (Exactly why can only be guessed at, but perhaps it is because although the dog cockle is edible, it does not taste as nice as the common cockle, *Cerastoderma edule*.) Often the presence of empty dog cockle shells will alert beachcombers to the nearby presence of living specimens, but they are not easy to find as they tend to live in coarse sand and gravel on the very lowest part of the shore. Although not eaten widely nowadays, in historical times dog cockles would often be gathered and cooked on an open fire, like chestnuts, and they were often found by archaeologists in Roman rubbish pits. It should be noted that this is not a true cockle (i.e. part of the Family Cardiidae) and that it has been the source of much confusion, with there once being an active debate about whether there are one or two British species. By my count it has been known by twenty-one different scientific names which is quite remarkable for such a common and distinctive shell. The dog cockle may be found buried in sand or gravel on the lowest part of the beach. They may be very common in some areas and can live gregariously offshore.

Description: L = 6.4cm. Circular or near circular, large and robust; taxodont hinge; equiv-alve; colour = yellow-brown with distinctive zig-zag patterning. Etymology: *Glycymeris* & *glycymeris* = a shellfish.

Chapter Ten

Mussels

Mussels

THE MUSSELS (Order Mytiloida = 'mussels') are a familiar sight to followers of French cuisine. They are a diverse order which range from the familiar edible mussel to larger, less rarely seen species such as the horse mussel (*Modiolus modiolus*). Mussels are common, often abundant, on most British rocky coastlines where some species (notably *Mytilus edulis*) may form wide, encrusting colonies that cover every inch of rock surface. The mussels are generally solid and triangular shaped; they usually attach themselves to rocks or other hard objects using byssus threads and although the larger species may sit in the open and can exist on very exposed coasts, smaller ones generally hide amongst seaweed, often in rock pools. Given their remarkable size range, finding mussel shells requires a variety of techniques, from simply walking the beach to sieving seaweeds from rock pools.

222 – *Adipicola simpsoni* (Marshall)

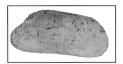

This small mussel leads a very specialist lifestyle. It was discovered in 1900 when a whale bone with two dozen bivalves attached to it was dredged from the seabed by fishermen between the Hebrides and Shetland Islands. The skull ended up in the possession of the Aberdeen shell collector James Simpson, who passed it on to the commercial printer and amateur conchologist, James Thomas Marshall who declared the bivalves to be a new species. All known specimens have been found on dead whale carcasses (apart from one that was found inside a piece of drifting pinewood). *Adipicola simpsoni* was one of the first organisms to be identified as a specialist feeder on whale carcasses but as such, it is unlikely ever to be found by amateur conchologists on the seashore.

Description: L = 2cm. Fragile, oblong, equivalve; dorsal margin straight, posterior much broader and more rounded than anterior; simple hinge; surface with fine concentric striations; interior pearly; colour = grey. Etymology: *Adipicola* = meaning unknown; *simpsoni* = after James Simpson.

223 – *Crenella decussata* (Montagu)

Described variously as being 'an exquisite gem of a mollusc' and 'a pretty little species', this minute shell has the look of an open fan when viewed using a microscope. A predominantly northern species that was first found in Dunbar, Scotland, and afterwards sent to the Devon–based conchologist George Montagu, who described them in the 1808 supplementary volume to his authoritative *Testacea Britannica*. *Crenella decussata* generally prefers to live just below the reach of the tide, but it can sometimes be found on the lower part of sandy shores around much of Britain (although it is less commonly seen in southern and south-eastern England). Its size makes it difficult to locate. Most specimens are recovered by sieving sediment, although its shells have been found inside the crop and stomach of sea birds.

Description: L = 0.4cm. Fragile, oval, equivalve; surface has approximately 50 distinct radiating ribs crossed by concentric lines producing a fan-like pattern; margin crenulate; colour = buff. Etymology: *Crenella* = a small notch; *decussata* = divided crosswise.

224 – *Crenella pellucida* (Jeffreys)

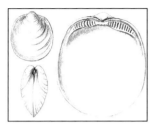

This is one of those contentious species that may not actually exist. First described by John Jeffreys in 1859 as *Limopsis pellucida* from specimens found in a Guernsey rock pool by Frederick Collings Lukis, it was, however, Jeffreys himself who afterwards withdrew the name, claiming that he had mistaken the larvae of *Rhomboidella prideaux* for a new species. Later studies appear to confirm that Jeffreys was in error but nobody could decide the exact nature of the mistake. Some believed that he had inadvertently described the larvae of one of the mussel family, while others believed the specimen to be the immature valves of the dog cockle (*Glycymeris glycymeris*). In recent decades the position has come full circle and the status of *Crenella pellucida* as a valid species has been revived with some modern reports coming from southern Europe and the Canary Islands. All this confusion makes it difficult to know where this animal may be found but it is alleged to live on the lower shore in sand and coarse sediment. (Illustration shows Jeffrey's original drawing).

Description: The controversy over this species means that it is difficult to find a reliable description of this species and the holotype illustration is rather indistinct. Etymology: *pellucida* = transparent.

225 – *Modiolarca tumida* (Hanley); Marbled Crenella

The living marbled crenella will typically be found embedded either within the body of an ascidian colony, or entangled amongst the rubbery holdfasts of oarweed (*Laminaria*). It is very particular about the location of its home and is capable of moving location. One naturalist observed: 'I have seen it, as if acting on a sudden impulse or a dislike of being watched, detach itself from its mooring and set out again on its travels to select a more sheltered or suitable spot'. It has since been noted that while this may be true of those specimens that are attached to bare rock, any that have made their homes within ascidians must remain where they are, although doubtless they are well protected by the mass of their host. It was first described by Sylvanus Hanley in 1843 and may be found on the lower shore all around the British Isles.

Description: L = 1.8cm;B = 1.1cm. Shell is small, thin with a highly angular outline; anterior part of the shell holds 15-18 broad ribs while the posterior has between 25 and 35 of the same; colour = light green with brown, red and purple patches. Etymology: *Modiolarca* = mussel-like *Arca*; *tumida* = swollen.

226 – *Modiolula phaseolina* (Philippi); Bean Horse Mussel

This small mussel takes its common and Latin name (*phaseolina* = like a kidney-bean) from the distinctive shape of its shell. The first scientific description of the bean horse mussel comes from a Sicilian specimen found in 1844 by Rudolph Philippi, but a British specimen had actually been found a year earlier in the Hebrides, though the shell was initially identified as being an immature common mussel (*Mytilus edulis*). It was not until 1847 that the Hebridian error was realised but by then it already had a name. The bean horse mussel has since been found around most of the British coastline, but it is not particularly common. It lives on the middle and lower parts of the seashore, attached to rocks and stones. There are also reports of it being found alive in areas of coarse sand.

Description: L = 2cm; B = 1.1cm. Small, triangular but with a rounded outline and rounded umbones; fine but irregular concentric growth lines; posterior is covered with many short, filamentous spines; colour = yellowish-brown. Etymology: *Modiolula* = mussel-like; *phaseolina* = kidney-bean.

227 – *Modiolus adriaticus* (Lamarck); Adriatic Mussel

First described by the controversial French pro-evolutionary scientist Jean-Baptiste Lamarck in 1819, who, by the time of this specimen's discovery, was almost totally blind. Perfect specimens of the Adriatic mussel will have a colourful pattern of reddish-brown rays that distinguishes it from all other mussels. It is well known from warmer southern European waters but generally uncommon in Britain, although it has been found in scattered locations in south-western England and southern Wales. It is delicate and lives attached to rocks offshore. Most specimens are gathered either by dredge or SCUBA divers.

Description: L = 3cm; B = 2cm. An elongate, irregular triangular shape; generally small and thinner than most mussels; many concentric growth lines; colour = light brown with rose-red rays across the posterior half. Etymology: *adriaticus* = Adriatic.

228 – *Modiolus barbatus* (Linnaeus); Bearded Mussel

The common and Latin name afforded by Carl Linnaeus (*barbatus* = bearded) in 1758 refers to the prominent, shaggy 'beard' that covers much of the shell within which may accumulate bits of shell, sand and other debris (a bit like the proverbial beard of an old mariner). Some pre-Victorian scientists believed that the beard and shell were separate organisms, with the former perhaps being 'some form of vegetable life'. The beard is actually made up of coarse bristles that emerge from the thin layer of skin (periostracum) which covers the outside of the shell. The bearded mussel was at one time thought to be very rare indeed, with specimens being highly prized by conchologists. It is certainly not common, nor easy to find, as it tends to hide among rocks or in the holdfasts of oarweed (*Laminaria*). The distribution is generally restricted to the middle and lower shore on southern and western coasts, with it being more common in the English Channel.

Description: L = 6cm (often less); B = 3.5cm. Shell is irregularly triangular with rounded umbones; posterior half of the shell is deeply serrated and has lines of thorn-like filaments which form its 'beard'; colour = red or yellowish-red. Etymology: *barbatus* = bearded.

229 – *Modiolus modiolus* (Linnaeus); Horse Mussel

By far the largest of the Mytiloida to grace the British shoreline, with some specimens being more than double the length of the next biggest mussel species. Historically known as the 'wry-beak', it is now commonly called the horse mussel and although fairly unpalatable, it was in times past eaten as a last resort by inhabitants of the Scottish islands who would wade into the water at low tide in search of large specimens. The horse mussel was also believed to steal bait from the lines of fishermen, a rumour that probably stems from the live shells having occasionally become snagged on their hooks. The largest specimens are rare and mostly known from deep water where they can grow to truly monstrous proportions. The biggest I know of measured a full 23 centimetres in length. One antiquarian remarked that it would make 'a dainty drinking-cup' or a 'pretty toy' for a mythical Nordic giant. Although generally sparse on the lower shore, the horse mussel may live gregariously in deeper water forming colonies of thousands of individuals. In some areas, especially the Irish Sea, horse mussel colonies were observed to cover several square miles of seabed, but in more recent times these have been disrupted by the action of trawling for scallops and other shellfish. The horse mussel is found all around the British Isles on the lower shore where it lives wedged in crevices, among *Laminaria* holdfasts or in coarse sediment.

Description: L = 12cm (sometimes more); B = 6cm. A large, solid shell that has distinctly blunted umbones; it is rhomboidal in outline; many fine concentric lines and ridges; colour = generally dark brown. Etymology: *modiolus* = mussel-like.

230 – *Mytilus edulis* (Linnaeus); Common Mussel

The common mussel will need no introduction to lovers of French cuisine as it is the principal ingredient of *moules marinière*. This is a colonising species that may, on certain beaches, coat every piece of available rock or other hard surface forming dense colonies that attract the attention of large mobile predators such as starfish. The sheer number of mussels on some coasts overwhelmed Britain's pioneering conchologists, many of whom professed puzzlement at the abundance of animals. The Eighteenth Century naturalist Thomas Pennant probably put forward the strangest theory to explain their numbers when he said: 'I think that the mussels were brought there by sea-birds to eat at leisure'. Another older myth includes the idea that the mussel gives birth to its young live, and also that they are a good source of gem quality pearls (neither is true). The common mussel is grown economically in many parts of Europe, usually in farms that consist of rows and rows of wooden poles driven into the beach to which the shellfish attach themselves. This industry dates back centuries when loose stones would pile up on beaches to encourage the mussels to grow so that they could be harvested and sold. In the 1840s Dr John Knapp, an Edinburgh naturalist, concluded that 400,000 shells a year were being consumed by the city's populace, but that the local fishermen were using some 3,456,000 shells to bait their crab pots and fishing lines. They are prone to natural disease and are sensitive to all types of pollution – in 1852 a virus killed off millions of mussels along the Norwegian coast, causing great hardship and even starvation in fishing villages. They are found all around Britain and most beachcombers should be able to obtain specimens with ease, even in areas where they do not form dense colonies.

Description: L = 6cm; B = 3cm. A solid shell which is roughly triangular in outline but with a rounded posterior edge; there are many fine concentric lines on the outside; inside is smooth and pearly; colour = purple or blue with brown and olive patches. Etymology: *Mytilus* = a mussel; *edulis* = edible.

231 – *Mytilus galloprovincialis* (Lamarck); Blue Mussel

The exact status of this species has been an often debated matter. Originally described as a separate species in 1819 by the French biologist Jean-Baptiste Lamarck, it was afterwards believed to be a variety of the common mussel (*Mytilus edulis*) from which it is hard to distinguish (the blue mussel has a larger, broader, flatter shell). In the 1850s John Jeffreys was emphatic that the two species were separate and claimed to have found them living side-by-side in the same locations. He was opposed by his older colleague William Clark who preferred to believe that the difference in shell shape was due to local variation. Jeffreys' view is at present accepted but, although known from Britain since early Victorian times, the blue mussel is more typical of the Mediterranean Sea and it is possible that the shell is a historical immigrant carried to northern Europe on the hulls of trading vessels. It has certainly spread to other parts of the world using this method and seems to be especially associated with historical or current shipping ports. It may be found on the lower shore around Britain attached to rocks using byssus threads but is localised. Illustration shows *Mytilus galloprovincialis* (left) with *M. edulis* for comparison (right).

Description: L = 7cm. Resembles a larger form of *Mytilus edulis* but has a rougher convex outer margin and concave hinge line; umbones are pointed and down turned. Etymology: *galloprovincialis* = French provincial.

232 – *Musculus costulatus* (Risso)

A rather attractive, if somewhat diminutive mussel shell which was first identified from the Mediterranean by the French pharmacist Joseph Risso in 1826 and not recognised from the British Isles until the 1850s. It is said to make itself 'a snug nest' among seaweeds and is known to be an early coloniser of artificial reefs such as are formed from shipwrecks or drilling platforms. It may be found low down on rocky or stony shores in the southern and western regions of Britain. There is a passing resemblance between *Musculus costulatus*, and some small mussel specimens that were recovered in 1855 from the crop of a Brent goose by Alfred Roberts of Scarborough. While Mr Roberts puzzled over the mussels, his wife attempted to cook the goose for lunch but discovered that the seaweed on which it had fed smelt so foul 'that bread and cheese had to be substituted'.

Description: L = 1.3cm. Fragile, equivalve; narrow; about 10 anterior ribs, 20 posterior with smooth area between; colour = purplish-brown, periostracum green. Etymology: *Musculus* = muscle; *costulatus* = slightly ribbed.

233 – *Musculus discors* (**Linnaeus**); **Green Crenella**

This unassuming mussel is a master of disguise, hiding itself away deep inside clumps of sea weed, or within the holdfasts of oarweed (*Laminaria*). Live specimens may be readily obtained from the short seaweeds growing within rock pools. They must be cut near the base and washed through a sieve (although dead shells will often be found amongst the debris that accumulates at the bottom of a rock pool). The naturalist and sea slug expert, Joshua Alder wrote of its habits: 'It generally prefers a stationary life and forms for itself a kind of nest or case by stitching together small seaweeds and corallines with its byssus threads. Here it remains waiting for food to come within its reach.' It is found on lower shores around Britain where it lives under stones and among coralline seaweeds.

Description: L = 1.5cm. Oval, broad, thin; 10-12 anterior ribs, 30-40 posterior ribs with smooth area between; fine concentric lines; colour = yellow-brown, periostracum green. Etymology: *discors* = inconsistent.

234 – *Musculus niger* (**Gray**)

Described in 1824 by the prolific English zoologist John Gray (1800-1875), *Musculus niger* is an Arctic species whose range extends to Scotland and northern England, where it lives offshore at depths of ten metres or more. Originally believed to be a variety of *Musculus discors*, this mussel was considered to be something of a rarity and was much sought after by Nineteenth Century collectors. In the 1840s *Musculus niger* was discovered to be relatively common on the oyster beds near the Frith of Forth, but its numbers soon diminished after local fishermen learned how much commercial shell dealers were prepared to pay for specimens.

Description: L = 5cm. Fragile, oval, equivalve; surface has approximately 50 posterior radiating ribs and 12 anterior ones with smooth area between; interior pearly; colour = dark brown or blue. Etymology: *niger* = dark.

235 – *Rhomboidella prideauxi* (**Leach**)

Considered to be rare, apart from at Lulworth Cove and Guernsey, where it is said to be 'tolerably common'. The species was named after Charles Prideaux who found the first shells in 1815 on the Devonshire coast and afterwards presented them to the British Museum. Prideaux lived near Plymouth and is said to have been an avid collector who often worked with the eminent local zoologists George Montagu and William Elford Leach (1791-1836). The latter says of Prideaux that 'he is decidedly Britain's best conchologist as far as relates to the knowledge of the species.' Many of Prideaux's specimens ended up in the British Museum, where Leach worked on them in a somewhat fanatic manner until his nervous breakdown of 1820. The small size of *Rhomboidella prideauxi* and its ability to hide among rocks makes it difficult to find, but it may be seen on the lower part of the seashore, though only in south-western regions and the Channel Islands. There are reports of dead shells being found in shell sand deposits.

Description: L = 0.3cm. Rhomboidal, swollen; 60-70 fine ribs, 12-15 distinctive ridges; colour = white, periostracum yellow. Etymology: *Rhomboidella* = a small rhombus; *prideauxi* = after Charles Prideaux.

Wing Shells and Fan Mussels

Wing shells and fan mussels that are not part of true mussels are in the Order Pterioida (= 'winged'), which is a small collection of distinctive shells that includes the largest British shelled mollusc, the fan mussel. They are generally rare and live offshore with most modern records coming from commercial fishermen who stray across specimens while trawling for scallops.

236 – *Pteria hirundo* (Linnaeus); Wing Shell

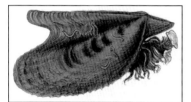

It is easy to deduce how the wing shell obtained its vernacular name for there is no other sea shell in Britain that looks quite like it. However, it is a rarity and was thought to be a warmer water species until the first specimen was recovered in the early Nineteenth Century by a Miss Hutchins in Bantry Bay, Ireland (she may be synonymous with the Irish botanist Ellen Hutchins; 1785-1815). The wing may be a means of better anchoring the animal into the soft sediment where it lives. But while common in the Mediterranean Sea, it is rare and sparsely distributed in Britain, though marginally more common in south-western England. It lives offshore, often in deep water, and is usually obtained by dredging.

Description: L = 7.7cm. Very distinctive because of elongate posterior ear; inequivalve, wing-shaped; interior pearly; colour = brown. Etymology: *Pteria* = winged; *hirundo* = a little bird.

237 – *Atrina fragilis* (Pennant); Fan Shell

Britain's largest shelled mollusc is also one of its rarest, so much so that when, in 2007, a specimen was found at low tide in the Bristol Channel, it made the national newspapers. The fan shell was something of a fascination to antiquarian naturalists, many of whom speculated about its lifestyle. Some believed it to be a predator that could trap and digest small fish inside its large shell; others thought that it could uproot itself and move location (neither is true). Although it may be found at low tide, most specimens are found offshore in quite deep water. They inhabit the same sort of ground as scallops and thus, are often caught in the nets of trawlers. It is said that in times gone by, Plymouth trawler men called the fan shell 'caperlonga', believed to be a corruption of *Cappa Lunga*, their Mediterranean name, and that the shells were responsible for tearing holes in their nets. Trawler men are probably the best source for these shells and those currently operating from Guernsey are said to pull up two or three a year. It is alleged to be good to eat, but its flesh is tough and requires several hours of stewing. There are isolated reports of another species of fan mussel, *Pinna rudis*, being found off south-west England but none have been confirmed. Illustration shows detail of beak area.

Description: L = 48cm; B = 24cm. Very large, triangular; brittle; equivalve; 8-12 radiating ribs and sometimes spines; colour = brown or black. Etymology: *Atrina* = meaning unknown; *fragilis* = delicate.

Chapter Eleven

File Shells

THE FILE SHELLS (Order Limoida = 'file shell') is an order of elongate shells which were once highly prized by conchologists and in some areas were over-collected, resulting in a collapse of local populations. Small, delicate and equivalve; when alive, file shells are notable for the numerous tentacles which protrude along their margin to give them a flame-like effect. This led John Jeffreys to remark that: 'The file shell, with its mantle studded with numerous eyes like the tail of a peacock, looks down upon the scallop as a poor blind creature'. They sometimes construct 'nests' under rocks and small spaces using large sand particles and shell fragments, and are most often encountered along the southern and western coasts of Britain.

238 – *Limaria hians* (Gmelin); Gaping File Shell

Once known as angels' wings in the Channel Islands, the gaping file shell is a notably attractive animal, whose numerous orange-red tentacles protrode through the gape of its shell giving it a flame-like appearance. It is not uncommon in southern and western regions where it lives beneath stones, or within seaweed holdfasts where it may form a 'nest' using byssus threads. Sometimes *Limaria hians* may occur in such large numbers that the nests form a mat across the seabed. In 1858 the conchologist Alfred Norman wrote that: 'Nothing can be more lovely than this animal, with its thousand delicate and beautifully ringed tentacula, each maintaining, as it were, a life independent of its neighbours, turning and twisting in every direction; the rich crimson foot and snow-white shell form an object that, to my eyes, is unsurpassed among the British mollusca.' Gaping file shells were commercially collected in large numbers during the Nineteenth Century but the animal had a defence mechanism against conchologists, as Mr Norman notes: 'It has a peculiar, tenacious and sickening odour: after handling a number of them it is no easy matter to remove the smell from the hands with soap and water; and so strong a hold has the nausacious smell had upon my olfactory nerves that a whole night has scarcely sufficed to remove the impression.' When disturbed the animal may sometimes swim by forcing jets of water through its valves.

> Description: L = 4cm; B = 2.5cm; shell is solid with a rhomboidal outline; around sixty prominent ribs; valves gape considerably on both sides when closed; in life the mantle has many orange-red tentacles which may be retracted when alarmed; colour = white or off-white; the nest may be 5 to 25cm in size. Etymology: *Limaria* = like a file; *hians* = gaping.

239 – *Limaria loscombi* (**Sowerby**)

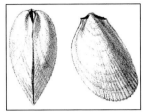

Named by George Sowerby the elder, after Clifton Wintringham Loscombe (1784-1853), who found the first specimen near Exmouth in 1823. As a young man, Loscombe inherited a fortune from a relation and afterwards, seems to have become something of 'a jack-of-all-trades' for although primarily a coin collector, he was a prolific author on a diverse range of subjects including seashells and wax seals. The snow white shell of *Limaria loscombi* and its relative fragility, made the shell an attractive proposition to conchologists. Specimens could be obtained only by dredging but in the process, many would become chipped or broken which made flawless shells something of a rarity. William Clark obtained a perfect living specimen, which he observed in an aquarium for several hours, and noted that it would rest for a few minutes before speeding through the water: 'It could cross a dish of six inches diameter whilst "one" could be counted,' he remarked. *L. loscombi* is alleged not to build nests in the same manner as *L. hians* but it does boast the same array of bright orange tentacles. It is rarely encountered on shore, and then generally in the south and west, although specimens from the west coast of Scotland are known; it lives among or under stones.

Description: L = 2cm; B = 1.4cm. Shell is thin, twisted to one side and extremely convex; fifty to sixty fine ribs of unequal size; colour = white. Etymology: *loscombi* = after Clifton Loscombe.

240 – *Limatula gwyni* (**Sykes**)

Originally described in 1863 by John Jeffreys as *Lima elliptica*, it was later discovered that this name had already been used two years earlier for a Jurassic fossil. In such circumstances, a new name must be selected and the task was left to Ernest Sykes who, in 1903, honoured its discoverer by using Jeffreys' middle name of 'Gwyn'. This shell seems to prefer colder waters and has been recovered from depths of over 2000 metres, although it does occur in coastal waters as well. It has been observed to live in many of the same locations as *Limatula subauriculata*, which it somewhat resembles. This is reputedly a rarely encountered species.

Description: L = 1.2cm; 0.7cm. Thin, elliptical, equivalve; 30-40 ribs, crossed by fine concentric striations; beaks prominent and extend beyond the hinge; hinge is straight; inside of shell has central furrow that matches one strong rib on exterior; colour = white/semi-transparent. Etymology: *Limatula* = small *Lima*; *gwyni* = after John Gwyn Jeffreys.

241 – *Limatula subauriculata* (**Montagu**)

First described by George Montagu in 1808, *Limatula subauriculata* appears to be a little remarked upon and little encountered shell that prefers the deep sea to inshore waters. Dead shells have occasionally been found on beaches but these are the exception rather than the rule. Most specimens are obtained by dredging over muddy ground in the south-west and west of Britain. Its tentacles are either white or pale pink in colour, and it is believed not to make a nest. Some specimens have been recovered from very deep waters (450 metres or more) and from locations within the Arctic Circle but it is rare in Britain.

Description: L = 0.7cm; B = 0.4cm. Thin, rather oblong, equivalve; twenty-four radiating ribs crossed by numerous fine striations; colour = white. Etymology: *subauriculata* = slightly eared.

242 – *Limatula subovata* (Jeffreys)

First described in 1876 by John Jeffreys, who discovered the first specimens during a deep-sea dredging expedition. It is a minute species about which there is very little additional information other than that it is not often seen, even by professional conchologists. It lives at great depths across the North Atlantic and Mediterranean and the one specimen I have seen was taken by a scientific research vessel from a depth of 2,200 metres. It was being auctioned with a starting price of £50 which I have taken to mean that it is exceedingly rare.

Description: L = 1.1cm. Etymology: *subovata* = sub-oval.

243 – *Limatula sulcata* (Brown)

Described by Thomas Brown in 1827, this was long believed to be a variety of *Limatula subauriculata,* but has more recently been treated as a separate species. The fragile shell is more rounded than *L. subauriculata* and somewhat resembles the snapped off end of a plastic teaspoon. It lives offshore in mud and silt in western regions and is rarely, if ever, encountered on the beach, even when dead.

Description: L = 1.3cm. Shell fragile, oval, equivalve with small ears; there are around 30 radiating ribs, one of which is usually thicker and will have a corresponding groove inside the shell; there are many fine concentric lines; single adductor muscle scar; colour = translucent with brown periostracum. Etymology: *sulcata* = furrowed.

244 – *Limea sarsi* (Lovén)

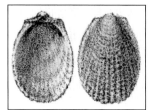

First discovered in Bergen in 1846 by Michael Sars, this distinctive and beautiful shell was not known from British waters until 1862 when two specimens were recovered in very deep water off the Shetland Islands. This is an exceedingly rare animal and is known from only a handful of British localities, and then only from deep waters and usually in Scotland. It is not known at all from the seashore.

Description: L = 0.3cm. Fragile, oval, equivalve. Surface dominated by around 24 strong ribs which are crossed by 21-30 broad concentric ribs; margin crenulate; colour = cream. Etymology: *sarsi* = after Michael Sars.

Chapter Twelve

Oysters and Scallops

THE OYSTERS (Order Ostreoida = 'oyster') contain not only the familiar edible species, but also several closely-related families including the scallops and the saddle oysters. In this list there are some iconic seashells, such as the great scallop (*Pecten maximus*) and some valuable economic species such as the flat oyster (*Ostrea edulis*) both of which have a long association with human civilisation. Eleven families occur worldwide but most are tropical or sub-tropical. Just three families, the oysters, scallops and saddle oysters, have representatives in British seas.

Oysters

The oysters (Superfamily Ostreacea) are a long established family which contains many species which are currently economically important or have been so in years gone by. The true oysters are characterised by a heavy, often asymmetrical shell that possesses a central adductor muscle scar. In life, they often attach themselves to rocks and may develop a very distorted shell shape as they grow around obstacles or uneven surfaces. Until recently, there was only one native British species of oyster but in recent times, additional species have been imported into Britain for commercial reasons.

245 – *Ostrea edulis* (Linnaeus); Common or Flat Oyster

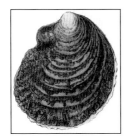 Entire books have been written about the commercial and cultural importance of the edible oyster. It was a staple part of the Roman diet and has at other times been the chosen food of both the rich and the poor. Oysters were at one time commercially harvested everywhere but especially along the east coast of England and in northern France. At its height, the oyster industry was very lucrative as is demonstrated by this description from the Channel Islands in the mid-Nineteenth Century: 'The islanders export not less than eight hundred thousand tubs [of oysters], each tub containing two English bushels [a bushel = 36 litres], and in some years thrice that quantity. As many as three hundred cutters have been employed upon them dredging. The oysters on the Jersey bank are of large size, and are sold from five to seven shillings the tub, or from three to four pence the dozen.' Oysters were especially popular with Victorian urbanites but over-fishing led to the import of foreign specimens – and a deadly parasite, *Bonamia ostreae*, which caused a collapse in native stocks. Although an Act of Parliament still protects the common oyster during its spawning season (May to August), most commercial fisheries currently stock their beds with the Portuguese oyster (*Crassostrea gigas*; see below) which is resistant to parasites. The common oyster may still be found on some beaches, where it is often cemented to the rocks on the lower shore. The larger free living animals, which are sometimes called 'horse's feet' because of their size, generally sit on the seabed, but they are rarely seen these days and usually live

offshore. Empty shells may be extremely common, especially in areas where the animals were once fished commercially.

Description: L = 7.5cm; B = 9cm. The mature animal has a heavy, thick shell; the left valve is larger and more convex than the right; it is rounded in outline with a foliated, almost scaly texture on the outside and a smooth interior; colour = generally a dull yellowish-brown. Etymology: *Ostrea* = oyster; *edulis* = edible.

246 – *Crassostrea gigas* (Thunberg); Portuguese Oyster; Pacific Oyster

The Portuguese oyster is one of a handful of introduced foreign species that has found British waters much to its liking. It was first imported in 1926 from Portugal as a replacement for the native edible oyster (*Ostrea edulis*) which had been badly affected by disease. The first commercial colony was in the River Blackwater, Essex, with several others following close behind. It was assumed that although the Portuguese oyster could survive in the colder British waters, it would not be able to breed as this required higher temperatures. However, a series of warm summers in the 1980s and 1990s did see the oysters reproduce in several places along the southern English coast. Fortunately, the resulting wild animals do not seem to have had an adverse effect on the local environment. Empty oyster shells may be found on beaches adjacent to commercial oyster farms, although these are usually from escaped individuals rather than locally bred specimens. The American oyster (*Crassostrea virginica*) is commercially farmed at a few locations in southern England and on Anglesey but has not been known to breed in the wild (yet).

Description: L = 20cm. Elongate, oval or tear-shaped; upper valve is flattened with a low round umbo; lower valve is more convex; shell is covered in several rows of coarse ridges giving it a rough, uneven margin. Etymology: *Crassostrea* = thick *Ostrea*; *gigas* = large.

Scallops

The scallops (Superfamily Pectinacea = 'scallops/comb shells') are a diverse collection of ornamentally attractive shells whose shape is familiar to most people. Scallops are usually asymmetrical, have well-developed ears, may be brightly-coloured and have a range of distinctive features such as spines and ridges. They live either freely on the seabed or by attaching themselves to hard substrates using byssus threads. Their shells are common on most British shores, although some of the smaller species may hide themselves in crevices or under stones.

247 – *Aequipecten opercularis* (Linnaeus); Queen Scallop

Although known these days as the queen scallop, this beautiful animal was once the 'common scallop' of the people, it being eaten in greater quantities than the larger great scallop (*Pecten maximus*) which itself, is often called the common scallop these days. It was widely fished but the largest commercial centre was at the Firth of Forth where, during the Nineteenth Century, tens of thousands of queen scallops were dredged annually. The queen scallop is especially notable for its ability to 'swim' for prolonged periods of time by flapping its shells together. This behaviour delights SCUBA divers, and was seen by some naturalists as a form of playfulness. 'Their motion is rapid and zig-zag,' wrote the Reverend David Landsborough in the 1850s, 'very like that of ducks in a sunny blink, rejoicing in the prospect of rain.' However, such swimming is not done for fun but as a defence mechanism which is designed to get the scallop out of the way of slow moving predators such as starfish. Although sublittoral in habit, the empty shells of Queen scallops may be found washed up on all British coastlines.

Description: L = 9cm. Circular; fragile; ears almost equal; around 20 ribs; crenulate margin; inequivalve; colour = high variable may include patterns or shades of red, pink, brown, orange and purple. Etymology: *Aequipecten* = equal to *Pecten*; *opercularis* = a pot lid.

248 – *Chlamys distorta* (da Costa); Humpback Scallop

This species was probably the shell that Dr James Wallace observed on the Orkney Islands in the 1690s which, according to him, were 'twisted and of an irregular shape'. Wallace wondered whether the 'odd strange tumbling that the tides make there can contribute anything to that frame'; but in truth, the characteristic distortion of the humpback scallop occurs in the adult animal after the right valve has been cemented to a rock surface, forcing the animal to become more convex in shape and distorting the profile of the whole shell. It is found on all British coasts on the lower shore and may sometimes be seen under the name *Talochlamys pusio*. Illustration shows *Chlamys distorta* with subadult shell (right).

Description: L = 5cm. Shell covered in numerous, fine, radiating, spiny ribs; ears unequal and on right valve may elongate. Etymology: *Chlamys* = mantle; *distorta* = distorted.

249 – *Chlamys islandica* (Müller); Icelandic Scallop

This is a moderately-sized Arctic species first described from Denmark by Otto Müller in 1776. Its empty shells are occasionally be found in the Shetland Islands and, more rarely, some North Sea coasts, but these are believed to be fossils and some consider the species not native to Britain. (Fossil specimens are generally very dark in colour while fresh shells are pink or white.) Outside of Britain, the Icelandic scallop is a commercial species that is fished in Scandinavia (especially Iceland) although stocks are reportedly dwindling in some areas. It is very rare in Britain.

Description: L = 6.5cm. Solid, circular, equivalve; surface possesses about 60 strong, radiating ribs and numbers concentric striations; anterior and posterior margin short and straight; central margin very rounded; one ear projects two thirds of distance to margin, the other very short with no byssal notch; colour = light brown with darker concentric banding. Etymology: *islandica* = Icelandic.

250 – *Chlamys varia* (Linnaeus); Variegated Scallop

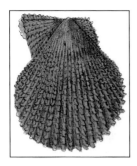

First described by Carl Linnaeus in 1758, this is probably the most common scallop species in the British Isles, and also one of its most attractive. Given its abundance, it is therefore something of a mystery as to why, in the 1830s, some collectors were paying £2 (= £140 today) for a perfect specimen. The inflated price could not be sustained and by the 1860s it was possible to obtain 50 such shells for the same price. The variegated scallop has been used as a food source in some parts of Britain and is still eaten in France, but it is not fished commercially. The animal gains its variegated name not from the overall shape but from the colour, which may include shades of white, red, pink, orange, yellow, green and purple in complex patterns, although single colour shells are also known. It occurs on the lower shore of all British coasts where it lives in coarse sediment or attached to rocks. Many living specimens are covered in sponges or other encrusting organisms.

Description: L = 6cm. Solid; anterior ear up to three times that of posterior; 25-35 strong, spine-laden ribs; crenulate margin; colour = very variable. Etymology: *varia* = variegated.

251 – *Palliolum striatum* (Müller)

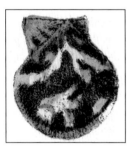

First discovered off the Danish coast in 1776 by the dredging pioneer Otto Müller, the almost paper thin shell of this small animal makes it difficult to obtain perfect specimens. Being an offshore animal, specimens were generally obtained using a dredge, often damaging the shells in the process. Consequently it was once a widely sought after commodity by collectors and scientists, a situation that was compounded by it having at one time been known under several different species names before being resolved into *Palliolum striatum* in the 1850s. One of the losers during this process was the naturalist Reverend David Landsborough (1779-1854), after whom the first British specimen of *Palliolum striatum* had been named by his friend Archibald Smith. Alas, the name *Pecten landsburgii* soon had to give way to the older (and thus valid) name given to it by Müller. It is generally not common and lives offshore in western and northern regions, often at considerable depth.

Description: L = 1.9cm. Fragile; anterior ear up to four times length of posterior; right valve has fine radiating lines and concentric lines; left valve very rough with many radiating, spine-laden ribs; colour = very variable includes white, pink and red-brown. Etymology: *Palliolum* = a small cloak; *striatum* = striated.

252 – *Palliolum tigerinum* (Müller); Tiger Scallop

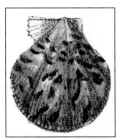

The tiger reference in both the common and species name refers not to any aggressive stance adopted by this scallop (which was first described by Otto Müller in 1776), but to the barred stripes which usually adorn its shell. It is highly variable in terms of its colour and its ornamentation, especially the ribs which may be of different height and width between specimens. Some naturalists have reported that on being disturbed, the animal will squirt a jet of water over 50 times its body length, but I have not seen this phenomenon reported in recent times. It is locally common around all British coasts and, though preferentially sublittoral in habit, may occasionally be found on the seashore.

Description: L = 2.5cm. A delicate shell; round with a smooth margin; surface looks almost smooth but in fact contains numerous very fine striations; colour = yellow, brown and purple which may occur as irregular streaks and blotches. Etymology: *tigerinum* = like a tiger.

253 – *Pecten maximus* (Linnaeus); Great Scallop, Common Scallop

This is the iconic scallop whose familiar shape has been used as a logo by countless seaside shops and cafés, as well as the international oil company Shell. This is also the commercial scallop that may be seen on the menu of most seafood restaurants and will sometimes be served up inside its shell, though this practice is rare these days. (Indeed, in times gone past restaurants would retain a supply of empty scallop shells into which the defrosted and cooked animal could be inserted; such shells can withstand repeated baking, washing and drying without ill-effect.) If familiarity does not immediately identify this animal, then its size will, for it is among the largest of the British shelled molluscs and may reach a length of twenty centimetres. It is a valuable commercial species which is traditionally obtained by raking a sandy seabed with large dredges. In some areas this practice was unregulated, leading to a collapse in numbers. In modern Britain, dredging is generally tightly-controlled, not just to preserve the scallops, but because of the serious damage it causes to other seabed life, especially delicate species such as corals. In some areas, scallops are now obtained by SCUBA diving, a practice that is much more sympathetic to the marine realm. It may be of interest to learn that the famous scallop logo of the Shell oil-company results from its founders, Marcus and Sam Samuel, who in 1897, used the profits from their London shell-dealing business to found the company – hence the company's name and logo which was initially a mussel shell, but was changed in 1904 to the now familiar scallop design. The great scallop lives offshore but its shells are often washed onto beaches or dumped there by trawlers. Otherwise, specimens may be obtained by having a friendly word with the local fishermen or fishmonger. Illustration shows *Pecten maximus*: left valve (top); right valve (bottom).

Description: L = 12cm. Easily distinguishable by its size and iconic scallop shape; it is a solid shell whose right valve is flat while the left is highly convex; each valve is rounded and has 15 or 16 solid ribs; reddish brown on the right valve, yellowish on the left valve. Etymology: *Pecten* = a comb; *maximus* = the largest.

254 – *Pseudamussium septemradiatum* (Müller)

Although known from Scandinavian waters in the 1770s, where it was described by Otto Müller, the first British report of this species was not until 1835, when Captain Thomas Brown was given a specimen taken from the Clyde Sea, Scotland. In Britain it is a northern species that is rarely encountered and which, even in the late Nineteenth Century, had yet to be seen alive by a British conchologist. It has been recovered alive since from deep water around the Scottish coast, but the animal is brittle and rarely encountered except in the Clyde area, where it has been dredged from muddy sea beds below 100 metres.

It is unlikely to fall into the hands of the average beachcomber, although it might be possible to follow in the footsteps of historical collectors and ask local fisherman to keep an eye out for specimens.

Description: L = 5cm. Fragile, circular, equivalve; shell dominated by around seven strong, smooth ribs; surface has fine radiating and concentric striations; colour = variegated with red, white, brown and purple. Etymology: *Pseudamussium* = meaning unknown; *septemradiatum* = with seven rays.

255 – *Cyclopecten greenlandicus* (Sowerby); Greenland Glass-Scallop

First described by the conchological artist George Sowerby in 1842, this was, for a while, assumed to be a variety of *Similipecten similis* or, in the words of one Victorian naturalist who was trying to gets to grips with the concept of evolution, 'a pure-blood descendant from the original stock'. It has since been recognised as a species in its own right but it is an Arctic form that would appear to be rare in Britain.

Description not available. Etymology: *Cyclopecten* = circular *Pecten*; *greenlandicus* = from Greenland.

256 – *Hyalopecten parvulinus* (Locard)

An abyssal species, the original specimen of which was taken from a depth of around 2000 metres during a French scientific dredging expedition in the early 1890s and which was afterwards described (with many other deep sea species) by Étienne Locard (1841-1904). I have been unable to find out much more than this and do not expect that this species is a feature of many shell collections worldwide.

Description not available. Etymology: *Hyalopecten* = glassy *Pecten*; *parvulinus* = minutely lineated.

257 – *Propeamussium lucidum* (Jeffreys)

In the late Victorian era a series of sea cruises were undertaken with the aim of sampling the deep-sea in order to see what sort of animal life lived there. *Propeamussium lucidum* was recovered during one such British voyage and then, in 1873, given to John Jeffreys who had taken a particular interest in deep-sea molluscs, believing that they played a role in the evolution of shallower water animals. This rare scallop has since been found across much of north Atlantic but it habitually lives at depths of hundreds of metres and so is rarely encountered, even by professional biologists. The animal has in recent years been recovered from underwater hills (known as seamounts) near Portugal but it will be unlikely to fall into the hands of amateur collectors.

Description: L = 1.5cm. Fragile, circular, inequivalve; left valve more convex, smooth with approximately 10 weak but distinct internal ribs; right valve larger with 8-10 internal ribs; ears about equal; shell very fragile; colour = pearly-white/transparent. Etymology: *Propeamussium* = resembles *mussium*; *lucidum* = clear.

258 – *Similipecten similis* (Laskey); Pygmy Scallop

First discovered in the Firth of Forth by Captain John Laskey, an avid northern naturalist who, at the turn of the Nineteenth Century, used his dredge to obtain marine specimens (see also *Angulus squalidus*). As one of our smallest bivalves, it had for many years mistakenly been identified as immature examples of other scallops, especially the great scallop (*Pecten maximus*). It is active and has been observed to 'flit like a bat' when introduced into an aquarium. The shell is widely distributed and is believed to be gregarious but, that said, it appears to be rarely reported, perhaps because of its size or because it lives just beyond the low tide mark.

Description: L = 1.1cm. Fragile, circular, equivalve; surface appears smooth but fresh specimens have numerous fine radiating and concentric lines; ears of equal size; colour = white, brown and yellow, often variegated or patterned. Etymology: *Similipecten* = resembles a *Pecten*; *similis* = resemblance (to the young of the great scallop).

Saddle Shells

Sometimes called jingle shells, the saddle shells (Superfamily Anomiacea) are oyster-like animals which adhere firmly to rocks using organic cement. They may quickly be identified by the large hole in the centre of the right valve through which, in life, pass calcified byssus threads which attach the animal to a rock surface. Of the three British species (all of which were described by Carl Linnaeus), just one occurs habitually on the seashore, where it may be common. Dislodging live animals is a near impossibility without causing damage. It is easier to gather empty shells.

259 – *Anomia ephippium* (Linnaeus); Saddle Oyster

Historically known as the jingle shell and first illustrated by the antiquarian naturalist Martin Lister in the 1680s. The saddle oyster is a problematic animal whose shape is hard to define with any degree of certainty because it will adopt the contours of the rocks, shells, stones and other objects to which it adheres. One French naturalist commented that of the 200 specimens he had in his cabinet, no two were alike. Some Nineteenth Century conchologists tried to overcome this hurdle by subdividing the species into a large number of varieties (subspecies) none of which are now widely used. However, despite such a great range of shapes and sizes, the saddle oyster is easily recognisable and its shells, alive and dead, are common around Britain.

Description: L = 6cm. Inequivalve, thin; right valve smaller and flatter than left; right valve has hole near to umbo; distinguished by three muscle scars in the left valve; surface rough; colour = white or pinkish. Etymology: *Anomia* = irregular; *ephippium* = a saddle cloth.

260 – *Heteranomia squamula* (Linnaeus)

In the Eighteenth Century this shell was thought to resemble a fish scale and was described as being 'about the size and shape of that of a carp or salmon'. For much of the Nineteenth Century it was lumped in with the highly variable saddle oyster (*Anomia ephippium*) either entirely, or as a variety (subspecies), but it is readily distinguishable by its smaller size and the possession of two muscle scars in the upper valve (the saddle oyster has three scars). Since the early the Twentieth Century it has been thought of a separate species and is known from most British coasts, where it lives on the lower shore and is common.

Description: L = 1.5cm. Shell small and irregularly circular; valves unequal; right valve flat and fragile while the left valve is convex and solid; irregular growth lines; colour = white or pinkish. Etymology: *Heteranomia* = spiny *Anomia*; *squamula* = scale (of a fish).

261 – *Pododesmus patelliformis* (Linnaeus)

Intermediate in size between the saddle oyster (*Anomia ephippium*) and *Heteranomia squamula*, it is alleged that this animal was considered to be a delicacy in Seventeenth Century France – although it cannot have made much of a meal. It is a widely distributed shell that lives offshore by attaching itself to hard objects, including large bivalves such as scallops. Like all members of this family, there has been much confusion over the correct scientific name of this animal. It has been afforded at least 15 different names in the past, which is around ten fewer than the saddle oyster (*Anomia ephippium*). It lives around Britain attached to rocks offshore.

Description: L = 4cm. Resembles *Anomia ephippium* but is smaller and with two separate muscle scars in left valve; muscle scars possess fine radial ribs; surface has fine radiating and concentric striations; colour = off-white or brown. Etymology: *Pododesmus* = bonded foot; *patelliformis* = like a limpet (*Patella*).

Chapter Thirteen

Venus Shells

T HE VENUS SHELLS (Order Veneroida = 'Venuses') is a large, highly diverse, order of bivalve molluscs that includes familiar shells as the cockles and razorfish, plus several lesser known but common families such as the hatchet shells and coin shells. Most Veneroida species possess symmetrical and solid shells with three teeth. Recent genetic research suggests that although many of the shells in this order look to be similar, they are in fact not closely related at all. One supposes that at some point there will probably be a major revision of the entire order. They are generally found on sandy shores where they burrow just below the surface.

Hatchet Shells and Lucines

The hatchet shells and lucines (Superfamily Lucinacea = 'lucines') are a collection of shells which sport broadly circular, colourless and generally small shells, some species of which may be quite common if somewhat localised in their distribution.

262 – *Loripes lucinalis* (**Lamarck**)

Described by Jean Baptiste Lamarck in 1818, *Loripes lucinalis* is often abundant in southern Europe but is less frequently seen in Britain where it is mostly restricted to southern and western coasts. It is small and almost perfectly circular, a property which helps distinguish it from the similar-looking, but less rounded, northern lucine (*Lucinoma borealis*). This species is absent from south-east and some southern coasts. It lives offshore on mud and sand but the shells are frequently washed on the shore.

Description: L = 2cm. Sub-circular, solid and convex; right valve with single cardinal tooth; exterior covered with numerous distinct concentric grow lines; colour = white. Etymology: *Loripes* = strap-shaped; *lucinalis* = likes *Lucina*.

263 – *Lucinella divaricata* (**Linnaeus**)

First described by Carl Linnaeus in 1758, this is one of our rarest bivalves. Once or twice each decade empty valves used to be dredged up in Britain, usually from the Cornish coast, but no living specimens have been forthcoming until 1950 when a specimen was dug up from the seashore on Tresco, Scilly Isles. Empty shells have been found in south-west England a number of times while in southern Europe, where it is more common, its abundance is said to have been increasing since the start of the 1990s. Specimens have been found on the beach in the south-west but it is very rare.

Description: L = 1.5cm. Solid, circular, equivalve; surface covered in numerous fine, wavy concentric lines which run from the posterior to anterior margin, these are crossed by distinct concentric striations; colour = white. Etymology: *Lucinella* = a small *Lucina*; *divaricata* = spread-out.

264 – *Lucinoma borealis* (Linnaeus); Northern Lucine

Originally described as the 'three-threaded white cockle'. Early Nineteenth Century naturalist George Montagu was surprised to discover that one of the easiest means of obtaining northern lucine specimens was in the fields near to Falmouth, onto which farmers routinely dumped seaweed for use as soil fertiliser. The similarity between the northern lucine and *Loripes lucinalis* has caused much confusion in the past and has even caught out very experienced professionals. In 1853 Silvanus Hanley reported that the northern lucine occurred abundantly near St Peter Port in Guernsey, which brought forth a comment from the local naturalist Frederick Lukis who said: 'I have never found a single specimen on the Guernsey coast although I have digged much in nearly every bay.' It was concluded that Hanley had made the schoolboy error of misidentifying *Loripes lucinalis* which is abundant in Guernsey. The northern lucine is generally common around most British sandy coasts on the lower shore where it may gregarious.

Description: L = 3.5cm. Equivalve; circular; numerous strong concentric ridges; two cardinal teeth in both valves; smooth margin; colour = dull white; periostracum brown. Etymology: *Lucinoma* = swollen *Lucina*; *borealis* = northern.

265 – *Myrtea spinifera* (Montagu)

Described by George Montagu in 1803, this is a generally local species that is more common along the western coasts of Britain. Its localised nature may be explicable by the discovery that this animal contains a large quantity of sulphur-oxidising bacteria within its gills which live symbiotically, and may allow it to exploit certain types of environments more efficiently. Equally well, a survey of the effect of effluent discharged into the sea from paper manufacturing factories found that *Myrtea spinifera* was much more abundant in the polluted areas. It is an offshore dweller that is generally found in depths of 10 metres or more. The empty shells are rarely found on shore.

Description: L= 2.5cm. Equivalve; oval/sub-triangular; around 50 fine concentric ridges which may become spiny on the dorsal margin; right vale has one cardinal tooth, left valve two cardinal teeth; external ligaments; colour =white often with pinkish interior. Etymology: *Myrtea* = meaning unknown; *spinifera* = prickly.

266 – *Thyasira croulinensis* (Jeffreys)

A rare shell that is found only in the far north of Britain and usually at depths of 10 metres or more (often considerably more). The first specimen was dredged in 1847 off the Hebrides by John Jeffreys and although its range extends to the Canary Islands, in Britain it is only known from Scotland.

Description: L = 0.3cm; H = 0.4cm. Fragile, oval-circular, equivalve; sculpture of numerous fine concentric striations with distinct growth stages; hinge line simple with no teeth; colour = white. Etymology: *Thyasira* = meaning unknown; *croulinensis* = from Crowlin Island, Hebrides.

267 – *Thyasira equalis* (Verrill and Bush); Equal Cleftclam

Described in 1898 by the Harvard zoologists Katherine Jeanette Bush, (1855-1937) and Addison Emory Verrill (1839-1926), this is said to be the commonest of the deep water *Thyasira* which occurs around Britain and prefers to burrow in clean silt and mud that is free from organic material. It generally lives in waters of 40 metres or more in depth and, in the right circumstances, can reach abundances of 200 specimens per square metre (although usually less). It appears to be sensitive to low oxygen levels and can suffer badly during the winter months when some deep water regions are cut off from the oxygen-rich water at the sea's surface.

Description not available. L = 0.7cm. Etymology *equalis* = equal.

268 – *Thyasira ferruginea* (Locard)

A minute bivalve that, when recovered, is often covered in a layer of encrusting rusty-looking material from which it derives its Latin name. It was first discovered in Crete and was described by Étienne Locard in 1886. It has a wide geographical range but, like many British *Thyasira*, is restricted to Scotland where it lives in sandy mud at a depth of 10 metres or more.

Description: L = 0.3cm; B = 0.25cm. Solid, circular, equivalve; marginally longer than broad; sculpture of fine concentric lines; often covered in red deposit; simple hinge with no teeth; colour = white often stained by red coating. Etymology: *ferruginea* = rusty.

269 – *Thyasira flexuosa* (Montagu); Wavy Hatchet Shell

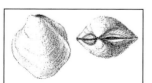

The most common and widely distributed of the British *Thyasira* species which may be found along all our sandy coasts, albeit at a depth of eight metres or more. It was first described by George Montagu in 1803. It is believed that his specimens came from a Devonshire beach.

Description: L = 0.9cm; B = 0.8cm. Equivalve; thin; squarish outline; fine concentric lines and growth stages; distinctive deep furrow from beaks to posterior margin; hinge without teeth; colour = white. Etymology: *flexuosa* = flexuous.

270 – *Thyasira gouldii* (Philippi); Northern Hatchet Shell

Named after the American medic and conchologist Augustus Addison Gould (1805-1866) who was a principal founder of the Boston Society of Natural History. *Thyasira gouldii* was first described in 1845, during Gould's lifetime, but following his death in 1866, a whole host of (mostly American) bivalves were afforded his surname in honour of his achievements. This is an Arctic species that is occasionally recovered from off the Scottish coast. It has featured in a number of seabed ecological surveys in recent years and is judged to be sensitive to disruptive events such as pollution and trawling. It is judged to be at risk of disappearing from British seas altogether, should there be any significant warming in the sea temperature due to climate change or other factors.

Description not available. Etymology: *gouldii* = after Augustus Gould.

271 – *Thyasira obsoleta* (Verrill and Bush)

Described in 1898 by Katherine Bush and Addison Verrill, this is a deep water shell that has been found off the north of Scotland. It appears to have been rarely encountered, even by the scientific community, but it may be more common below about 300 metres. Most specimens have been recovered as part of ecological survey work in the North Atlantic.

Description not available. Etymology: *obsolete* = shabby/worn out.

272 – *Thyasira pygmaea* (Verrill and Bush)

Another species that was first described by Harvard duo and *Thyasira* experts Katherine Bush and Addison Verrill. Not uncommon on mud and silty sand across the entire Arctic and sub-Arctic region, but its preference for deeper waters (usually greater than 30 metres) places it out of the reach of amateur conchologists. It is common around oil rigs in the northern North Sea and in some of the Scandinavian fjords. It is gregarious and usually found in the company of other small bivalves including various species of *Tellina*, *Yoldiella* and other *Thyasira*.

Description not available. Etymology: *pygmaea* = dwarfed.

273 – *Thyasira subtrigona* (Jeffreys)

Another rare, and generally deeper water *Thyasira* species, whose preference for colder waters restricts it to the far north of Scotland. It was first described by John Jeffreys in 1858 but there has been much debate since as to whether this is a true species or a misidentification. Jeffreys gathered his specimens off the Shetland Islands in very deep waters and it has received only sporadic British reports since then, although some specimens are known from as far south as the Azores. It is very unlikely to be found by beachcombers.

Description: L = 0.2cm; B = 0.1cm. Fragile, oblong, equivalve; distinguished from other species by elongate outline; anterior margin more rounded than posterior; sculpture of fine concentric lines; simple hinge with no teeth; colour = white. Etymology: *subtrigona* = nearly triangular.

274 – *Diplodonta rotundata* (**Montagu**)

Shortly after its discovery by George Monatgu in 1803, this shell was described as being 'portly and protuberant'. One naturalist even wondered whether the rounded shape of the adult shell was due to gluttony during its younger years. 'Good living will doubtless tell on the *Diplodonta*,' he remarked. This is an offshore shell whose distribution is mostly restricted to the south and west of England but it may be locally common. It lives offshore in shallow to moderate depths but the shell is robust and I have found concentrations of empty shells washed up on some beaches. Some books describe a variety (*Diplodonta rotundata* var. *eddystonia*) that was recovered from off the Eddystone Lighthouse in the 1890s but it is now generally considered to be synonymous with its parent species.

Description: L = 2.3cm; B = 2.5cm. Equivalve; circular; fine concentric lines; two cardinal teeth in each valve; smooth margin; ligament external; colour = white/yellow. Etymology: *Diplodonta* = double-toothed; *rotundata* = rounded.

Coin Shells

There are two rather disparate superfamilies (Galeommatacea and Cyamiacea) covered by this broad title which, while only loosely related, often possess shells that are small, dull coloured but often solid and ornamented. Some species are quite specialised in their distribution and may be found only on certain coasts or in the company of particular animals.

275 – *Galeomma turtoni* (**Sowerby**)

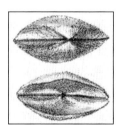

'We dredged this up in the English Channel, alive, during a gale of wind,' wrote George Sowerby the elder about his discovery of this shell in 1825. Described as looking like 'beautiful pearls', the first specimen was given by Sowerby to the pioneering British conchologist William Turton but it proved to be extremely rare in the British Isles, with only isolated examples being dredged off Cornwall and Devonshire and so, as conchology became a popular pastime, its monetary value rose to a guinea (£1) per specimen. In the 1840s it was discovered that *Galeomma turtoni* could be readily obtained at very low water on one particular beach on the island of Herm leading to the conchological equivalent of a gold rush. Within a matter of years the beach at Herm had been stripped clean of specimens causing the species to be declared 'almost extinct' by 1897. Such was the value of the animal that one person employed to dredge for specimens was accused of stealing the shells for his own profit. To judge by the descriptions of some of Victorian *Galeomma turtoni* collecting trips to Herm, the numbers have not recovered from the blow dealt to them by the shell collecting community. The living animal prefers rocky coasts where it lives under stones and among seaweed, sometimes attached by byssus threads but it remains rare.

Description: L = 1.3cm. Shell thin; transversely oval; equivalve; gaping widely in front; surface longitudinally striated and decussated; beaks minute, acute; cartilage pits under the beaks, small; no hinge teeth; ligaments internal; colour = white. Etymology: *Galeomma* = cat's eye; *turtoni* = named after Dr Turton.

276 – *Kellia suborbicularis* (Montagu)

George Montagu named this shell in honour of the Reverend Matthias Joseph O'Kelly, an Irish naturalist and great friend of many conchologists, including Montagu and William Turton. It was once said of O'Kelly that: 'There was not in the country a better collector of zoological subjects'. In the 1860s a description of *Kellia suborbicularis* greatly upset John Jeffreys who passionately disliked the use of the word 'teeth' to describe the projections in its hinge area. 'Anyone but a conchologist may well ask why these hinge processes are called "teeth",' mused John Jeffreys, 'seeing that they are not homologous to the teeth of vertebrate animals, and that they are always placed at the back, instead of in front, of a headless creature.' He bitterly concluded that the word 'had become household and is unchangeable'. Why *Kellia suborbicularis* should have sparked this thought, rather than the hundreds of other bivalve species who are described as having 'teeth', must remain a mystery. The shell itself may be dug up on the lower shore and has been found in many places around Britain but is more common in the west and south; it has been found inside the stomachs of haddock.

Description: L = 1cm. Equivalve; oval, rounded; fine concentric lines; right valve one cardinal tooth; left valve two cardinal teeth; colour = white, periostracum fawn. Etymology: *Kellia* = after Matthias O'Kelly; *suborbicularis* = nearly orbicular.

277 – *Lasaea adansoni* (Gmelin)

First discovered near Sandwich, Kent, the original 1784 illustration provided by its finder, George Walker, proved to be woefully inadequate and so the glory of naming it went to George Montagu in 1803. Montagu named it *Lasaea rubra* (after its red colour) but in the 1970s it was found that the German naturalist Johann Gmelin had originally described the species in 1791, so the name has recently been changed to *Lasaea adansoni*, after the Scottish-French naturalist Michel Adanson, (1727-1806). This is one of our smallest bivalves and, although reasonably common around Britain, it wedges itself into crevices, old shells and other inaccessible places, and is generally only retrievable with much patience. Empty shells may be recovered by sieving but identification usually requires a microscope or powerful hand lens.

Description: L = 0.3cm. Equivalve; minute; oval; fine concentric and radiating lines; left valve with one cardinal tooth, one lateral tooth; right valve with one anterior and posterior tooth; colour = white tinged with red and green, periostracum yellowish. Etymology: *Lasaea* = probably means 'little shield'; *adansoni* = after Michel Adanson.

278 – *Semierycina nitida* (Turton)

Another minute bivalve, first described by William Turton in 1822, that inhabits offshore waters below about 15 metres in depth and which is known from around all the British Isles. Live specimens are active and have been observed to climb the glass wall of an aquarium 'as fast as any gastropod'. The animal has been described as being quite gelatinous, an observation which led one naturalist to direct a quote from Shakespeare at this species: 'a liquid prisoner, pent in walls of glass'. Empty shells may be washed onto the shore and found using a sieve.

Description: L = 0.3cm. Equivalve; sub-circular; numerous fine concentric lines; pit marks near to beaks; right valve one cardinal tooth and two anterior and posterior teeth; left valve one cardinal tooth and one anterior and posterior tooth; colour = white. Etymology: *Semierycina* = half Venus; *nitida* = *shining*.

279 – *Lepton squamosum* (Montagu)

'This is certainly the prince of British bivalves,' wrote William Clark in 1835. 'The snow white colour of both animal and shell sheds over this interesting creature the inexpressible charms of purity and elegance.' It is indeed a handsome shell, but Mr Clark's elation may also have been due to his having obtained a living specimen which was considered very rare following George Montagu's original description in 1803. 'This scarce shell is very rarely obtained entire, dead single valves being the usual condition of cabinet specimens,' wrote Edward Forbes in 1853, a statement with which others concurred. The problem may have been that, unknown to these collectors, this species is symbiotic and is usually found inside the burrows of the callianassid prawns *Upogebia deltaura* and *Upogebia stellata*. This tends to localise its occurrence and has restricted the general distribution to the lower shores of southern and western Britain. Most conchologists have to accept the battered, empty shells that are washed up onto beaches in the areas where it occurs.

Description: L = 1.3cm. Shell thin and brittle with a square outline with rounded corners; equivalve; very fine concentric and radiating lines overlain by numerous fine pits; small central cardinal tooth in each valve; colour = white. Etymology: *Lepton* = thin; *squamosum* = scaly.

280 – *Devonia perrieri* (Malard)

A rare and small bivalve which attaches itself to the sea cucumber *Leptosynapta inhaerens* in the south of Britain and also *Leptosynapta bergensis* which occurs further north. Both these hosts may be found burrowing in sand low on the seashore as well as offshore. It was named by the conchologist Eugène Malard, probably after the French echinoderm expert Jean Perrier, (1844-1921) or possibly his brother Rémy (1861-1936) who, as well as echinoderms, was interested in nudibranch molluscs (sea slugs). Although known from around Britain, its occurrence is patchy.

Description: L = 0.5cm. Fragile, oblong, equivalve; surface with concentric striations and growth stages; simple hinge; colour = white. Etymology: *Devonia* = Devonian; *perrieri* = probably after Jean Perrier.

281 – *Epilepton clarkiae* (Clark)

Named in 1852 by William Clark as a tribute to his wife who, to judge by his writings, must have spent a majority of their marriage with her husband either on the seashore or in a boat dredging the seabed. It is probably our smallest species of bivalve, reaching just 2mm in size, and thus it escaped the notice of scientists until 1852, even though it may be found on the beach. Clark found his specimens in Exmouth but it was not long before other conchologists, alerted to the animal's existence, were finding it in other locations across Britain. It is restricted to the southern and western regions and may be found very low on the shore in sand or among seaweed. In general you will need to sieve sediment and then use a microscope to recover and identify any specimens, whether living or dead.

Description: L = 0.2cm; B = 0.25cm. Minute, thin and oval; numerous fine concentric lines and radiating lines; colour = pale yellow or white. Etymology: *Epilepton* = akin to *Lepton*; *clarkiae* = after Mrs Clark.

282 – *Montacuta donacina* (Wood)

Originally described from a fossil specimen found at Sutton in 1851 by the English geologist Searles Valentine Wood (1798-1880), it was later found to be a living inhabitant of modern seas, although its relationship with other members of this family baffled conchologists for a decade or so. It still sports the same name that was afforded by Wood and has been dredged from localities in the North Sea and also off Shetland. It is rare.

Description: L = 2.5cm; B = 2cm. Fragile, oblong, inequivalve; right valve more rounded; slight posterior gape; surface with numerous concentric striations; colour = pale yellow with radiating pink rays. Etymology: *Montacuta* = after George Montagu; *donacina* = resembles *Donax*.

283 – *Montacuta substriata* (Montagu)

A small and delicate shell that may be found living within the anal spines of the burrowing sea urchins *Spatangus purpureus* and *Echinocardium flavescens,* on which it may sometimes occur abundantly. It took William Clark a while to separate some live specimens from the spines of an urchin he had dredged up and afterwards he observed that the animal strode defiantly about his aquarium in search of a new home. Its restricted habitat was recognised in the early Nineteenth Century and was the source of some amazement among scientists who did not then have many solid examples of animal symbiosis. Despite its specific requirements, *Montacuta substriata* is widely distributed about Britain and empty shells are not uncommon if slightly tricky to find. It generally lives offshore but it has been found on echinoids dug up on very low spring tides.

Description: L = 0.3cm; B = 0.35cm. Equivalve; oval but irregular; approximately 12 radiating lines with few concentric lines; growth lines distinct; no cardinal teeth but one lateral tooth in each valve; colour = white. Etymology: *substriata* = slightly striated.

284 – *Mysella bidentata* (Montagu)

In 1803, George Montagu found this small bivalve nestling inside holes that had been drilled into old oyster shells. He assumed that the mollusc was making these holes and this myth was perpetuated until the late 1850s when it was found that a sponge was responsible for the damage. In fact, *Mysella bidentata* does not habitually live within old oyster shells (although it has been found there) but usually in association with the brittle star *Acrocnida brachiata* which buries in muddy sand low on the shore. It has been found on most British coasts but is rather uncommon.

Description: L = 0.3cm. Equivalve; rhomboidal; fine concentric lines; both valves with one anterior and posterior tooth; colour = white. Etymology: *Mysella* = meaning unknown ; *bidentata* = two-toothed.

285 – *Mysella dawsoni* (Jeffreys)

In 1864, John Jeffreys was sent a handful of minute shells by Robert Dawson, an amateur conchologist from Aberdeenshire. Among them was a single valve that could not be identified. Jeffreys was also stumped and admitted that 'I cannot identify it with any known species, whether living or fossil'. He did not want to describe it as a new species on just one dead specimen, but suggested that if any more examples came to light then it should be called *Montacuta* (but now *Mysella*) *dawsoni* after its discoverer. It was Mr Dawson who came to the rescue after dredging three more specimens which allowed Jeffreys to validate the name. It was not until several years later, while on a scientific cruise, that Jeffreys himself encountered more examples of this species but they were dredged from very deep waters in the Atlantic, an event that he believed to be 'quite remarkable'. More recently, doubt has been cast as to whether this deep water species could really have found its way into shallow waters off eastern Scotland but until Mr Dawson's specimens can have been proved to have come from elsewhere, this remains on record as being a very rare British species.

Description: L = 0.3cm. Solid, triangular, equivalve; shell smooth with growth stages; hinge straight; margins rounded; colour = white. Etymology: *dawsoni* = after Robert Dawson.

286 – *Tellimya ferruginosa* (Montagu)

Described by George Montagu in 1803, this shell is considered to be rare by some conchologists and to be simply localised by others. Like other species in this family, *Tellimya ferruginosa* is specialised in its habitat and generally associated with the burrowing sea urchin *Echinocardium*. It has also be found living on its own, in which case it is often coated in a layer of thick, reddish crust from which it derives its species name. The nature of this crust has been a matter of debate by naturalists, the perceived conclusion being that it was faecal matter that had accumulated due to the animal's sedentary lifestyle, although in fact, it is an inorganic deposit. It is widely distributed around Britain but localised. It may be found onshore, often in the burrows of *Echinocardium*, but has also been recovered from the stomach of haddocks.

Description: L = 0.75cm; B = 0.5cm. Equivalve; internal ligament; concentric lines; right valve with one cardinal tooth, left with one anterior tooth; colour = white but often covered in red encrustation. Etymology: *Tellimya* = *Mya*-like *Tellin*; *ferruginosa* = rusty.

287 – *Arculus sykesi* (Chaster)

Sometimes a shell may totally escape the attention of conchologists and then be discovered by two people at the same time. Such is the case with this species which was first dredged off the coast of Guernsey in 1893 by James Marshall who immediately recognised that it was a new species and proposed calling it *Lepton pusillum*. However, Marshall did not get into print quick enough and in the meantime, another specimen was discovered by George

William Chaster, an obsessive dredger of the seabed, who published a description and thus had the honour of naming it. This is one of our smallest and rarest bivalves and since its identification there have been few further discoveries and only a handful from the British mainland in Cornwall and south Devon. It is said to live offshore in association with the tanaid crustacean *Tuberapseudes echinatus* and may be considered very rare.

Description: L = 0.16cm. Shell fragile, equivalve and circular; evenly spaced concentric ridges; small cardinal tooth in each valve; colour translucent. Etymology: *Arculus* = little circle; *sykesi* = after Ernest Sykes.

288 – *Neolepton obliquatum* (Chaster)

This southern European species has just one known record from the northern Irish Sea where it was dredged in the early Twentieth Century. Based on this, *Neolepton obliquatum* was included on lists of known British species for several decades until, in the 1960s, the English conchologist Norman Tebble queried the Irish records. It remains on many lists of British species although its claim to be a native shell is tenuous.

Description not available. Etymology: *Neolepton* = new *Lepton*; *obliquatum* = sideways.

289 – *Neolepton sulcatulum* (Jeffreys)

This animal has followed much the similar history of *Arculus sykesi* in that it was first dredged off Guernsey in the 1850s and was for two decades considered to be endemic to the island until, in 1874, further specimens were found off south-west England. It is a southern European species whose northerly range just clips the extreme south of Britain. Although often found at low water in the Channel Islands, among coralline and other seaweeds, it is very rare on the British mainland and known only from Cornwall, the Scilly Isles and the Isle of Man.

Description: L = 0.16cm. Shell fragile, inequilateral and broadly circular; numerous concentric lines and visible growth lines; colour = white. Etymology: *sulcatulum* = slightly furrowed.

Astartes

The astartes (Superfamily Astartacea = 'scale-like') are generally triangular in outline and quite solid. They were the cause of much anguish with early conchologists, many of whom tried to split the various species into a myriad of subspecies so that by the time John Jeffreys came to look at them, in 1865 he was forced to remark, 'I do not know a more puzzling study.' Matters have improved somewhat since then with many of the various varieties and forms of Victorian times having been streamlined into several coherent species.

290 – *Astarte crebricostata* (Forbes)

An Arctic species that, as far as I am aware, is known only from some very degraded specimens that were dredged off the coasts of the Hebrides and Shetlands during Victorian times and afterwards handed to, and named by, Edward Forbes. Historical conchologists did not consider it to be truly native to Britain and I have been unable to find any further records of its occurrence on our shores.

Description not available. Etymology: *Astarte* = a goddess of the Moon; *crebricostata* = numerous ribs.

291 – *Astarte sulcata* (da Costa)

Named by Emanuel da Costa in 1778 and widely distributed around Britain, although it seems to be rarer in the south than the north. The animal has been described as 'inactive' and 'anti-social', preferring to live in isolation rather than gregariously, and when found alive it may occasionally be encrusted with minerals. It lives offshore in mud and gravel, generally below five metres, but empty shells may be washed up on the beach.

Description: L = 2.7cm; B = 2.8cm. Solid, equivalve, triangular; 2four–five0 strong ribs; right valve has two cardinal teeth, the left three; margin finely crenulate; colour = white. Etymology: *sulcata* = furrowed.

292 – *Goodallia triangularis* (Montagu)

First described in 1803 by George Montagu and named after Sir Joseph Goodall (1760-1840), a renowned amateur conchologist and the provost of Eton College. Although commonly discovered on all of Britain's coasts, Victorian conchologists seemed only to procure empty shells, a living specimen having eluded them until at least the 1870s. It is speculated that this lack of living animals might be because the animal is heavily predated upon by gastropods such as the European sting winkle (*Ocenebra erinacea*). In 1822, William Turton proposed moving this species from its original genus of *Astarte* to *Goodallia*, but the idea was considered 'ill-based' by his fellow conchologists. It was not until the late Twentieth Century that Turton's generic name was adopted. Although it lives in shallow water offshore, empty valves may be commonly found on the beach and may be gathered by carefully sieving coarse sediment.

Description: L = 0.3cm. Minute, solid, equivalve, triangular; surface has very fine concentric lines; inside margin crenulate; both valves have two cardinal teeth; colour = white, periostracum brown/yellow. Etymology: *Goodallia* = after Joseph Goodall; *triangularis* = triangular.

293 – *Tridonta borealis* (Schumacher)

Named in 1817 by German zoologist Heinrich Schumacher (1757-1830), this is an Arctic species that has given a headache to many conchologists and is known by at least ten other scientific names. Worn shells have been gathered from northern Scotland but it has not been recovered alive, or even close to the shore, in Britain and is thought doubtful to be a native species.

Description: L = 4cm. Solid, sub-triangular, equivalve; distinguished by large size and smooth margin; sculpture of numerous concentric lines; colour = dark brown. Etymology: *Tridonta* = three-toothed; *borealis* = northern.

294 – *Tridonta elliptica* (Brown)

Tridonta elliptica was one of several ascribed subspecies of *Astarte sulcata* that existed in mid-Victorian times. The practice of splitting one species into several 'varieties' (subspecies) based upon minor differences was frowned upon in the early Nineteenth Century but became very popular by the 1850s. When writing about *Tridonta elliptica*, John Jeffreys defended the copious splitting of species by saying, 'I need not apologise for particularising so many varieties as all naturalists are agreed as to the utility of this mode of discrimination; the time has gone when varieties were not regarded.' The fashion for varieties did not much outlive the Victorian era and during the Twentieth Century many scientists started re-examining the definition of species. Most varieties were adsorbed back into their parent species but some, including *Tridonta elliptica*, were found to have a basis in fact and were deemed to be species in their own right. *Tridonta elliptica* is an Arctic shell that is most common offshore in sand, gravel and mud around Scotland and in the Irish Sea.

Description: L = 3cm. Solid, triangular, equivalve; 30 or fewer strong concentric ridges with finer concentric striations between; margins rounded; inner margin smooth; colour = white, periostracum brown. Etymology: *elliptica* = elliptical.

295 – *Tridonta montagui* (Dillwyn)

A sub-Arctic species that is chiefly known from the North Sea where it lives at depths of 70 metres or more. Although known from Arctic regions, this is a relatively recent addition to the known list of British species. Its deep water habitat makes it unlikely that specimens will come into the possession of amateur conchologists.

Description: L = 1.3cm. Resembles *Tridonta borealis* but is smaller with 40 or more strong concentric ribs; inner margin smooth; colour = white, periostracum is brown. Etymology: *montagui* = after George Montagu.

Cockles

The superfamily Cardiacea (='heart-like'), or cockles, are a broad family of solid, ribbed shells that are often ornamented with spines or blunt tubercles. Their shells are familiar to many holiday-makers as well as to lovers of pickled shellfish. The larger species are edible but only one (*Cerastoderma edule*) is common enough to be commercially harvested. Although most species live offshore, their shells are frequently washed onto the beach, while on some low lying coasts the edible cockles (*Cerastoderma edule*) may be found in its tens of thousands.

296 – *Acanthocardia aculeata* (Linnaeus); Spiny Cockle

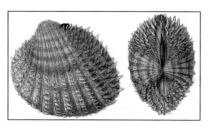

A large, solid and distinctive shell that burrows offshore but which may be found washed up on the beach, often in a fairly worn state. Britain represents the northerly edge of its geographical range and for a while it was believed to occur only in Devonshire. In the 1850s, a craze for offshore dredging increased its range to much of south and south-west England, although there are reports from Scotland, including the Hebrides. It is our largest species of *Acanthocardia* but is generally rather rare and only likely to be found as empty shells along the seashore.

Description: L = 8.4cm; B = 8cm. Large, very solid, equivalve; 20-22 prominent ribs with distinct spines connected to one another by low ridge; margin strongly crenulated; colour = yellow. Etymology: *Acanthocardia* = spiny *Cardium*; *aculeata* = thorny.

297 – *Acanthocardia echinata* (Linnaeus); Prickly Cockle

First described in the Sixteenth Century by the French physician William Rondelet (1507-1566) as the *concha echinata* (prickly shell). This historical name was utilised two centuries later when Carl Linnaeus gave it a full scientific description in 1758. The Eighteenth Century naturalist Otto Friedrich Müller believed that the living animal consisted of little more than a huge foot. This is certainly the impression one gets on seeing live specimens trying to dig themselves into the sand. It may occasionally be found on the shore at the very lowest point of large spring tides but in general it lives below the tide mark down to considerable depths. It is found on all of Britain's sandy coasts and its empty shells will often be found washed up.

Description: L = 5.5cm; B = 5.7cm. Large, sub-orbicular, solid; 18-20 strong ribs with individual, unconnected spines; inside of shell possess deep crenulations; colour = yellow. Etymology: *echinata* = prickly.

298 – *Acanthocardia tuberculata* (Linnaeus); Rough Cockle

For nearly a century, *Acanthocardia tuberculata* was also known as *Acanthocardia rustica* after Carl Linnaeus accidently described the same animal under two different names. Usually the older name will have priority but in this instance both were given in the same 1758 publication and it was not until the 1860s that *Acanthocardia tuberculata* was generally accepted as the official title, it being more descriptive. Although superficially similar to the other British *Acanthocardia* species, the distinct spines, which are not jointed by a ridge, make it instantly identifiable. Such small details are important in defining a species and bring to mind the warning offered by John Jeffreys that: 'More harm has been done to science by a slight and consequently vague diagnosis than by too great a prolixity of detail.' This animal is relatively rare and is found only in the south and west of England where its empty shell may occasionally be washed onto sandy shores.

Description: L = 8cm; B = 7.5cm. Large, solid, equivalve; 21-22 strong ribs with tuberculate spines that are flattened (more spatulate) near the margin and sharper towards the beak; colour = light brown. Etymology: *tuberculata* = tuberculated.

299 – *Cerastoderma edule* (**Linnaeus**); **Common Cockle**

The common cockle was first described by Carl Linnaeus in 1758 and is familiar both for its distinctive heart-shaped shells, which may be found in abundance in some areas, and also for its soft-body which is cooked, pickled and eaten across the entire country. The common cockle prefers beaches which have a low gradient and fine sediment. On some sand flats they can occur in such abundance that they may be collected, usually using rakes or other devices, and sold commercially. This industry has been historically important in many parts of Europe and continues to be so today but it is not without danger. In February 2004, 23 Chinese cockle-gatherers lost their lives when cut off by the incoming tide at night in Morecambe Bay. The edible quality of the cockle has been written about since historical times. It is thought that the molluscs roasted on an open fire in one of Aesop's fables were cockles whose audible fizzing caused a boy to say, 'O wicked creatures, are you singing while your houses are being burnt!' As well as being eaten, the empty shells were used in the building and chemical industries as a source of lime. Most collectors experience little difficulty in finding cockle specimens which may be obtained both alive and dead on most sheltered sandy beaches and estuaries.

Description: L = 4.1cm; B = 4cm. Solid, heart-shaped, equivalve; 22-28 strong ribs with very fine but broad spines; inside margin crenulate; colour = white or off-white. Etymology: *Cerastoderma* = horny skinned; *edule* = edible.

300 – *Cerastoderma glaucum* (**Poiret**)

Cerastoderma glaucum is almost identical to the common cockle (*Cerastoderma edule*), save for a few features such as a shorter ligament and a smoother shell. The two species are most readily distinguished by habitat: *Cerastoderma glaucum* prefers brackish waters which tends to isolate it from the fully marine common cockle. The species has been the source of much confusion. For many years it went under the name of *Cardium lamarcki*, the original specimen of which was found in Devonshire, but it has not been seen there since. The exact status remained a matter of debate until the 1970s when a series of intensive studies established that there were physical and lifestyle differences between the two and that, furthermore, the species had first been described in the 1780s and should more correctly be called *Cerastoderma glaucum*. It is known to occur in various brackish habitats across most of Britain excepting the North Sea. Unlike the common cockle, it may be found amongst vegetation and often anchors itself using a byssus.

Description: L = 5cm. Differs from *Cerastoderma edule* by having a thinner shell, smoother surface, more crenulate interior and a shorter ligament. Etymology: *glaucum* = bright and gleaming.

301 – *Clinocardium ciliatum* (**Fabricius**); **Hairy Cockle**

First described by the Danish zoologist and explorer Otto Fabricius in 1780, the hairy cockle is an Arctic species that was unknown from the British Isles until recently when some live specimens where taken from the Hebrides. It is a small and attractive shell that lives offshore but it is rarely seen in the British Isles.

Description: L = 2.6cm. Solid, equivalve; resembles *Cerastoderma edule* but is smaller, more swollen with finer ridges; interior glossy with inner margin crenulate; colour = white. Etymology: *Clinocardium* = angled cockle; *ciliatum* = hairy.

302 – *Laevicardium crassum* (Gmelin)

Described in 1791 by the German medic and naturalist Johann Gmelin, the large, very distinctive empty (and often worn) shells of this robust cockle are frequently washed onto the seashore from deeper waters. It is known from around the entire British coast and, while not usually abundant, is tolerably common in areas of sand and gravel. It is a shallow burrower and is frequently obtained alive using a dredge. 'It is capable of considerable leaps,' wrote one observer, 'often springing out of the vessel in which it is placed when in captivity.'

Description: L = 8cm. Large, solid, equivalve; distinguished by smooth shell with 40-50 faint ribs which are more prominent at the margins; margin crenulate; colour = brown or yellowish. Etymology: *Laevicardium* = perhaps means left-handed *Cardium*; *crassum* = fat.

303 – *Parvicardium exiguum* (Gmelin); Little Cockle

Another of Johan Gmelin's discoveries, this small species of cockle has turned up in an assortment of odd places including 'the interior of the hardest stones' and pieces of driftwood. Like most cockles, its usual habitat is the sandy seabed where it makes a shallow burrow. It occurs all around Britain, low down on the shore, but can tolerate moderately-low salinities in estuarine areas. Illustration shows *Parvicardium exiguum* with detail of shell surface.

Description: L = 1.4cm; B = 1.4cm. Solid, swollen, equivalve; 20-22 ribs with short, somewhat arched spines on anterior and posterior margins but none in central region; colour = white or yellow, periostracum brown. Etymology: *Parvicardium* = smaller cockle; *exiguum* = little.

304 – *Parvicardium minimum* (Philippi)

As its Latin name implies, this is the smallest of the British cockles, large specimens of which barely reach a centimetre in diameter. It is easily confused with several other small species, most notably *Parvicardium ovale* and *Parvicardium scabrum*, the obvious difference being with the nature and number of ribs, although a good hand lens will be needed to see this. It is more common in the north and west, becoming rarer in the south and absent from much of the North Sea and English Channel. An offshore burrower, its shells are robust and may be washed up onto the beach. Illustration shows *Parvicardium minimum* with detail of shell surface.

Description: L = 1cm; B = 1cm. Shell fragile and circular; 28 to 32 radiating ribs each with numerous flattened spines giving it a texture like the fine side of a cheese grater; colour = white. Etymology: *minimum* = smallest.

305 – *Parvicardium ovale* (Sowerby)

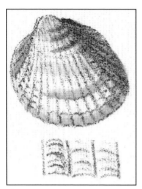

Two hundred years ago, when microscopes and hand lenses were optically substandard, small cockle specimens were the source of much trouble. Many were obtained dead from the beach and had key features that were broken and worn away. As a consequence, specimens from the same species would be given different names by different naturalists. Trying to unravel this tangled mess caused later conchologists many problems as they would often only have brief descriptions and sketches with which to work. The frustration this caused occasionally comes across in their writings. Edward Forbes, when trying to discern what his forerunner William Turton meant with his description of *Cardium elongatum*, was vocal on the matter saying, 'Turton's original inadequate description is unaccompanied by any figure which might enlighten us as to what was actually intended'. Forbes eventually sorted out the chaos and discovered that the oldest valid name was *Cardium fasciatum* ('banded cockle') but, alas, this title was already in use by another species. As a compromise the name *ovale* was adopted by George Sowerby the younger. This is an offshore species but empty shells are not uncommon on sandy shores around all of Britain. Illustration shows *Parvicardium ovale* with detail of shell surface.

Description: L = 1.3cm. Solid, swollen, oval, equivalve; 24-26 ribs with broad, flattened spines on the anterior margin, and pointed, sharp spines on posterior margin, no spines in central region; rows of fine pits between ribs; colour = yellow. Etymology: *ovale* = oval.

306 – *Parvicardium scabrum* (Philippi)

'In strict justice this species ought to be called *roseum*,' wrote John Jeffreys, referring to several pink-coloured specimens he had obtained from southern England and the Channel Islands. Others were amazed that a shell which is so common could have escaped the attention of conchologists until the opening decades of the Nineteenth Century. It was supposed that the little shell must have been mistaken for sub-adult specimens of the common cockle (*Cerastoderma edule*). Like *Parvicardium ovale*, the original name assigned to this species by Rudolph Philippi in 1844, *Cardium nodosum* ('knotty cockle') was already in use requiring the assignment of a new name, *scabrum*. It lives offshore around all Britain but empty shells may be washed onto the beach. Illustration shows *Parvicardium scabrum* with detail of shell surface.

Description: L = 1.3cm. Solid, sub-oval, equivalve; 26-28 ribs all of which bear spines, those on anterior margin broad and low while those on posterior are more pointed; no pits between ribs; colour = white. Etymology: *scabrum* = scratched.

307 – *Plagiocardium papillosum* (Poli)

Named in 1795 by Josepho Poli from an Italian specimen, *Plagiocardium papillosum* was not discovered in British waters until the 1850s when Frederick Collings Lukis dredged some specimens from the coasts of Sark and Guernsey. Since then, it has been found in Cornwall and Devon, where it is extremely rare, but it has only been found with any regularity in the Channel Islands. The gift of several perfect specimens by Lukis caused John Jeffreys to expound on the difference between true naturalists and those who collected shells for profit: 'The naturalist loves science for its own sake, and not for the childish pleasure of acquiring many rare species or even a unique specimen. The naturalist is never selfish or covetous, his only craving being for the sympathy of others who have the same tastes of himself. The mere collector is not so intellectual or estimable.' This is an offshore species and, as explained above, a rare one at that. Very worn specimens have been found on the shore but most are obtained using a dredge. This is probably our rarest cockle species. Illustration shows *Plagiocardium papillosum* with detail of shell surface.

Description: L = 1.4cm. Solid, swollen, equivalve; 24-26 ribs each with broad, irregular, white tubercles; distinctive rows of broad pits between the ribs; interior glossy; colour yellow, sometimes stained with red, brown or purple. Etymology: *papillosum* = covered in papillae.

Trough and Otter Shells

The trough and otter shells (Superfamily Mactracea = 'a kneading trough') are a collection of large, often robust, molluscs, many of whose species may be found around much of the British coastline. Commonly referred to simply as 'clams' the trough and otter shells are generally easy to recognise by their distinctive shape. Most species may be found on the lower part of sandy and muddy shores although some, notably the otter shells, can bury themselves to quite a depth.

308 – *Lutraria angustior* (Philippi)

Named in 1844 by Rudolph Philippi, the deep-burrowing habit and preference for offshore waters means that *Lutraria angustior* is more commonly found on the beach as empty shells which are often worn and battered. This is the smallest and rarest of the three British *Lutraria* species, occurring only in the south and south-west and living offshore, often in deep water. It is rarely encountered in Britain, where it is restricted to the south and south-west. It is more typical of the warmer waters of southern Europe.

Description: L = 10.1cm. Shell, solid with broad gape at ends; elliptical with straight margins; fine concentric lines and ridges; colour = light brown. Etymology: *Lutraria* = otter-like; *angustior* = constricted.

309 – *Lutraria lutraria* (Linnaeus); Common Otter Shell

A generally mud-loving species (although it does occur in sand and gravel), the common otter shell is most often found in estuaries but obtaining live specimens is a mucky business as they must be dug from their deep burrows using a fork. In 1803, George Montagu described the art of finding an otter shell. 'It is rarely obtained alive and then only by digging and that only when the tide is unusually low. Their place of concealment is generally known by a dimple on the surface, through which they can eject water to a considerable height, though the shell is frequently buried two feet beneath.' The common otter shell is known from all British coasts and will most often be found as empty shells, although live specimens can be dug on the lower part of the beach.

Description: L = 13cm. Large, solid, elliptical; both ends have a gape; surface has very fine concentric lines; the pallial line separated from pallial sinus; colour = yellow-white, periostracum is brown. Etymology: *lutraria* = otter-like.

310 – *Lutraria magna* (da Costa); Oblong Otter Shell

An offshore species first described by Emanuel da Costa in 1778 but whose distribution is restricted to southwest England and which is likely only to be found as empty shells. This and other *Lutraria* species were widely eaten in the past and were even considered to be a delicacy in some parts of the British Isles. On the island of Herm they were referred to as 'clumps' with the live shells being roasted on an open fire and the shells afterwards discarded. Otter shells are rarely eaten in Britain these days but they may occasionally be seen on restaurant menus in some Mediterranean countries. Obtaining specimens is usually a mucky business (one conchologist commented that he had 'become a mudlark' in pursuit of otter shells) but sometimes nature does lend a hand. In September 1993, for example, a severe storm in Torbay, Devon, left thousands of live otter shells stranded on the beach, much to the amazement of locals.

Description: L = 12.8cm. Solid, elongate; equivalve; smaller than other Lutraria with concave dorsal margin and rounded ventral margin; pallial line confluent with pallial sinus; colour = white, periostracum brown. Etymology: *magna* = larger.

311 – *Mactra glauca* (Born); Five Shilling Shell

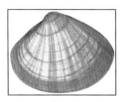

The five shilling shell was once highly prized by collectors, so much so, that specimens could be sold for several shillings a piece (hence the name). Although known from southern Europe, it was not until 1801 that the first British shells came to attention of conchologists. These originated from a Miss Pocock who recovered empty shells from the sands at Hale Beach, Cornwall, and afterwards sold them on to collectors. In the 1820s, William Turton was given a battered shell that had been dredged off Guernsey and, a few years later, live specimens were dug by Frederick Lukis from a small cove on the nearby island of Herm. This confirmed that the five shilling shell was native to Britain and since then, it has been commonly found in the Channel Islands and rarely in Cornwall and Devon. It is most plentiful on Jersey where, in the 1860s, a professional dealer on the island offered 40 pence [about £11 today] for as many specimens as could be obtained. The local fishermen inundated him, and for several years afterwards the price of the shells was severely depressed by the resultant glut. I have obtained specimens in Jersey by digging in fine sand at the lowest point of the largest spring tides. Their large size makes them unmistakable, but the fragility of the shells means that empty specimens tend to be rather battered. Frederick Collings Lukis noted that 'when the tide recedes it buries itself two or three inches in the sand; and when the tide rises it bestirs itself to reveal its hiding place.'

Description: L = 10cm; B = 7.5cm. Large, solid, elliptical, equivalve, not swollen; may be distinguished by large size which exceeds all other *Mactra*; surface has fine concentric lines; fresh specimens possess a brown, satin texture periostracum; colour = off-white with darker rays. Etymology: *Mactra* = a kneading-trough; *glauca* = blue-grey.

312 – *Mactra stultorum* (Linnaeus); Rayed Trough Shell

'It ranges from one end of the British Isles to the other without restriction,' wrote Sylvanus Hanley in 1853 of this commonly occurring shell. Indeed, so common is it that in many areas it was an important source of food for humans, fish and seabirds. In 1861, a harbour channel in Newhaven was being deepened using an industrial steam dredger but as the sediment was churned up, so thousands of rayed trough shells were disturbed and washed onto the beach, much to the delight of the local inhabitants. The Newhaven fishermen also took advantage of this bonanza by clustering their boats around the steam dredger to haul up both the shells and fish that were being thrown up with the sediment. This is a common shell around Britain that burrows in sand and gravel low on the beach. Obtaining specimens, live or empty, should not present too much of a problem. In older books it is usually referred to as *Mactra corallina*, a name that is now defunct.

Description: L = 5cm; B = 3.8cm. Fragile, swollen, equivalve; left valve has two teeth conjoined to form an inverted 'V' shape; colour = buff with brown rays, periostracum brown. Etymology: *stultorum* = foolish.

313 – *Spisula elliptica* (Brown)

Although frequently occurring on the seashore, the five known British *Spisula* species are difficult to identify with certainty. *Spisula elliptica* is a case in point. It very closely resembles *Spisula solida* and has at various times been a subspecies of it. However, the two are quite distinct and, in the words of Edward Forbes, *elliptica* may be distinguished 'by its lesser solidity, more productive shape and above all by the absence of those regular sulci that roughen the dorsal margin of *Spisula solida*'. Some conchologists could not see this difference, including John Jeffreys, who lumped *S. elliptica* with *S. solida*. He anticipated the howls of despair from his scientific colleagues and even wrote a mock letter of complaint to himself: 'Who can possibly doubt *Spisula elliptica* being a species? Well! I wonder where all this innovation will end!'

Description: L = 3.1cm; B = 1.8cm. Solid, triangular, equivalve; in left valve cardinal teeth joined to form inverted 'V' shape which is half the length of hinge plate; fine concentric lines; colour = off-white, periostracum brown. Etymology: *Spisula* = possibly meaning thick or compact; *elliptica* = elliptical.

314 – *Spisula solida* (Linnaeus); Thick Trough Shell

A very common shell around Britain on all sandy shores and one that used to be widely eaten in Devon and Cornwall, and which may still be served up as part of a *fruits de mer* in northern France. As both its Latin and vernacular name imply, the thick trough shell is robust and may be found living on most of our shores, including quite exposed ones, while the empty shells may survive prolonged transportation. Beachcombers should have little difficulty in obtaining empty specimens while living ones may be found by raking in areas of coarse sand or by digging.

Description: L = 4cm; B = 3.5cm. Solid, equivalve; resembles *Solida elliptica* but may be distinguished by inverted 'V' formed by cardinal teeth in left valve which is less than half length of hinge plate and by dorsal area which has fan-shaped patterning; colour = off-white, periostracum brown. Etymology: *solida* = solid.

315 – *Spisula subtruncata* (da Costa)

Once known as the 'lady cockle' in Belfast and simply as 'aikens' in lowland Scotland, this abundant animal has at times been harvested commercially in some northern regions both for human consumption but also, in later years, to feed pigs. It is around the same size as *Spisula elliptica* but is generally more oval in outline and is truncated along one margin. Like other *Spisula* species, this is common around all of Britain and may be found in vast numbers on some seashore areas. There is one further, rare, species *Spisula ovalis* which is not covered here.

Description: L = 2cm; B = 1.25cm. Solid, small, swollen, equivalve; distinguished from other *Spisula* by its truncated anterior and posterior margins, prominent beaks and by the pallial sinus which is very shallow; many concentric lines and prominent growth stages; colour = off-white, periostracum brown. Etymology: *subtruncata* = somewhat truncated.

316 – *Donacilla cornea* (Poli)

A large shell that lives in southern Europe and the Mediterranean Sea where it may reach densities of 3,000 per square metre. Over the years, there have been several reports of *Donacilla cornea* from British waters but most have been dismissed as exotic shells that have been accidentally transported here by fishing boats returning from southern voyages. However, the northern range of this species is currently considered to be southern England, although I am unaware of the exact details of any finds.

Description: L = 8cm; B = 2.5cm. L = 8cm. Solid, sub-triangular, flattened, equivalve; sculpture of fine concentric striations, growth stages clear; colour = white with brown streaks. Etymology: *Donacilla* = a small *Donax*; *cornea* = horny.

Razorfish

The razorfish (Superfamily Solenacea = 'razorfish') possesses an elongate, brittle shell that cannot easily be mistaken for any other type of bivalve. The empty shells are a common sight on sandy beaches while the live animal, which hides itself within a vertical burrow, is rarely seen for, once disturbed, it will dig downwards at such an extraordinary rate that it may be impossible dig out. The razorfish is a common source of food and, aside from the British fishing methods which are described below, I should add the following method used by Italian fisherman in the early Nineteenth Century: 'On finding a razorfish hole, the fisherman leans on his stick and feels about in the sand for the animal', he then 'catches and holds it between his big toe and the next'. Apparently the animal may struggle so violently that injuries to the fishermen's feet were common place.

317 – *Solen marginatus* (Pulteney); Grooved Razorfish

First named in 1799 from Dorset by Richard Pulteney, the grooved razorfish (like most members of this family) was once gathered for food but is now more commonly dug by fishermen for bait. Salt is sometimes used to entice the animals from their burrows as this extract from a 1712 manuscript describes. 'The *Solen* lie in their holes nearly vertical and their places are marked by perforations shaped like keyholes. The fishermen endeavour to tempt them out by putting salt on their tails. The salt penetrating the perforation reaches and irritates the siphons, and the *Solen*, annoyed and pained, rises suddenly to clear itself of the nuisance. His vigilant human enemy watches the moment and seizes the opportunity.' The practice of tipping salt into razorfish holes continues today and is an effective means of catching razorfish. It is widely believed that on sensing the salt the mollusc rises to the surface, thinking that the tide has come in but it is more probable that the salt severely irritates the animal, causing it to vacate its burrow. Originally named *Solen vagina* because of its sheath-like structure (*vagina* = a sheath or scabbard), it was for many years assumed that the grooved razorfish was the female counterpart to the male pod razorfish (*Ensis siliqua*) which, needless to say, it is not. It lives on the lower shore and in some areas may be abundant with empty shells being commonly cast higher up the beach. It is generally rare or absent from northern areas and the North Sea.

Description: L = 12.5cm; B = 2.1cm. Fragile, tubular, equivalve; dorsal and ventral margins straight, gape on posterior and ventral margins; constriction on anterior margin; adductor muscle scar stretches three-quarters of shell length; colour = yellow. Etymology: *Solen* = Razorfish ; *marginatus* = marginated.

318 – *Ensis americanus* (Gould); Jack Knife Clam

A native species of North America that was supposedly introduced to Europe as larvae in tanker ballast water. It was first recorded in Britain in 1989 on Holme beach, Norfolk, and has spread rapidly along the eastern and southern coasts. It is also said to be abundant in some parts of Essex and Norfolk. Its effects on the native species are not yet understood but it is theorised that *Ensis americanus* may prefer finer sediment to some of our existing species and thus might not be in direct competition. It is common in many lowland parts of northern Europe and is expected to spread further afield within Britain.

Description: L = 17cm. Fragile, equivalve; straight dorsal margin, curved ventral margin; may be distinguished from *Ensis arcuatus* by its greater breadth and ventral margin which is distinctly more curved towards the anterior; colour = greenish yellow and brown. Etymology: *Ensis* = scimitar; *americanus* = American.

319 – *Ensis arcuatus* (Jeffreys)

Once believed to be a subspecies of the pod razorfish (*Ensis siliqua*), *Ensis arcuatus* is smaller, more fragile and with a curved ventral margin. Its abundance on some shores illustrates another method by which these animals may be captured. 'The mode in which a dishful of these esculents may be rapidly gathered by children, might be successfully imitated by conchologists, for other than culinary purposes,' observed Sylvanus Hanley. 'A narrow wire, sharpened at one end, is thrust into the sand and passing between the valves, the barbed portion fixes itself in the animal, forcing it to the surface.' This technique is still in use today, with the wire implement often being fashioned from an old coat-hanger. It is common on the lower shore around the entire British coast.

Description: L = 15.2cm; B = 1.9cm. Fragile, large, equivalve; straight dorsal margin and gently curved ventral margin; both ends gaping; colour = white with brown and red blotches. Etymology: *arcuatus* = curved.

320 – *Ensis ensis* (Linnaeus); Common Razorfish

Named by Carl Linnaeus in 1758, the curved shell of *Ensis ensis* bears a resemblance to an old-fashioned cut-throat razor and thus gave this entire family of bivalves their common name. Like all the animals in this family, the common razorfish possesses a powerful, flexible foot that will hang suspended below the shell. This led some early conchologists to believe that the razorfish animal was too large for its shell, but in fact the foot is an organ that ordinarily lies within the shell but which can be filled with fluid, vastly and instantaneously increasing its size. It is the expansion and contraction of the foot that allows the razorfish to pull itself down through soft sand at such a prodigious rate. Indeed, they may burrow so fast that it is impossible to catch up with them using a large garden fork. It is for this reason that those indulging in the art of razorfishing must walk slowly and carefully across the sediment, so as not to alarm the animals into digging deeper within the sand. The common razorfish is, as the name suggests, frequently encountered on the lower shore around Britain's coastline.

Description: L = 1.25cm; B = 9.25cm. Fragile, narrow, equivalve; ventral and dorsal margins curved to same extent; anterior end rounded; adductor muscle scar runs almost full length of shell; colour = white with brown orange streaks. Etymology: *ensis* = scimitar.

321 – *Ensis siliqua* (Linnaeus); Pod Razorfish

In Seventeenth Century Yorkshire the pod razorfish was known as the 'hose-fish' and would be traditionally caught on low spring tides at night by candlelight. The antiquarian naturalist that recorded this, Martin Lister, added that the animals could be made into a delicious sauce which tasted like shrimp. In contrast, a century later the Italian conchologist Giuseppe Poli commented that the animal tasted 'so acrid that none but the poorest would use this kind for food'. Despite this poor review, the pod razorfish is still eaten in some countries and, in my experience, it tastes a little like squid. In modern Britain this species is widely used for fish bait, and in some areas size restrictions apply in order to conserve numbers. It is the largest British razorfish and is commonly found on all coasts where it buries deeply in sand. Its empty shells are often washed up, although finding intact large specimens can be problematic.

Description: L = 20cm; B = 2.5cm. Large, fragile, equivalve; dorsal and ventral margins straight; posterior and anterior ends not rounded but truncated in straight line; colour = cream with brown/orange streaks. Etymology: *siliqua* = a pod.

322 – *Pharus legumen* (Linnaeus)

A small, rounded razorfish that is considered to be relatively localised along the south-western and western coasts of England and Wales. Although found on the lower shore, it is rarely encountered and the delicate shells do not stand up to much battering by waves and currents, although there have been historical instances of dozens of individuals being cast up on the shore following storms. It is one of the two razorfish species (the other being *Phaxas pellucidus*) that is not commonly eaten, although I expect it may be used as bait if encountered by fishermen.

Description: L = 13cm. Fragile, pod-shaped, equivalve; straight ventral margin, the dorsal margin is curved towards the posterior and slightly concave towards the anterior; shells tapers to the anterior; end rounded; colour = off-white. Etymology: *Pharus* = an Egyptian lighthouse; *legumen* = a bean-pod.

323 – *Phaxas pellucidus* (Pennant)

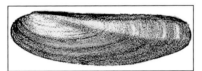

The smallest of our native razorfish, this delicate shell was discovered on the Welsh coast in 1770 by the botanist Reverend Hugh Davies (1739-1821) who sent his specimens to his friend Thomas Pennant. *Phaxas pellucidus* is an offshore species which unlike most razorfish, ventures beyond the shallow coastal waters into depths of a kilometre or more. Its shell is very delicate and does not stand up to much wear and tear which lessens the probability of a beachcomber obtaining a perfect dead specimen. It is widely distributed and can live in a variety of muddy and sandy sediments.

Description: L = 3.7cm; B = 1cm. Fragile, equivalve; dorsal margin straight, ventral margin highly curved; posterior end very rounded, anterior end truncated in a near straight line; colour = cream with brown streaks. Etymology: *Phaxas* = possibly after an Ancient Greek character; *pellucidus* = transparent.

Tellins and Wedge Shells

The Tellins (Superfamily Tellinacea = 'a tellin') is a large, diverse and often beautiful group of shells that burrow shallowly in loose sediment on the lower part of the beach. They have been known since the days of ancient Greece and were frequently gathered for food. Most species are widespread and will be found on the seashore, alive or as empty shells.

324 – *Angulus squalidus* (Pulteney)

First named in 1799 by the Dorset naturalist Richard Pulteney, *Angulus squalidus* is restricted to the south-western and western coasts of Britain where it is uncommon. The lone report of a specimen from Dunbar, in the North Sea, was so far outside the species' usual range that it was dismissed by one Victorian conchologist who cryptically commented that Dunbar was, in his opinion, 'a hotbed of spurious molluscs'. This statement was justified with the comment that many shells reported from Dunbar were actually tropical in origin. This was probably a complaint against the achievements of Captain John Laskey, an early Nineteenth Century naturalist who actively collected shells in the Dunbar region but whose studies were afterwards subject to a deal of revision. *A. squalidus* is an offshore dweller that is said to occur 'sparingly' and whose empty shells are rarely seen on the beach.

Description: L = 4.5cm; B = 2.7cm. Solid, flattened, inequivalve; right valve more swollen and rougher texture than left; rounded anterior margin, elongate posterior margin tapering to point; cruciform muscle scars sometimes visible on posterior dorsal area; colour = variegated or banded with orange, yellow and pink. Etymology: *Angulus* = angular; *squalidus* = rough.

325 – *Angulus tenuis* (da Costa); Thin Tellin

'Helplessly stranded amid seaweeds and foam, they lie in the rays of the setting sun, wet and glistening, ruby, gold, amber and opal. These pretty wrecks always accompany a storm and afterwards the sea puts on a sorrowful face, as if repenting the havoc that he made.' This was John Jeffreys' view of the mass stranding of thin tellin shells that would be seen on many British beaches. The animal is indeed vulnerable to storms and strong currents. It is a shallow burrower and lives higher up the beach than most bivalves and so is easily dislodged. Emanuel da Costa named this specimen in 1778 and, as Jeffreys' description implies, the thin tellin is both common, widely distributed and very pretty: many children will gather them when on holiday and the beachcomber should have little difficulty in obtaining specimens.

Description: L = 3cm. L = 2.5cm. Fragile, flattened, triangular, inequivalve; right valve larger than left; distinct concentric lines; colour = variegated or concentrically banded with red, white, orange and yellow. Etymology: *tenuis* = thin.

326 – *Arcopagia crassa* (Pennant); Blunt Tellin

Described by Thomas Pennant in 1777, this is a solid, robust shell that burrows in sand on the lower shore. It has been known as a native British species for some centuries and was originally believed to be restricted to the south-west of England, although it has since been found in most regions apart from the southern North Sea and eastern English Channel. If unearthed, it will rapidly rebury itself and has been observed always to rest on its left side when in sediment. It has been collected for food but it is not especially common on the seashore and may generally be found alive only on the lowest spring tides although empty shells may be washed higher up the beach.

Description: L = 5.25cm; B = 4.5cm. Solid, oval, flattened, inequivalve; right valve larger than left and more swollen; distinctive lone crenulations on posterior part of the ventral margin; many concentric ribs and radiating lines; colour = white with rays of brown/orange. Etymology: *Arcopagia* = probably meaning leaf-tipped; *crassa* = solid.

327 – *Arcopella balaustina* (Linnaeus)

This is an attractive shell that is common in the Mediterranean and which was only discovered in Britain when the shell collector George Barlee dredged a specimen from Bitterbuy Bay, Ireland, in the 1850s. Other specimens followed from Scotland, Guernsey and Cornwall, but the shell was considered very rare in Britain and by the 1860s was fetching up to £5 (about £300 today) a specimen on the collectors' market. It remains rare to this day and, as a denizen of deeper waters, is unlikely to be encountered by the casual beachcomber, although there are reports of fragments having been washed up in south-west England.

Description: L = 2.2cm; B = 1.9cm. Fragile, oval, swollen, equivalve; irregular concentric ridges; margin smooth; colour = white with red-brown rays. Etymology: *Arcopella* = possibly meaning hidden-tip; *balaustina* = pomegranate-coloured.

328 – *Fabulina fabula* (Gmelin)

Apparently known to the historical Dutch as 'sny boontje', this is a small but generally common shell around all British coastlines and is said to occur 'wherever the coast exhibits a long expanse of sand'. First described in 1791 by the German botanist Johann Gmelin, this species resembles *Angulus tenuis* but whole specimens may be identified by checking the surface of the two valves. The right valve will be covered with concentric lines and oblique striations, while the left is far smoother and without any striations. This is an inhabitant and shallow burrower on the lower shore and beachcombers will have little difficulty in obtaining specimens.

Description: L = 2.1cm; B = 1.3cm. Fragile, flattened, triangular, inequivalve; right valve more swollen than left; many fine concentric lines but right valve is also obliquely striated; colour = white tinted with orange. Etymology: *Fabulina* = like a small-bean; *fabula* = a small-bean.

329 – *Gastrana fragilis* (Linnaeus)

A southern European shell that was first described by Carl Linnaeus in 1758. It is common from the Mediterranean Sea up to Brittany, but its presence in British waters is rare and localised. As late as 1853 its known British range was from the Irish coast but in the following decade a number of examples were dredged from various localities from Cornwall to the west coast of Scotland. Although uncommon, *Gastrana fragilis* can live in sand on the lowest part of the beach and empty specimens do occur on the seashore.

Description: L = 4.5cm; B = 3.1cm. Fragile, swollen, wedge-shaped, equivalve; irregular fine concentric ridges with many radiating striations; colour = white, periostracum brown. Etymology: *Gastrana* = turgid; *fragilis* = brittle.

330 – *Macoma balthica* (Linnaeus); Baltic Tellin

Once described under the name *Tellina rubra* by Emanuel da Costa, an Eighteenth Century British conchologist who steadfastly ignored the Linnaean system for naming species in favour of his own convention. The Victorian conchologist Edward Forbes discarded da Costa's name because it 'emanates from an author who, having wilfully passed over the just claims of his predecessors in nomenclature, has forfeited the right of challenging for himself the law of priority'. In 1853, Forbes proposed that the name *solidula* be used but in fact, both he and da Costa had got it wrong as the oldest name is *balthica*, as given by Carl Linnaeus in 1758. This is a mud-loving species that can lie several centimetres below the surface and which lives on the middle and lower part of the shore. It can tolerate low salinities and may be especially common in estuaries and mud-flats where empty shells may be readily obtained. As the name implies, it is found across much of northern Europe, including the Baltic Sea.

Description: L = 2cm; B = 1.75. Solid, oval, swollen, equivalve; very fine concentric lines; colour = very variable and often banded with white, crimson, yellow and purple. Etymology: *Macoma* = possibly 'hair of the Turkish goddess Ma'; *balthica* = Baltic.

331 – *Moerella donacina* (Linnaeus)

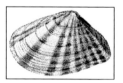

Described variously as 'elegant' and 'Britain's prettiest tellin shell', some specimens of this small shell have beautiful pink rays which radiate across its surface while others are less patterned or even dull. As with so many species that are common in southern European, the northerly range of *Moerella donacina* only just clips the British Isles with it being commonly found only in south-west England, although specimens do occur along the west coast as far north as the Orkneys. It prefers to burrow into coarse sand and is not known to live on the seashore. Empty specimens may be found on the beach but the shell is brittle and subject to wear and tear by the elements.

Description: L = 2.5cm; B = 2cm. Fragile, oblong, inequivalve; right valve more swollen than left; anterior margin rounded, posterior tapering and slightly gaping; many fine concentric striations; colour = white with pink radiating rays. Etymology: *Moerella* = small *Moer*; *donacina* = resembles *Donax*.

332 – *Moerella pygmaea* (Lovén)

The nature of this shell puzzled many conchologists, some of whom did not think it to be a species in its own right, but instead a dwarf form of *Moerella donacina*. Some even felt that the two species were mutually exclusive northern and southern subspecies, even though their ranges overlap to a considerable degree. In fact, there are consistent differences, most notably that *M. pygmaea* is more solid, more convex and with a finer surface sculpture. It adopts the same habitat as *M. donacina* but is generally more common in the northern parts of Britain and especially off eastern Scotland.

Description: L = 0.8cm; B = 0.5cm. Small, fragile, oblong, inequivalve; similar to *Moerella donacina* but smaller with rounded posterior margin and pallial sinus that occupies two-thirds of length; colour = very varied, sometimes rayed and bright with white, yellow, pink and orange. Etymology: *pygmaea* = dwarfed.

333 – *Donax variegatus* (Gmelin)

First described in 1791 by Johann Gmelin, it has always surprised me that this beautiful and comparatively large shell, which is a rich brown and cream colour with a distinctive white ray, does not have a vernacular name (or at least one of which I am aware). Edward Forbes rated it as one of Britain's prettiest shells, saying, 'its vivid tinting presents one of the few exceptions to that tameness of colouring which characterises the shells of the less sunny climates of Europe'. It is restricted to south-western coasts and is only commonly encountered in the Channel Islands. In 1685, Martin Lister pictured a shell that had been collected in 'Garnsey' (Guernsey) and it was from there that most Victorian collectors obtained their specimens. It lives on the lower shore where it lies buried in sand. Empty shells may be found in those areas where it occurs.

Description: L = 3.8cm; B = 2cm. Fragile, wedge-shaped, flattened, glossy, equivalve; surface almost smooth; interior often stained violet; colour = pale brown, yellow with distinctive white and red-brown rays. Etymology: *Donax* = a species of fish ; *variegatus* = variegated.

334 – *Donax vittatus* (da Costa)

Named by Emanuel da Costa in 1778, the athletic ability of this animal has been much admired for if the shell is dug from the sand it will use its foot to jump and twist about the beach until it finds a suitable resting place. It is common around most of Britain and is found 'wherever there exists a wide range of unmixed sand'. The shell may be variously and attractively coloured with white, yellow, brown and purple but its small size makes this hard to appreciate. Empty shells are commonly found on sandy shores.

Description: L = 3cm; B = 1.8cm. Solid, wedge-shaped, glossy, equivalve; many fine radiating lines; margins crenulate; interior often stained purple; colour = variegated with radiating or concentric bands of brown, purple, yellow and white. Etymology: *vittatus* = banded.

335 – *Azorinus chamasolen* (da Costa)

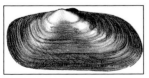

Although first described as a British species by Emanuel da Costa in 1778, this large and distinctive shell seems to have escaped the notice of many Victorian conchologists, few of whom mention it in their writings, even in passing. The majority of records seem to come from the Irish Sea where it is dredged from muddy locations (often in thick, sticky mud). It is certainly not one of our commonest shells and, aside from being restricted to the southern and western coasts, it lives offshore, often in deep water. I suspect that empty shells are rarely found on the shore.

Description: L = 6.5cm; B = 3cm. Shell solid, equivalve and oblong in shape; gapes widely at the posterior and anterior margins; surface possesses fine concentric lines and ribs;

right valve with two spine-like cardinal teeth, the left valve with just one; colour = white with brown periostracum. Etymology: *Azorinus* = after the Azores; *chamasolen* = clam-razorfish.

336 – *Gari costulata* (Turton)

First dredged off the coast of Torbay by William Turton in 1820s, this small shell is not common (although neither is it very rare) but its offshore habitat means it is not often seen on a beach. Turton was pleased with his original specimens, recording that, 'of this nonde-script and most beautiful shell we have taken by the dredge four fine specimens, three of which were living ones'. It is known from around the British Isles, although it appears to be quite localised with some people referring to it as being 'one of our rarest bivalves' while others think it to be common. The truth lies somewhere in-between these two extremes.

Description: L = 2.5cm; B = 1.6cm. Fragile, flattened, oval, equivalve; posterior area has 12-20 strong radiating ribs; many fine concentric lines; colour = rose or white with purple rays. Etymology: *Gari* = possibly meaning spear; *costulata* = slightly-ribbed.

337 – *Gari depressa* (Pennant); Large Sunset Shell

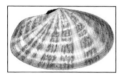

The sunset shells derive their common name from the coloured rays that radiate obliquely across the surface of the shell giving the impres-sion of stunning sun set. The historical name for *Gari depressa* was for many years the 'setting sun shell' and this was reflected in its Latin name which, for a few decades, was *vespertina* (= 'belonging to the evening'). Although small, the shell may be locally abundant in muddy sand on the lower shore and was once gathered commercially and eaten in Ireland. One visitor to Kenmare, Country Kerry, recalled that 'heaps of their shells may be seen about the huts of the peas-antry'. It is found around most of the British Isles, although it may be rarer in the North Sea and eastern English Channel. It is quite common, and after rough weather quantities of their shells may be washed up on the beach. To obtain live specimens, dig in fine or muddy sand on the lowest part of the beach.

Description: L = 6cm; B = 3.1cm. Solid, flattened, oblong, equivalve; concentric striations and fine radiating lines; pronounced posterior gape; anterior rounded, posterior trun-cated; colour = cream with purple rays. Etymology: *depressa* = compressed.

338 – *Gari fervensis* (Gmelin); Faroe Sunset Shell

Quite distinctive and commonly found on most European coasts including all the British ones. It laboured under several different names during the Nineteenth Century and there was a minor battle as to whether the Latin name should be spelt *fervensis* or *ferroensis*. The former eventually won the day as this was the original spelling used by Johann Gmelin in 1791. This is a shallow burrower in clean sand and both living and empty shells may be found with reasonable frequency. There are records of specimens being recovered from the stomachs of small members of the shark family, such as dog fish.

Description: L = 4.5cm; B = 2.5cm. Rounded anterior but posterior is sharply truncated; a distinctive ridge runs from the umbo to the posterior margin; fine concentric striations and distinctive growth lines; colour = variable white, pink, yellow and purple, often rayed. Etymology: *fervensis* = from the Faroe Islands.

339 – *Gari tellinella* (Lamarck)

This species was not recognised as being British until several years after the French botanist-cum-zoologist Jean-Baptiste Lamarck had described it in 1818. Prior to this time, it was probably mistaken as a sub-adult of the large sunset shell (*Gari depressa*). It was for many years regarded as rare, something that in later times was considered quite strange given its relative abundance on some coasts. It is the only British species of *Gari* that habitually lives offshore, although its empty shells may be cast onto the beach. It is rare or absent from much of the North Sea and the eastern English Channel.

Description: L = 2.8cm; B = 1.5cm. Solid, flattened, oblong, glossy, equivalve; dorsal, anterior and posterior margins rounded, ventral margin straighter; inside is white; colour = white or yellow with rays and bands of purple, pink and orange. Etymology: *tellinella* = small *Tellin*.

340 – *Solecurtus scopula* (Turton)

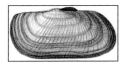

Once rated as one of the rarest British shells. Edward Forbes commented that he usually only saw 'single specimens in the cabinets of collectors'. The first British specimen was dredged from Exmouth by William Clark and later handed to William Turton. It is more common than Forbes and others supposed, although it does tend to be localised in its distribution. In the 1850s, the Reverend Richard Dennis was one of many conchologists who travelled to the tiny Channel Island of Herm in search of specimens. He was rewarded with the discovery of two live specimens of *Solecurtus scopula* which he watched with fascination before concluding that they were in fact bullies: 'I looked at them, really travelling at a great rate for molluscs, and without the least respect for their neighbours' comforts, walking over and upsetting all the weaker shellfish that were with them.' This is principally an offshore species, although there are rare reports of specimens being found low down on sandy shores. It is restricted to the western and southern coasts where its occurrence is localised.

Description: L = 6cm; B = 2.1cm (usually much less). Solid, oblong, equivalve; anterior and posterior margins rounded and gaping; around 45 strong radiating striations which are restricted to the posterior and middle regions only; many concentric lines; colour = white. Etymology: *Solecurtus* = a short *Solen*; *scopula* = scorpion.

341 – *Abra alba* (Wood)

This small shell, described by William Wood in 1802, is a lover of muddy environments and may occur in abundance in estuaries, sheltered bays, harbours and other muddy environments. It is notably active and is capable of dragging itself through the mud to find a more advantageous position. It is chiefly a littoral or shallow water species, and so the recovery of a specimen during a deep sea dredging expedition in 1847 caused a rush of excitement, during which a Russian conchologist almost knocked over a French colleague. 'Excuse me,' said the Russian. 'But I had become intoxicated by the sight of the molluscs!' *Abra alba* may be found around the British Isles, both alive and dead.

Description: L = 2cm; B = 1.25cm. Fragile, oval, equivalve; dorsal margin very rounded, anterior margin more pointed than posterior; fine concentric lines; colour = white. Etymology: *Abra* = pretty; *alba* = white.

342 – *Abra longicallus* (Scacchi)

Described from the Mediterranean Sea in 1834 by Archangelo Scacchi, who was then a young Italian zoologist with a fascination for dredging and seashells. *Abra longicallus* is a deep water shell that did not enter the list of known British species until the early Twentieth Century when live specimens were dredged off north-west Scotland. It is small and is extremely rare in water shallower than around eighty metres, although it may be quite common in deeper water sediments and has even been recovered from sections of sea floor that are nearly five kilometres in depth. In Britain it is best known from Little Minch and Loch Fyne in western Scotland but I am not aware of any recent finds. The beachcomber will be highly unlikely to find specimens on the seashore.

Description: L = 2cm; B = 1.6cm. Fragile, flattened, oval, inequivalve; left valve more swollen than right; fine concentric and radiating lines; colour = white. Etymology: *long-icallus* = long and hard.

343 – *Abra nitida* (Müller)

Described from Denmark by Otto Müller in 1776, this animal hides itself well from the conchologist as it not only lives offshore, but also prefers to bury itself within 'slimy mud', an environment that few divers or dredgers opt to search. Although widespread in its geographical distribution, it is not common and is rather localised in its occurrence. It may be found in water that is only a few metres deep (although it has been recovered from depths of 300 metres) and empty shells may occasionally find their way on shore. I have found dead examples by sieving shell gravel.

Description: L = 2cm; B = 1.1cm. Fragile, oblong, flattened, glossy, equivalve; fine concentric lines; colour = white, sometimes with flecked surface. Etymology: *nitida* = glossy.

344 – *Abra prismatica* (Montagu)

George Montagu, who described this species in 1803, was able to see some fresh specimens which retained their outer skin (periostracum). From this he observed an iridescence and so named the animal after its prismatic lustre. Unlike many of the British *Abra*, this species is not restricted to muddy environments but is more commonly found in fine sand. It is widely distributed and may occasionally be found on the lower shore, although it is most often recovered in water of a few metres' depth.

Description: L = 2cm; B = 1cm. Resembles *Abra nitida* but is narrower, less rounded (especially on anterior margin) and with a shallower pallial sinus; colour = glossy white. Etymology: *prismatica* = prismatic.

345 – *Abra tenuis* (**Montagu**)

In 1859, the conchologist Frederick Collings Lukis recounted how he had stumbled across an unexpected abundance of *Abra tenuis* when dredging a tidal pond: 'I sifted the weeds at the time of nearly high tide, while the sea water was rushing into the pond; and I imagine that the active *Abra* was rising to the surface of the mud to imbibe the fresh stream from the sea, and thus became entangled in the weeds to be transferred to my sieve, an easy prey.' Lukis found dozens of specimens but his experience highlights the localised nature of this species which, although often abundant is generally an uncommon shell that seeks out muddy areas with a reduced salinity. It does not live offshore and is rarer in the north and northwest of Britain. Its empty shells may be found in abundance in those areas where it lives. It is a favourite food of fish and seabirds.

Description: L = 1cm; B = 0.75cm. Small, fragile, triangular, flattened, equivalve; fine concentric lines; anterior margin more rounded than posterior; colour = white, often iridescent. Etymology: *tenuis* = thin.

346 – *Ervilla castanea* (**Montagu**)

Originally described in 1803 by George Monatgu, this minute and easily overlooked shell was for decades only known from dead and worn specimens, all of which came from Cornwall. By the 1820s, it was assumed that the shell was not native to Britain but had been brought here from foreign climes by a ship wreck in the Cornish region. Then further specimens were recovered from the Scilly and Channel Islands and, finally, a live animal was recovered from near Penzance, Cornwall, by Robert MacAndrew in the 1840s. Its rarity is probably a function of both its restricted occurrence, its small size and its preference for deep water (usually below 50 metres). Most beachcombers are unlikely to encounter specimens during their littoral sojourns.

Description: L = 1.2cm; B = 0.7cm. Small, solid, flattened, glossy, equivalve; concentric lines with clear growth stages; colour = red-brown sometimes with darker rays. Etymology: *Ervilla* = a small *Erva*; *castanea* = chestnut-coloured.

347 – *Scrobicularia plana* (**da Costa**); **Peppery Furrow Shell**

'It principally inhabits sludgy or muddy places, buried to the depth of five or six inches,' remarked George Montagu in 1803. Known as 'mud hens' in Devon, the peppery furrow shell can be difficult to obtain but it is large and common enough to have been used as a food source in historical times. Montagu believed that it tasted bitter while others describe it as being quite piquant. It is probably because of its sharp taste that it acquired its original Latin name of *piperata* (= peppery) and also colloquial name. A lover of stiff, sticky mud, this shell is rarely sought these days and even in historical times there were few collectors who would venture into estuaries and other filthy places to obtain living animals. 'Cabinets are usually only furnished with worn specimens washed up after rough weather,' muttered Edward Forbes in 1853. It is littoral, can tolerate low salinities and is especially common in estuaries. Empty shells are common.

Description: L = 7.8cm; B = 6.4cm (usually less). Large, fragile, flattened, oval, equivalve; irregular concentric lines and ridges; large internal ligament; prominent crescent-shaped chondrophore; colour = white but often stained by mud, periostracum brown. Etymology: *Scrobicularia* = little trench; *plana* = level or plain.

Heart Cockles

Grouped together in this section are three species from the superfamilies Arcticacea (= 'Arctic') and Glossacea (= 'tongue'), two of which are large and very robust while the other is exceedingly rare.

348 – *Arctica islandica* (**Linnaeus**)

The size and solid nature of this shell make it quite unmistakable. Although common in most parts of Britain, I have only ever come across two examples. The first was an empty, whole shell that floated past me while I was swimming in a bay in Jersey; the second I dug up in a Hertfordshire garden while planting potatoes (evidently a present from a previous occupant). As a sub-Arctic species, this large shell was a favoured food in northern Europe and, in historical times, was the generic 'clam' of Shetlanders and went by the name of 'krok-fishur' in Iceland, where it is regarded as a delicacy. It burrows in soft sediment on the lowest part of the beach and is easily dislodged by bad weather. In some parts of Scotland and Scandinavia impromptu feasts would occur after stormy weather cast up large numbers of *Arctica islandica* onto the shore. Its first depiction was by Martin Lister in the late Seventeenth Century and its size and abundance ensured that it received a description in Carl Linnaeus' 1758 pioneering work on the classification of animal life, *Systema Naturae*. Although often stated as being common around the whole of Britain, it may be rarer in south-western England. Empty shells can be found onshore but they may be surprisingly brittle. It is also known as a fossil from many Ice Age sediments.

Description: L = 13cm; B = 12cm. Large, solid, sub-circular, equivalve; many fine concentric lines; smooth pallial line; margin smooth; colour = light brown. Etymology: *Arctica* = Arctic; *islandica* = Icelandic.

349 – *Coralliophaga lithophagella* (**Lamarck**)

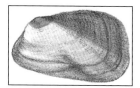

A southern species that was originally discovered in the Mediterranean by the French naturalist Jean-Baptiste Lamarck. During the 1850s, several specimens were recovered in Brittany leading John Jeffreys to implore fellow conchologists to 'search for *C. lithophagella* on our southern shores and especially in the Channel Islands'. It was Jeffreys himself who was to be successful when, a short while later, he and his friend Frederick Collings Lukis were dredging off the east coast of Guernsey and there found 'a young and perfect specimen of *Coralliophaga lithophagella*'. A few years later, a dead specimen was recovered in the same locality by Edward Waller but, as far as I'm aware, it has not been seen in the British Isles since (this is probably because dredging for specimens is now a rare pastime). It is an offshore species that lives in coarse gravel and is one of the rarest British seashells.

Description: L = 1.9cm; B = 0.9cm. Fragile, wedge-shaped, equivalve; posterior margin narrow and pointed, ventral margin wide and truncated; ventral margin straight, dorsal curved; fine concentric ridges; colour = light brown. Etymology: *Coralliophaga* = coralline eater; *lithophagella* = small rock eater.

350 – *Glossus humanus* (Linnaeus); Heart Cockle

Described as 'a rare and noble shell' by William Turton, this large, robust shell is unmistakable because of its prominent and highly incurved umbones. Although now landed with the Latin name of 'human tongue' (*Glossus humanus*), it is more popularly known as the heart cockle because of its characteristic heart-shape when viewed side on. The heart cockle is localised in its distribution and is chiefly known from the western and southern coasts of Britain where it lives offshore, and may occasionally be found in some abundance. It prefers muddy environments and, when studied alive by the Reverend James Bulwer in 1826, was observed to be completely oblivious to changes in light, sound, pressure and other external stimulation. However, when Bulwer dropped a particle of sand into its open valves, the animal emitted a jet of water that squirted right out of the aquarium. In historical times it was commonly procured from fishermen who would keep any shells they dredged to sell to passing tourists or conchologists. It is rarely seen onshore and is most commonly found in the Irish Sea and off the Cornish and Devonian coasts. Illustration shows *Glossus humanus* with detail of beak region.

Description: L = 10cm; B = 9.5cm. Large, solid, equivalve; distinguished by twisted beaks and shell's heart-shape when viewed from the side; colour = off-white. Etymology: *Glossus* = tongue; *humanus* = human.

Venus Shells

The Superfamily Veneracea (= 'Venus shells') are solid, distinctive and often pretty. Some of the larger species are (or were) gathered for food although they are rarely abundant enough to permit commercial fishing. Their empty shells may be commonly encountered on sandy beaches, but on spring tides fishermen may be observed using long rakes to comb them from loose sandy sediment in certain areas.

351 – *Callista chione* (Linnaeus); Smooth Venus

This large, attractive shell was named after the mythical Chione, whom the Roman poet Ovid described as the beautiful daughter of Daedalion in his *Metamorphoses*. Its chestnut coloured shell is a favourite among conchologists and collectors alike, and has had much attention devoted to it. In 1791, the Sicilian naturalist Guiseppe Poli was so enamoured with his specimens of *Callista chione* that he not only wrote a lengthy essay on its beauty, but also declared it to be a delicacy, even providing a recipe for cooking it. The shell is indeed attractive and not uncommon in the west and south-west of Britain but it is not easy to come by specimens. The animal lives in waters of a few metres depth or more where it burrows in sand. The shells are rarely cast onto the beach and in days gone past, most collectors obtained specimens either by dredging or by asking trawler men to keep those that came up with their nets.

Description: L = 7.5cm; B = 6.8cm. Large, solid, oval, equivalve; smooth surface with numerous very fine concentric lines; colour = brown with darker rays. Etymology: *Callista* = most beautiful; *chione* = a character in *Metamorphoses*.

352 – *Chamelea gallina* (Linnaeus)

This shell is highly variable in its size and general shape, so much so, that for nearly a century most British conchologists called it by the name *Venus striatula* and did not recognise that it was the same as the Mediterranean species *Chamelea gallina*. In 1863, and after a decade of debate on the mater, John Jeffreys corrected the mistake but by then the number of different names used for this one species had reached ten. The situation was not aided by unscrupulous shell dealers who would doctor specimens by dying them different colours or altering their shape in order to catch out 'ignorant collectors'. The shell may be found on all British coasts. It burrows in sand on the lowest part of the shore and may be discovered by digging or raking. Empty shells may be commonly found onshore and are distinguished by their highly ridged surface.

Description: L = 3.2cm; B = 2.8cm. Solid, triangular, swollen, equivalve; numerous strong concentric ridges with fine striations between; colour = off-white with three brownish rays. Etymology: *Chamelea* = unblemished; *gallina* = a hen.

353 – *Circomphalus casina* (Linnaeus)

'The shell is remarkably pretty,' wrote John Jeffreys, 'but is almost totally devoid of colour.' He is correct, for although this small shell does not retain much patterning, its compact shape and regular concentric ribbing provides a pleasing symmetry that has attracted collectors and conchologists to it for centuries. It is widely distributed about Britain, but might be rarer on the southern North Sea. It is an offshore burrower and tends to be local in its occurrence, but empty shells may occasionally be found on the beach. Good specimens make an attractive addition to any collection.

Description: L = 4.3cm; B = 4cm. Solid, circular, equivalve; strong concentric ridges which are broader and flattened (but not tuberculated) on the anterior margin; lunule heart-shaped; colour = yellow-white with brown rays. Etymology: *Circomphalus* = circular phallus; *casina* = a nymph.

354 – *Clausinella fasciata* (da Costa); Banded Venus

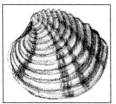

In 1838, the Cornish naturalist Jonathan Couch remarked that the banded venus was an active animal that on occasion would walk across the seabed and hop into crab pots. A few decades later other conchologists disputed this: 'The animal is inactive and does not seem to be fond of exhibiting itself to the curious malacologist,' was the opinion of one. Like many venus species, *Clausinella fasciata* is notably attractive and has received its fair share of compliments. 'The elegance of its shape and the variety and brilliance of its painting are unsurpassed in any other British bivalve,' wrote John Jeffreys before adding, 'like many a wild flower, however, it is too common to be thought much of.' Live specimens may occasionally be discovered on the lowest part of the shore but it is generally a shallow water dweller. Empty shells are generally common but, being small, must be searched for carefully. It may be found on all British coasts.

Description: L = 2.2cm; B = 2cm. Solid, flattened, triangular, equivalve; many alternating large and small ridges; colour = pink, red, yellow, brown which may be formed into attractive streaks and rays. Etymology: *Clausinella* = small *Clausina*; *fasciata* = banded.

355 – *Dosinia exoleta* (Linnaeus); Rayed Artemis

First mentioned by Martin Lister in the 1690s, it was a specimen from Guernsey (plus one from Norway) that formed the basis of Linnaeus' original 1758 description. Widely distributed, it may be found on the lower shore in coarse sand and gravel and is large enough to be gathered up and eaten in some areas. Empty shells are common and in some areas may be found washed quite high up the shore. It is quite pretty and often patterned with coloured rays.

Description: L = 5cm; B = 4.8cm. Solid, circular, flattened, equivalve; numerous concentric ridges; clear growth stages; colour = white with bands and rays of brown and pink. Etymology: *Dosinia* = meaning unknown; *exoleta* = worn away.

356 – *Dosinia lupinus* (Linnaeus)

Similar to the rayed artemis (*Dosinia exoleta*), but smaller with a more convex shape and generally lacking the coloured rays that give *Dosinia exoleta* its common name. Opinions vary as to its distribution which, although countrywide, is sometimes said to be mutually exclusive to that of the rayed artemis (i.e. where one occurs, the other does not). This may stem from *Dosinia lupinus* preferring slightly finer sediment but I have encountered both species sharing the same section of sandy seashore. Like the rayed artemis, *Dosinia lupinus* is generally inactive and prefers to burrow deeply. It may generally be found by digging, although empty shells are not uncommonly found upon the beach.

Description: L = 4cm; B = 4cm. Solid, circular, flattened, equivalve; numerous fine concentric ridges and fine radiating lines; colour = off-white with light yellow patterning. Etymology: *lupinus* = wolf-like.

357 – *Gouldia minima* (Montagu)

At the turn of the Nineteenth Century this was one of the rarest British shells and was highly sought after by collectors. The great naturalist George Monatgu had to make do with specimens that were 'very small and in poor condition' while a majority of conchologists could only dream of owning an example of this shell. As with many shells that were once deemed rare, the situation was reversed by the mid-Victorian era when naturalists started to rake the offshore seabed with their dredges and trawls. 'Large and beautifully coloured British examples now decorate all our best cabinets,' said Edward Forbes in 1853. *Gouldia minima* may be found on all British coasts where it lives just offshore, either on the surface of the seabed or buried shallowly. It would appear to be locally common and the empty shells may be washed onto the beach.

Description: L = 1.4cm; B = 1.3cm. Small, solid, circular, equivalve; numerous broad concentric ridges; colour = variable and patterned with white, yellow, red and brown. Etymology: *Gouldia* = after John Gould; *minima* = smallest.

358 – *Irus irus* (Linnaeus)

This variable, unusual animal probably took its name from the shaggy, ragged appearance of its shell which is most often found wedged into narrow rock crevices or among the holdfasts of oarweed (*Laminaria*). It is the prominent concentric ridges that are most notable and which give it such a distinctive appearance. The shell is generally oblong in shape but this may vary depending on the nature of the cavity into which it is wedged. Although very common in southern Europe, it is seldom seen in our region and is known mostly from the southern and western coasts. It may be searched for on rocky shores on the lowest of spring tides. Empty shells are generally reported to be more common than living specimens.

Description: L = 2.5cm; L= 1.25cm. Fragile, oblong, equivalve; shell often distorted; surface dominated by around 16 strong concentric ridges which, in fresh specimens, are raised, between these may be finer concentric striations; colour = white, sometimes with brown staining. Etymology: *Irus* = a mythical beggar; *irus* = ditto.

359 – *Mercenaria mercenaria* (Linnaeus); Quahog

A large and distinctively robust bivalve that originates from the east coast of North America where it was once used as a form of currency among native tribes and is currently prized as a food source. The first British specimen of a quahog was discovered in 1864 from the Humber estuary, although how it got there is uncertain. In the subsequent decades a number of attempts were made to establish commercial colonies of quahogs without success and it appears that it disappeared from Britain around 1907. In 1925, a barrel of quahog spats was imported from New York and an attempt was made to establish a breeding population in Southampton, close to the water outlet from a power station. The animals did not thrive until the late 1940s when a series of severe winters decimated a number of local burrowing shellfish, giving the quahogs an opportunity to usurp their ecological niches. It has since spread along adjacent parts of the south coast and has also been found in Blackwater, Essex, although it is occasionally reported from other parts of Britain. The Southampton quahogs have been commercially fished since the 1960s but in recent years overfishing has seen numbers decline markedly. The quahog buries itself deep within mud or muddy sand and is especially common on estuary flats, where they can tolerate reduced salinity. Empty shells may be washed on shore but those seeking specimens will need to travel to the south coast to obtain them.

Description: L = 13cm. Large, solid and very distinctive; broadly oval outline; ornamentation of concentric lines, some of which form ridges, and fine radiating lines; lunule is heart-shaped; colour = shell is off-white with brown or greyish periostracum; some specimens have zig-zag markings at the margins. Etymology: *Mercenaria* = commercial.

360 – *Tapes aureus* (Gmelin); Golden Carpet Shell

First depicted by Martin Lister over three hundred years ago, the golden carpet shell may typically be found living just below the low water mark (although live specimens are known on the beach). It is the smallest of the carpet shells but is nonetheless gathered for food in France and some parts of southern Britain. It can survive in a wide range of sediment types, including mud, sand and coarse gravel and may be locally abundant (although rarer in most of Scotland). Empty shells are commonly washed ashore.

Description: L = 3.8cm; B = 3.3cm. Solid, oval, equivalve; concentric ridges and lines and radiating striations; colour = white or light brown with a complex pattern of brown and purple streaks, rays and blotches. Etymology: *Tapes* = a tapestry; *aureus* = golden.

361 – *Tapes decussatus* (Linnaeus); Chequered Carpet Shell

In the Seventeenth and Eighteenth Centuries this shellfish was known as 'purrs' in some parts of Britain (although exactly which parts is not clear) and was widely eaten in most parts of its range. The French and Channel Islanders still eat this species which is known locally as 'palourde', a name which can also be applied to carpet shells in general. Some years back an attempt was made to farm beds of 'palourde' along the east coast of Jersey but the venture was not financially successful and the shellfish are now gathered as a hobby by locals. In most areas this is the commonest and most easily obtained of the carpet shells which burrows in sand or gravel from the middle of the beach downwards. Empty shells are common and distinctive.

Description: L = 5cm; B = 4.5cm. Solid, oval-squarish, equivalve; concentric striations and radiating ribs intersect to form a cross-hatched pattern, especially on the anterior and posterior areas where they may become tuberculate; colour = white with purplish-brown spots, rays or zigzags. Etymology: *decussatus* =cross-hatched.

362 – *Tapes philippinarum* (Adams and Reeve); Pacific Carpet Shell, Manila Clam

An introduced species from the Pacific Ocean that has colonised parts of the Italian coast and which was introduced into Poole Harbour, Dorset, for aquaculture in 1988. The Pacific carpet shell adapted well to conditions there and by the mid-1990s it was so abundant that licenses to gather and sell the clams commercially were granted to over 30 fishermen. Around 250 tonnes of the shellfish are collected and sold annually but the shell remains largely restricted to Poole, although it is expected to spread further along the coast in time. The Pacific carpet shell is a similar size to the chequered carpet shell (*Tapes decussatus*) but it may be distinguished by its orange foot and the black and white markings on the shell. It lives in the mid to lower part of the shore and any effects on local ecology have yet to be fully assessed.

Description: L = 6cm. Large, solid, oval-triangular, equivalve; strong concentric lines crossed by radiating lines forming decussate patterning; colour = off-white with distinctive black and white rays, streaks and blotches. Etymology: *philippinarum* = Filipino.

363 – *Tapes rhomboides* (Pennant); Banded Carpet Shell

Recognised and eaten in Britain since at least 1685, this robust bivalve is often strikingly patterned with streaks and zig-zags of reddish purple. Although it is common on seashores around Britain, naturalists held the shell in high regard. 'Its elegant shape and bright and variegated painting help to redeem a collection of our native shells from the common opprobrium that they are poor and dingy compared with foreign shells,' wrote one authority. At one time the banded carpet shell was divided into several subspecies, some of which were thought to be localised to particular parts of the British Isles. However, as with many historical taxonomic subdivisions, these observations have not withstood the test of time and the differences have been re-adsorbed into the coherent name *Tapes rhomboides*. The shell is widespread and may be dug up in sandy areas at low water. It can be locally abundant and empty shells may be found washed high up on the shore.

> Description: L = 6cm; B = 5cm. Solid, oblong, equivalve; numerous concentric striations but no radiating ribs; surface smooth towards the beaks; colour = off-white with patterning of yellow, pink, brown and red. Etymology: *rhomboides* = rhomboidal.

364 – *Timoclea ovata* (Pennant); Oval Venus

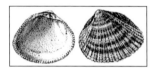

A common and widespread shell that, as its name implies, is egg-shaped in outline. It is small and has a coarse sculpture that, to the naked eye, can make it resemble a small cockle. However, under the hand lens or microscope the shell displays the classic features of a venus and has a rough but entrancingly regular pattern of ribs and concentric lines. The original scientific description made by Thomas Pennant in 1777, consisted of just 17 words, concluding with the observation that it was 'the size of a horse bean'. A century later, conchologists were devoting over a thousand words to its description, thus illustrating the immense progress that had been made in the zoological sciences between the Eighteenth and Nineteenth Centuries. The oval venus is widespread around Britain and, while preferring shallow offshore waters, it may occasionally be found living in sand on the lower shore. Its empty shells are found on the beach but, as noted above, a hand lens is usually necessary to secure an identification.

> Description: L = 1.7cm; B = 1.4cm. Small, solid, flattened, equivalve; numerous concentric striations crossed by around 50 radiating ridges creating a tuberculate pattern; colour = yellow-white. Etymology: *Timoclea* = possibly an Ancient Greek woman; *ovata* = egg-shaped.

365 – *Venerupis senegalensis* (Gmelin); Pullet Carpet Shell

This large, edible, bivalve has been known under a variety of names about Britain. In Devonshire it was known as a 'puller' and at the other end of the country, Shetlanders called it 'kullyak', a name allegedly derived from the Norse word for a haddock. Indeed, in the early Nineteenth Century the Shetland based naturalist Dr Arthur Edmondston was a promoter of the pullet carpet shell as a food source and claimed that it tasted better than oysters (few agreed with him). These days the pullet carpet shell is not widely eaten in Britain but remains a delicacy in France where it is often grilled with garlic butter. For many decades it was known to British conchologists under the species name *pullstrata* (meaning a pullet) but in recent years this has been corrected to the older and more valid *senegalensis* (from Senegal). This also demonstrates the geographical spread of the species. The pullet carpet shell is common around most British coasts where it buries in shallow sand, often in association with large rocks and stones. It may be found on the lower shore and empty shells are common.

Description: L = 4.3cm; B = 3.8cm. Solid, rhomboidal, equivalve; numerous concentric ridges which may be irregular or rough posteriorly, these are crossed by fine radiating ribs; colour = white with reddish brown markings especially at the anterior. Etymology: *Venerupis* = rock Venus; *senegalensis* = from Senegal.

366 – *Venus verrucosa* Linnaeus; Warty Venus

The genus *Venus* at one time held a dozen or more different British species but over the centuries the attention of conchologists has whittled this number down to just one, the warty venus. Anciently known as the 'Cornwall heart cockle' its distribution is restricted to the south and western coasts of Britain where it lives on the lowest part of the shore buried in coarse sand and gravel. It has been eaten in the past and is still a gastronomic delicacy in northern France and the Channel Islands. As a boy in Jersey I would accompany my father on many low water fishing expeditions where, armed with a metal-pronged rake, we would gather a small basket of 'praire' (as *Venus verrucosa* is known locally) from banks of loose sand. The shell is extremely robust so that when the metal prongs encountered one the rake would make a distinctive 'ping' alerting us to the whereabouts of our prey. The empty shells are remarkably resistant to wear and tear and may be found cast up on the beach some distance from their point of origin. The tough, highly ridged exterior immediately distinguishes the warty venus from any of the other shells in this family.

Description: L = 5cm; B = 4.5cm. Solid, swollen, circular, equivalve; easily distinguished by its thick shell and rows of strong concentric ridges which become warty and spiny at the margins, these are crossed by fine radiating lines; colour = yellow-brown. Etymology: *Venus* = the goddess of love; *verrucosa* = warty.

367 – *Turtonia minutum* (Fabricius)

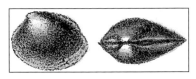

This tiny animal may be super-abundant where conditions are right. One recent British study recovered some 60,000 specimens from a single cubic metre of sediment which means that literally millions may occur in some places. Even so, at just two millimetres in breadth, what is surely Britain's commonest bivalve managed to escape the attention of several prolific collectors and conchologists including William Turton, the man after whom the genus was later named. It was first identified from Greenland in 1780 and is extraordinarily widespread, being found in Arctic, temperate and subtropical seas across the world. The little bivalve lives by attaching itself to seaweed, rocks and other objects between the tide marks. Discovering specimens is not difficult provided you have a keen eye and a hand lens but identification is best secured using a microscope. Empty shells are very common in sediment from which they may sieved and picked using a damp 00 gauge paintbrush.

Description: L = 0.25cm; B = 0.2cm. Minute, oval and thin; three cardinal teeth per valve; fine concentric lines and distinctive growth lines; colour = brown. Etymology: *Turtonia* = named after William Turton; *minutum* = minute.

368 – *Petricola pholadiformis* (Lamarck); American Piddock

The American piddock is an accidental immigrant to British waters from its native North America when, in the Nineteenth Century, it was introduced with the oyster *Crassostrea virginica*. The first British report came from 1890 in the River Crouch, Essex, but it was afterwards recognised from a number of locations along the southern and eastern coastlines, usually in areas where oysters are commercially farmed. It is not a true piddock (see Chapter 15) and lives on the lower shore by boring holes in soft rock, wood and other substances. In some parts of Europe it has replaced native piddock species, especially *Barnea candida*, although this is not thought to have happened in Britain. It is large and easily recognisable but is localised in its distribution. Perfect examples of empty shells are rarely seen on the beach but they may be found wedged inside its hole. It is not a true piddock but it does closely resemble members of that family.

Description: L = 6.5cm. Fragile, oblong, equivalve; concentric striations crossed by around 40 ribs that may display flattened spines in anterior area; two cardinal teeth in the right valve and three in the left valve colour = off-white, periostracum brown. Etymology: *Petricola* = possibly means rock stalk; *pholadiformis* = like a piddock.

369 – *Mysia undata* (Pennant)

Once described as 'inelegant but peculiar', this thin, fragile shell lives just offshore where it burrows in soft sediment, a habit that has left it vulnerable to the seabed disruption that results from commercial trawling. Empty shells are not common on the beach but they may occasionally be found, although perfect specimens are hard to come by. It is found around the entire British coastline.

Description: L = 3.4cm; B = 3.1cm. Fragile, circular, equivalve; numerous concentric lines; margins smooth but undulating; interior glossy; colour = white or pale yellow. Etymology: *Mysia* = meaning unknown; *undata* = wavy.

Chapter Fourteen

Gape, Basket and Flask Shells

WITHIN THE Order Myoida (= 'mya shells') there are two suborders. This chapter covers the Suborder Myina which contains the gape, basket and flask shells, a large group of distinctive bivalve shells that burrow in soft sediment or bore their way into wood or soft rock (the second suborder is covered in Chapter 15). Although widespread in their geographical occurrence, most Myina species are highly specialised and must be searched for in the appropriate medium.

Gape Shells

Although common on some coasts, gape shells (superfamilies Myacea = 'Mya shells'; and Gastrochaenacea = 'ventral gape') are deep burrowers and are generally only encountered as empty shells. They are distinctive because of the large opening (gape) that exists even when the shell is closed shut.

370 – *Mya arenaria* (Linnaeus); Sand Gaper

The sand gaper occurs across the entire northern hemisphere and has been used as an important source of food in many countries including China, Japan, Europe and North America where, in the 1850s, some 5,000 bushels (a bushel = 36 litres) a year were being exported from Boston annually. It was once eaten (and used as fish bait) in Britain and is historically known as the 'old maid' on the south coast and the 'cock brillion' in Northern Ireland. The animal burrows deeply in many types of soft sediment and may tolerate very low salinities, allowing it to occur in large numbers in estuaries, from whence it has been commercially harvested at low tide. It is alleged to live for several decades and may be found around the British Isles where it reaches peak abundance in estuaries. Live shells must be obtained by digging (a long fork is needed as some specimens may lay half a metre or more deep). Empty shells are not uncommon and may be distinguished by their size and convex nature.

Description: L = 15cm; B = 7cm. Large, solid, elongate, inequivalve; right valve is highly convex, the left somewhat less so; chondrophore large and projecting in left valve; surface covered in numerous concentric lines; growth stages visible; no teeth in the hinge; colour = off-white, periostracum brown. Etymology: *Mya* = the Greek term for these shells; *arenaria* = sand-dwelling.

371 – *Mya truncata* (Linnaeus); Blunt Gaper

Described as having a rich, creamy flavour, the blunt gaper has been collected and eaten for thousands of years in many parts of Europe. It is not just humans who seek it out. The stomachs of cod abound with the remains of this animal. They have even been found inside walruses causing some historical naturalists to speculate that these large mammals would rake the sand with their tusks in search of a meal. Described as the 'broad pholade muscle' in the Eighteenth Century, the blunt gaper has many regional vernacular names including 'smirslin' in Shetland which is allegedly derived from the Norse word for butter (a reference to its taste). Although not very tolerant of low salinity water, the blunt gaper is commonly found in estuaries where it buries at least 30 centimetres in depth and may be discovered by digging at low tide. Like most species of gaper, once dug up, the animal cannot bury itself and must lie exposed to the elements and potential predators. Empty shells may be found on the shore but in my experience they are often quite worn which perhaps reflects the energy needed to expose them from their deep burrows.

Description: L = 6.5cm; B = 5cm. Solid, oblong, swollen, inequivalve; right valve more convex than left; posterior margin straight, gaping and truncated; spoon-shaped projecting chondrophore; numerous concentric lines with fine radiating lines; colour = off-white, periostracum brown. Etymology: *truncata* = truncated.

372 – *Sphenia binghami* (Turton)

William Turton named this species after Major-General George Ridout Bingham (1777-1833), a successful commander during the Napoleonic wars whose heroic deeds were current at the time of this shell's discovery. Although related to the deep burrowing *Mya* species, *Sphenia binghami* has eschewed a life in sediment for the security of wedging itself into small holes and narrow cracks. This offers a great deal of protection but limits the animal's size, with most specimens barely reaching a centimetre in breadth. In areas of soft rock it may frequently be found inside the holes made by piddocks and other boring bivalves but almost any confined space will suit, including the tangled holdfasts of oarweed (*Laminaria*). Rare on the lower shore, it is common in shallow water but finding and extracting specimens can be a time consuming and protracted affair. A penknife and long tweezers are handy for this.

Description: L = 0.6cm; B = 1.25cm. Thin, oblong but outline irregular inequivalve; right valve larger and more convex than left; posterior rounded and slightly gaping; surface undulating and covered in concentric lines; colour = white. Etymology: *Sphenia* = meaning unknown; *binghami* = after George Bingham.

373 – *Corbula gibba* (Olivi); Basket Shell

Once described as being 'one of the commonest bivalves found around the British Isles', the basket shell is only abundant in localised areas, though it may be found on sandy shores around all of Britain. The accidental export of this species has led to ecological concerns in areas of Australia where, over a period of four decades, it has become gregarious in some south-eastern areas. Finding specimens, live or dead, is not difficult in most places and is simply a matter of digging and sieving sand or muddy gravel on the lowest part of the shore. It may immediately be identified by the unequal shape of its two valves, the right of which is much larger and more convex than the left.

Description: L = 1.5cm; B = 1.3cm. Small, solid, triangular, inequivalve; right valve much larger and overlaps left which is often covered in thick periostracum; anterior margin extremely rounded; many concentric striations with only a few fine radiating lines; colour = white or red-brown, periostracum brown. Etymology: *Corbula* = little basket; *gibba* = gibbous.

374 – *Gastrochaena dubia* (Pennant); Flask Shell

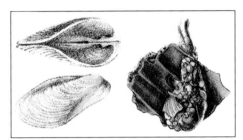

This rock-boring animal has been afforded some supernormal abilities, including the idea that it could carve holes in solid granite as suggested by George Montagu in 1803. Even at the time, this was thought highly unlikely and was confirmed a few years later by Frederick Corbin Lukis who noted that in hard rock regions the flask shell was reduced to living inside old oyster shells. That said, this animal has been observed to tunnel its way into most types of sedimentary rock, including hard sandstones, and derives its vernacular name from the flask-shaped excavation it creates. The French naturalist Frédéric Cailliaud even dared to eat some specimens but declared them to be 'insufferably acrid' with a taste like bitter cucumber. The flask shell is restricted to southern and western coasts and is generally to be found below the tide marks. It is most commonly found in soft rocks but specimens have been obtained from within the empty heavy shells of large molluscs such as oysters. It is not often found on shore and, in times gone by, most specimens were obtained using a dredge. Illustration shows *Gastrochaena dubia* with an image of its burrow.

Description: L = 2cm; B = 0.8cm. Fragile, triangular, equivalve; characterised by broad gape on the anterior ventral margin; surface rough and irregular with concentric lines; no teeth in hinge; colour = off-white, periostracum brown. Etymology: *Gastrochaena* = ventral gape; *dubia* = doubtful.

Rock Borers

The Superfamily Hiatellacea (= 'little gapers') are a family of shells that has generated much debate over the years. Exactly how many species there are and how they may be related is still problematic to conchologists. In the absence of consensus I have included the three species below, but opinions differ on the subject. Contrary to their common name, most species do not actively tunnel into rock but may instead be found in stiff mud or inside the vacated holes of other boring molluscs, such as piddocks.

375 – *Hiatella arctica* (Linnaeus); Wrinkled Rock Borer

The British *Hiatella* has been the subject of intense debate for over a century and a half and even now it is still uncertain whether there is just one variable species or several separate ones. As someone who does not readily enjoy the splitting of species, I have included just one here, *Hiatella arctica*, but in other works you may also see the species

Hiatella rugosa and *Hiatella gallicana*. Although described as a rock borer, this animal does not make holes for itself but inhabits the vacated excavations of other boring molluscs such as the piddocks. It may also wedge itself into other small spaces where it can hide very effectively, its only outward sign being the leathery siphons. It is a common animal which may be found low down on the shore but also offshore in very deep water. It is said that as one generation dies, so one of its children, which nestle within its shell, will utilise the vacant hole (a bit like inheriting a family home). Extracting the shells from the hole is often problematic as they will be wedged tight against the sides. Empty shells are rarely seen loose on the shore.

Description: L = 3.5cm; B = 1.5cm. Solid, oblong, often inequivalve; general rectangular outline but the shape varies depending on the space it inhabits; posterior gape; double ridge from beaks toward posterior which may be spiny; surface uneven with concentric lines; colour = white, periostracum light brown. Etymology: *Hiatella* = little gaper; *arctica* = Arctic.

376 – *Panomya arctica* (**Lamarck**)

A northern species that has been found, usually at considerable depth, in the North and Irish Seas. In the early Nineteenth Century it was trawled up with regularity from the Dogger Bank after which the empty shells would be used as household ashtrays and grease pots. However, this practice stopped when the fishermen discovered that there was a commercial market amongst conchologists. It is not a littoral species and lives offshore in muddy sand. As such, it is unlikely to be encountered on the beach, alive or dead.

Description: L = 7.5cm; B = 5cm. Solid, oblong, inequivalve; right valve just larger than left; posterior margin is truncated and has a gape; sculpture of fine concentric lines; distinct furrow in the middle of both valves; colour = white, periostracum is brown. Etymology: *Panomya* = complete *Mya*; *arctica* = Arctic.

377 – *Saxicavella jeffreysi* (**Winckworth**)

A relatively recent discovery, it was first described in 1930 by Harold Winckworth (1878-1947). It is small and, while being widespread in its distribution, it lives offshore in sand below about 10 metres in depth and is considered rare. Most specimens are obtained by dredging but there is at least one record of an empty shell being found on shore. It is one of several species that are named in honour of John Gwyn Jeffreys, an eminent conchologist who held a particular interest in deep sea molluscs.

Description: L = 1cm; B = 0.6cm. Fragile, oblong, equivalve; gape at posterior and anterior margins; posterior of shell rounded and very swollen; dorsal margin straight, while ventral margin slopes; sculpture of fine concentric lines; colour = white, periostracum white-yellow. Etymology: *Saxicavella* = small rock borer; *jeffreysi* = after John Jeffreys.

Chapter Fifteen
Piddocks and Shipworms

THE PIDDOCKS AND SHIPWORMS (suborder Pholadina = 'hidden in a den') are a large suborder of molluscs that can tunnel into soft substrates such as wood, some sedimentary rocks and stiff mud. They may occur in large numbers and were a considerable nuisance to wooden piers, ships' hulls, etc., which could be rendered structurally unsound by their tunnelling in just a few years. Their occurrence around Britain is generally governed by the availability of a suitable material in which these shellfish can bore. Thus, on some parts of the Dorset coast the soft shale may be peppered with holes while in granitic areas such as the Scilly Isles, Cornwall and parts of Scotland, these molluscs are almost entirely absent.

Piddocks

The piddocks (Superfamily Pholadacea) are a distinctive and attractive collection of bivalves that typically use their serrated wedge-shaped shells to bore into wood or soft rock. A surprisingly diverse number of species has been reported from the British Isles, many of which are not native but have arrived from tropical climes inside lumps of driftwood, cork and other materials (these foreign species are not included here; for a full list see *Annals and Magazine of Natural History*, v.6: pp.121-127, 1860). They were once common in wooden piers and ships but the increasing use of concrete, stone and fibreglass may be responsible for a noticeable decline in the reporting of these animals from some parts of the country.

378 – *Barnea candida* (Linnaeus); White Piddock

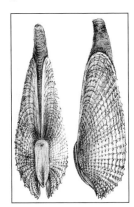

First noticed in the late Seventeenth Century by Martin Lister, this small piddock is capable of boring into a variety of substances from peat and wood to chalk and shale. There are even historical records of it having been found in hard igneous and metamorphic rocks such as granite and gneiss but, based on modern observations, this seems somewhat unlikely. The white piddock may be found around all of Britain on the lower shore but its occurrence is largely governed by the availability of suitable rocks or other substances into which it can tunnel. Thus, and like most boring molluscs, it tends to be rare in hard rock areas (such as the far south-west and parts of Scotland) and more common where soft rocks occur. I have seen parts of the Dorset coast where the soft shale and limestone are peppered with holes made by this mollusc. Empty shells are common but extracting them from the holes in one piece may be problematic.

Description: L = 4.3cm; B = 2.5cm. Fragile, swollen, oblong, equivalve; posterior gape; no cells (septa) on hinge plate; many concentric ridges and radiating ribs which form into spines in posterior area; colour = white. Etymology: *Barnea* = after Daniel Henry Barnes; *candida* = white.

379 – *Barnea parva* (Pennant); Little Piddock

Much of what has been said about the habitat preferences of the white piddock (*Barnea candida*) may be applied also to the little piddock. However, the geographical distribution is more restricted with the little piddock being known only from the south and south-west coasts of England. Like most piddocks, the shell is brittle and it is difficult to obtain whole specimens. This was a source of frustration to many early collectors whose display cabinets contained only fractured specimens. The little piddock tends to be quite localised in its distribution but it is reportedly common in parts of south Devon. Empty shells are fragile and do not survive for long once the animal has died.

Description: L = 4.6cm; B = 2cm. Fragile, swollen, oblong, equivalve; broader and more rounded than Barnea candida; posterior and ventral gapes; smooth tubercle on hinge plate; numerous concentric ridges and radiating ribs forming a strong reticulate pattern except in anterior area; colour = off-white. Etymology: *parva* = small.

380 – *Pholas dactylus* (Linnaeus); Common Piddock

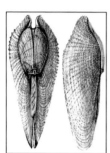

Historically known as the 'stone piercer', the common piddock may occur in abundance where conditions suit. It is especially prolific in soft, but coherent, materials such as peat, marl and packed sand but may also tunnel into wood and sedimentary rocks. In 1863, a storm on the Tenby coast was estimated to have dislodged and killed 15,000 individuals while one historical survey of the peat at Saundersfoot found more than 100 shells in a metre square. The common piddock has been used as a food source and for fishing bait both in Britain and abroad, although the practice of gathering them commercially seems to have long-since ceased. It is by far the largest of the British piddocks and has, in exceptional cases, found to reach a length of 24cm. The living animal is phosphorescent and has been observed to glow with a green-blue light at night. It is only found on southern and western coastlines where it may be locally very common on the lower shore.

Description: L = 12.5cm; B = 4.3cm (sometimes more). Large, fragile, swollen, equivalve; distinguished by size; anterior and posterior gapes; surface with many concentric ridges and around 40 radiating ribs which are concentrated in the anterior region to form sharp spines; row of cells (septa) below the beak; colour = white. Etymology: *Pholas* = hiding within a den; *dactylus* = finger-like.

381 – *Pholadidea loscombiana* (Turton); Paper Piddock

Named by William Turton after the dedicated but now forgotten Exmouth naturalist Clifton Loscombe, a gentleman scientist who, during the early Nineteenth Century, collected and then distributed many shell specimens from the south coast of England, including this species of which he was the discoverer. Like its fellow piddocks, this species is a borer but it appears to favour soft media and is known mostly from stiff mud, peat and clay and only rarely from soft rocks such as poorly cemented sandstones. In Britain it is known only from the south and west coasts where it lives on the lower shore but is generally uncommon or rare. It is one of the few piddock species that is known to live in deep water environments (most piddocks are either littoral or live just offshore). The young shells are morphologically very different to the adult and have been the source of much confusion. The Nineteenth Century scientist who originally described this species, William Turton, initially believed that the young and adult forms were separate species.

Description: L = 4cm. Fragile, oblong, equivalve; distinguished in the adult form by a cup-shaped appendage (known as the siphonoplax) attached to the posterior; anterior margin rounded and, in subadult form, gaping but this closes in adult; left valve has prominent chondrophore, right less so; colour = white. Etymology: *Pholadidea* = Pholas-shaped; *loscombiana* = after Clifton Loscombe.

382 – *Zirfaea crispata* (Linnaeus); Oval Piddock

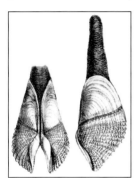

Described by James Petiver in the early 1700s as the 'furrow-rib'd pholade mussel', the oval piddock is a large and widespread species that may be found around all of Britain. It is known to bore into quite hard rocks, such as schist, but may also be found in peat and soft wood. It has reportedly been used as a food of last resort by hard-pushed coastal communities in Scotland and is generally believed to be rarer in southern England where it has to compete with the common piddock (*Pholas dactylus*).

Description: L = 8cm; B = 4.5cm. Solid, swollen, sub-oblong; equivalve; furrow runs from beak to ventral margin; anterior margin angular and pointed; ventral and posterior gapes; about 20 concentric ridges which form into spines in the anterior area; colour = white. Etymology: Etymology: *Zirfaea* = possibly after a Greek magician; *crispata* = curled.

383 – *Xylophaga dorsalis* (Turton); Wood Piddock

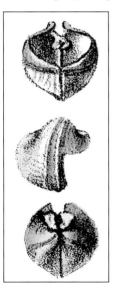

A strictly wood-boring mollusc that may be found living in wooden piers, floating tree trunks and other submerged timber. The first known specimens were recovered from the planking of a wreck that had been submerged for half a century off Torbay but most examples of this shell come from floating logs or driftwood which bring this animal within the reach of the beachcomber. The wood piddock is generally an offshore dweller and may live at considerable depths. It has even been found tunnelling its way into submarine telegraph cables. It may be found all around Britain and should be searched for among any driftwood that is cast up onto the shore.

Description: L = 1.5cm; B = 1.3cm. Small, fragile, globular, equivalve; shell divided by double ridge and deep groove; anterior gape only; anterior region possesses complex pattern of concentric ridges while posterior is smooth; colour = off-white. Etymology: *Xylophaga* = wood-eating; *dorsalis* = back.

384 – *Xylophaga praestans* (Smith)

First discovered in wood that was collected off the Northumberland coast in 1903, this is a rare shell that is known from only a handful of localities in Europe. It lives offshore and may be considered as one of Britain's rarest and more inaccessible molluscs.

Description: L = 2cm; B = 1.9cm. Small, fragile, globular, equivalve; resembles *Xylophaga dorsalis* but is larger with more pronounced posterior gape and broader more distinctive ridging in the anterior region. Etymology: *praestans* = meaning unknown.

Shipworms

Shipworms (Family Teredinidae = 'borer') are wood-boring bivalves that create long calcareous-lined tubes, the far end of which houses the animal. Once a serious menace to wooden-hulled ships, the shipworm is more rarely seen these days and tends to be restricted to wooden structures such as piers and floating logs.

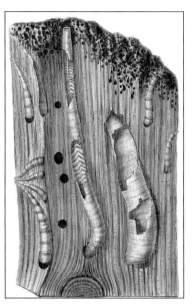

385 – *Teredo navalis* (Linnaeus)

Once called the 'Dutchman's pest', this shipworm was the bane of historical sea captains who had little choice but to watch as this destructive organism chewed its way into their wooden hulls causing them to become weakened and water-logged. Although well-known to seafarers, it was not much studied by British conchologists leading John Jeffreys to remark that 'it is extraordinary that the animal of such a common species has not been described by any author'. Part of the problem is that the shell is rarely accessible and may live deep within the timber at the end of a tunnel (which may be 30 centimetres or more long) that is lined with a calcareous sheath; thus, the process of removing the animal from its home often led

The calcareous-lined tubes of the shipworm used to be a menace to sailors.

to its destruction. In 1859, a Dr Berloren of Holland kept shipworms in an aquarium for several months and noticed that over time the animals became 'tame' and would not withdraw themselves in reaction to loud noises or sudden bright light, as once they had. (He also noticed that they 'seemed to prefer the sunny side of the jar'.) Although very common all around Europe in historical times, *Teredo navalis* is considerably rarer these days as its one time habitat (untreated wooden ships and piers) has greatly decreased, forcing it to survive in driftwood and the occasional standing wooden structure. Finding and extracting specimens can thus be quite an arduous process.

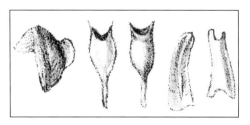

Description: L = 0.75cm; B = 0.75cm. Small, fragile, globular, equivalve; profile shape resembles a horse's saddle; pallets of two parts and are shaped like a tulip; numerous ridges on anterior lobe and concentric lines on posterior disc; colour = white. Etymology: *Teredo* = a borer ; *navalis* = of ships.

386 – *Lyrodus pedicellatus* (Quatrefages)

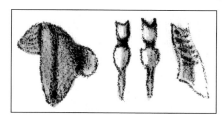

Originally discovered in the north of Spain, there have been rare reports of this species from the Channel Islands and Plymouth, where it has been found boring into wooden piers and shipwrecks. In the Nineteenth Century this small animal caused much trouble in Alderney where a landing stage was discovered to be riddled with its holes after just two decades in the sea. However, in recent years it has only rarely been reported which is perhaps a consequence of a decline in the sort of obsessive conchologist who would make themselves present when a land stage was being dismantled and the increasing use of stone and concrete to construct piers.

Description: L = 0.5cm; B = 0.5cm. Very similar to *Teredo navalis* but pallets consist of three distinct parts with a distinct constriction near the top. Etymology: *Lyrodus* = meaning unknown; *pedicellatus* = pallet-stalked.

387 – *Nototeredo norvegica* (Spengler); Common Shipworm

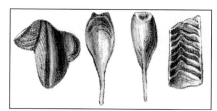

The presence of so many foreign shipworms in European waters, brought here by ocean-faring vessels arriving from tropical ports, led to speculation that *Nototeredo norvegica* was not native to the British Isles but a recent immigrant. This debate began shortly after the discovery of *Nototeredo norvegica* in British waters in the early Nineteenth Century, and was still going strong in the 1850s when specimens were being recovered from all over Britain. By this time, few conchologists were in doubt that the animal was established and breeding here but the question still remained: Had it been imported or not? Sylvanus Hanley noted that *Nototeredo norvegica* was more common in northern England than the south, something that he found odd for a supposedly tropical immigrant, and a few years later John Jeffreys discovered that this species featured in *Museum Wormarium*, a 1655 work by the Danish antiquarian Olaf Worm. By the 1860s, consensus favoured it being native and, far from being rare, as many collectors had once believed, it was common if somewhat localised in occurrence. *Nototeredo norvegica* may be found around all the British Isles but it only tunnels into submerged standing timbers (i.e. not floating wood) and may construct tubes that are many centimetres in length, making them difficult to find and extract. In the past, most specimens were procured from piers and landing stages after the wooden timbers had been removed from the sea (in some cases the need for removal was caused by the shipworm's destructive tunnelling); there is now a general absence of wooden piers but finds are still reported from shipwrecks and the wooden poles used as part of mussel and oyster farms.

Description: L = 1.6cm; B = 1.5cm. Fragile, globular, equivalve; generally distinguished by larger size and tube length which may be 30cm long or more; anterior and posterior gapes; anterior lobe and disc serrated, posterior disc smoother with concentric lines; pallets lozenge-shaped with short handle; colour = white. Etymology: *Nototeredo* = southern *Teredo*; *norvegica* = Norwegian.

388 – *Psiloteredo megotara* (Hanley)

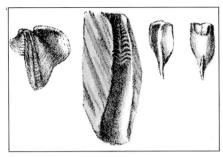

'The united valves . . . have fancifully been compared to a helmet,' wrote Forbes and Hanley in 1853. 'The middle fang shaped portions constituting the headpiece, the two trigonal areas composing the crown, and the posterior auricle forming a kind of crude ornament, or support for the crest.' When viewed in profile, one can see their point and this is particularly true of *Psiloteredo megotara* which has the appearance of a Roman soldier's headwear. *Psiloteredo megotara* was first identified in a sub-adult form from Torbay in 1822 by William Turton but it was not until a wooden pier in Kent had been almost entirely destroyed by its tunnelling that the adult from was recognised in 1853. It is found both in floating timber and standing wooden structures, such as piers, and is generally widespread about the British Isles. A majority of recent specimens were taken from wood, cork and other flotsam and jetsam washed onto the seashore.

Description: L = 1cm; B = 1cm. Similar to *Nototeredo norvegica* but smaller with pallets that are narrower, have larger auricles and which have a semi-circular hole in the end that exposes the laminations within; colour = white. Etymology: *Psiloteredo* = smooth *Teredo*; *megotara* = great-eared.

Chapter Sixteen

Lantern
and Pandora Shells

HELLS WITHIN the Order Pholadomyoida are generally thin, white and inequivalve. They are mostly offshore species and are quite rare around much of Britain. The three main sub-groups are the lantern shells, Pandora shells and the septibranchs.

Lantern Shells

The lantern shells (Superfamily Thraciacea = 'sea nymphs') are generally flattened and oval in shape, much like an old-fashioned oil-lamp (hence the name). Only a handful of British species is known, most of which may be found on all our coasts, usually on the lowest part of sandy shores or just offshore. The empty shells are surprisingly robust and may be found on many sandy shores.

389 – *Thracia convexa* (Wood)

A globular, small shell that is widely distributed about the British Isles but rather localised in its occurrence. It was considered to be one of Britain's rarest bivalves by early Victorian collectors but it was later discovered that its preference of burying deep in sticky mud offshore had placed it beyond the attention of many conchologists. Most specimens were obtained using a dredge but were frequently dead and poorly preserved. Many conchologists relied on obtaining fossil specimens, recovered from glacial deposits (which were more common than living examples) for their display cabinets. It is a rare shell and not commonly known from the seashore.

Description: L = 6cm. Fragile, swollen, oval-triangular, inequivalve; right valve larger and more swollen than left; sculpture of fine concentric lines; surface smooth but irregular; distinctive hole in the beak of left valve; hingle simple with no teeth; colour = pale yellow-brown. Etymology: *Thracia* = a sea nymph; *convexa* = convex.

390 – *Thracia distorta* (Montagu)

The smallest of the British *Thracia* and the only one that makes its home inside narrow crevices and cracks, where its shell may become distorted through constricted growth. Perhaps because it sometimes inhabits the vacant holes of piddocks, *Thracia distorta* was at one time believed to be a boring mollusc but this notion had gone by the 1840s. It is widely distributed about Britain but generally rare and can be quite tricky to find. Empty shells are known from the seashore and have been found inside small rocks that have been dredged from deeper waters.

Description: L = 2cm; B = 1.5cm. Fragile, convex, inequivalve; right valve more convex; umbo of left valve punctures right; outline variable and often irregular; colour = white. Etymology: *distorta* = distorted.

391 – *Thracia phaseolina* (Lamarck)

This is a notoriously difficult species to identify with certainty as it very closely resembles *Thracia villosiuscula*, the distinguishing characteristic being the direction of slope of the posterior truncation (*phaseolina* = 'downwards and forwards'; *villosiuscula* = 'upwards and forwards') and the microscopic coarseness of the shell surface (*villosiuscula* is coarser). These differences were first noticed in the 1820s but have proved to be the bane of conchologists (amateur and professional) ever since, leading to confusion as to the exact distribution of both species. However, modern studies reveal that both species are widely distributed about Britain and may be found on the lower shore in sand and gravel, sometimes living in close proximity. Empty shells occur on the seashore but they are brittle and do not stand up to much of a pounding by the sea.

Description: L = 2.75cm; B = 1.5cm. Thin, oblong; anterior rounded, posterior truncated; fine concentric striations; colour = white or cream. Etymology: *phaseolina* = a kidney bean.

392 – *Thracia villosiuscula* (MacGillivray)

One of only a handful of shells to be described by Scottish ornithologist William MacGillivray, *Thracia villosiuscula* is identical to *Thracia phaseolina* in almost every respect. There is little new that can be added here and so I refer you to the aforementioned species's entry.

Description: L = 2.5cm. Very similar to *Thracia phaseolina* and is generally identified by its noticeably coarser surface texture which can only be seen using a hand lens or microscope. Etymology: *villosiuscula* = meaning unknown.

393 – *Thracia pubescens* (Pulteney)

A large but rarely encountered shell that lives offshore in the west and south of Britain (although there is an isolated record from the North Sea). It is a warmer-water species better known from southern Europe and the Mediterranean and was at one time widely desired by conchologists who prized its size and rarity. Most specimens were dredged from soft sediment but its empty shells are known from the seashore, although apparently this is a rare occurrence. Initial reports from the Irish Sea were discounted, but recent discoveries confirm that it is resident as far north as the Isle of Man.

Description: L = 8.9cm. Brittle, inequivalve; right valve larger and more convex; rounded anterior with posterior truncated; colour = white or cream. Etymology: *pubescens* = fully-grown.

394 – *Cochlodesma praetenue* (Pulteney)

Once known as the 'thin spoon-hinge' because of a spoon-shaped feature (a resilifer) in the hinge area of the shell, this is generally an offshore species that may occasionally be taken on very low tides all around the British coast. It burrows into a wide range of soft sediment, from mud to gravel, and has been dredged from depths of over 100 metres. Its empty shells may be found on shore but it would appear to be more common offshore.

Description: L = B = 3.8cm. Fragile, oval, inequivalve; right valve larger and more swollen than left; both valves with crack on posterior side of beak; sculpture of numerous fine concentric lines; hinge simple with spoon-shaped pit behind beak; colour = white. Etymology: *Cochlodesma* = bonded hood; *praetenue* = very thin.

Pandora Shells

The Pandora shells (Superfamily Pandoracea = 'Pandora shells') are distinctive, attractive shells whose pearly interior and fragile shells caught the attention of many historical conchologists. They are generally found on sandy shores but their shells are easily broken and in most areas whole specimens are hard to come by.

395 – *Lyonsia norvegica* (Gmelin)

Originally identified in Britain in the late Eighteenth Century at Tenby, Wales, by the local conchologist William Lyons (although some credit the young Irish conchologist Ellen Hutchins), this is an uncommon shell that occurs principally on the western and southern coasts where it lives just offshore. It is a cosmopolitan Atlantic animal that may be found from the chilly Arctic waters around Iceland down to the sub-tropical Canary Islands. It was rumoured in Victorian times that the finest specimens were to be dredged off the Dorset coast. Such claims of localised shell beauty were often made but few, if any, have stood up to the test of time. It is conceivable that empty shells might find their way onto the shore but their fragile nature suggests that this is probably a rare occurrence.

Description: L = 4.25cm; B = 2.25cm. Fragile; nearly equivalve; left valve marginally more convex; anterior rounded with posterior sharply truncated and gaping; coarse radiating lines and fine concentric lines; colour = white. Etymology: *Lyonsia* = after William Lyons; *norvegica* = Norwegian.

396 – *Pandora inaequivalvis* (Linnaeus); Pandora Shell

A localised species that lives on sheltered, sandy beaches on southern and western coasts but which is only common around Jersey and Guernsey. The Pandora shell is distinctive and attractive and is noted for its ability to squirt water when disturbed. I have witnessed this several times but have not seen the display witnessed by the conchologist H.K. Jordan who measured one water jet at a height of 40 centimetres. It was believed to be extremely rare or absent from the British mainland until the 1840s and is still considered to be a desirable shell by many collectors. Empty shells may be washed on shore and, being white, are easy to spot against the sand but they are often disarticulated and worn. Living specimens are much rarer.

Description: L = 3.1cm; B = 1.5cm. Fragile, oblong inequivalve; left valve convex, right valve flat; anterior portion rounded, posterior elongate and tapering; internal ligament; colour = white, interior pearly. Etymology: *Pandora* = a mythical woman; *inaequivalvis* = unequal valves.

397 – *Pandora pinna* (**Montagu**)

Although once believed to be a variety, or even a sub-adult, version of the Pandora shell (*Pandora inaequivalvis*), this is a species in its own right and one which is far more common and widespread. The main (and immediately obvious) distinction is between the two outlines of the shell which, in the case of *Pandora pinna*, is more rounded and blunt. How the two could ever be confused was a source of mystery to some: 'No species of *Pandora* can be more radically different,' wrote Forbes and Hanley in 1853, but this did not stop several highly experienced conchologists from lumping them together in the coming decades. It is an offshore species that prefers sand but it is rarely found in waters less than 15 metres and more frequently much deeper than this. Empty shells are very rare onshore and most specimens are taken using a dredge.

Description: L = 1.8cm; B = 1cm. Greatly resembles *Pandora inaequivalvis* but is smaller with pointed anterior and more truncated posterior. Etymology: *pinna* = a feather.

Septibranchs

The septibranchs (= 'chambered gills') were once a separate order of molluscs that contained the Superfamilies Poromyacea (= 'transitional mya') and Cuspidariacea (= 'pointed') but they have more recently been included within the same order as the lantern and Pandora shells. They are noteworthy as being one of the few types of truly carnivorous bivalve which live by sucking in minute crustaceans (which are usually dead) that are then crushed and digested by their powerful stomachs. They are commonly associated with deep-sea areas where there is not enough food for other bivalves to survive and are rarely seen close to shore. There are only a few British species, none of which is likely to be found by the casual beachcomber.

398 – *Poromya granulata* (**Nyst and Westendorp**)

A rare and little encountered species that lives at depth off the north Scottish coast. Although identified from Scandinavia in the 1830s, it was not until the early 1850s that a British specimen was dredged in 70 metres of water off the Isle of Skye. The finder was that most unstoppable of practical conchologists, John Jeffreys, who was praised for his 'distant and laborious dredgings [which have] enriched natural history with many rare and interesting discoveries'. It remains a rare British shell with, to my knowledge, only a handful of reports all from the north of Scotland. It is most unlikely to be seen by the casual beachcomber.

Description: L = 1.3cm. Fragile, swollen, oval, inequivalve; right valve more swollen than left; sculpture of indistinct concentric lines; posterior margin truncated; right valve has a cardinal tooth which occurs before a narrow chondrophore; colour = cream or off-white. Etymology: *Poromya* = a transitional *Mya*; *granulata* = granulated.

399 – *Cuspidaria abbreviata* (Forbes)

This was first described from the Aegean Sea by British conchologist Edward Forbes in 1843, but it was not until several years later that Robert McAndrew hauled up some dead shells in Loch Fyne, western Scotland at a depth of around 100 metres. Immediately afterwards, George Barlee found 'seventy to eighty individuals' at the same location and, later recovered more specimens from off the Shetland Islands. However, since then the shells have only been found a few times more and always off the western Scotland coast between depths of 80 and 300 metres.

Description: L = 1cm, B = 0.7cm. Fragile, swollen, triangular, equivalve; posterior margin has elongate 'spout' which gapes and has a deep furrow leading towards the beaks; sculpture of around 12 evenly spaced, broad, concentric lines; colour = white, periostracum is brown. Etymology: *Cuspidaria* = pointed; *abbreviata* = shortened.

400 – *Cuspidaria cuspidata* (Olivi)

A rare but distinctively-shaped bivalve that was first described in 1792 but which was not discovered in British waters until 1829, when James Gerard dredged an example from the Firth of Forth. Although it can occur in relatively shallow waters of 30 metres, it is more often recovered from considerable depths and although specimens are known from most parts of the British coast, there are relatively few modern reports. Specimens have only ever been obtained using deep-water dredging techniques.

Description: L = 2cm; B = 1.1cm. Fragile, swollen, equivalve; distinguished by posterior margin being drawn into narrow, projecting spout which gapes; sculpture of numerous fine concentric lines; colour = white, periostracum is brown. Etymology: *cuspidata* = pointed.

401 – *Cuspidaria rostrata* (Spengler)

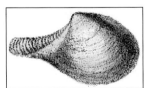

Exceedingly rare and known only from very deep water off Scotland. Up until late Victorian times, it was known only from dead shells. Since the Second World War there have been only a handful of British specimens, all taken in deep water on the very margins of the UK's territorial waters.

Description: L =1cm; B = 0.6cm. Fragile, flattened, equivalve; distinctive because of posterior spout which is almost half total shell length and because the shell width is narrow; colour = white, periostracum is brown. Etymology: *rostrata* = beaked.

402 – *Cuspidaria costellata* (Deshayes)

Not known from British waters until 1845. This is a shallower water species than most *Cuspidaria* but it still lives below 20 metres and is even then rarely seen. Known occurrences all cluster around the Scottish and northern Irish coastlines but there have only been a few live reports during the last half century. As with most of the British *Cuspidaria*, fine specimens were much desired by both scientists and commercial dealers but only a few ever made it onto the market with a majority staying in the hands of the conchologists that found them.

Description: Fragile, glossy, swollen, equivalve; may be distinguished by the possession of around 20-30 radiating ribs which become widely spaced toward posterior margin; dorsal margin crenulate; colour = white, periostracum light brown. Etymology: *costellata* = fine-ribbed.

Chapter Seventeen

Other Molluscs of Interest

I N ADDITION to the seashells described in the previous sections, you may encounter other types of mollusc on the seashore which, due to a lack of space, cannot be covered in this book. This chapter will therefore offer a brief introduction some of our other British molluscs.

Chitons

The chitons, or coat-of-mail shells, form the exclusively marine Class Polyplacophora (meaning 'many-plated'). They are generally small (under 5cm in length) and secretive, hiding themselves under rocks or in old shells low down on the seashore or in shallow water. Chitons are easily recognisable by their elongate shape, flattened profile and the row of

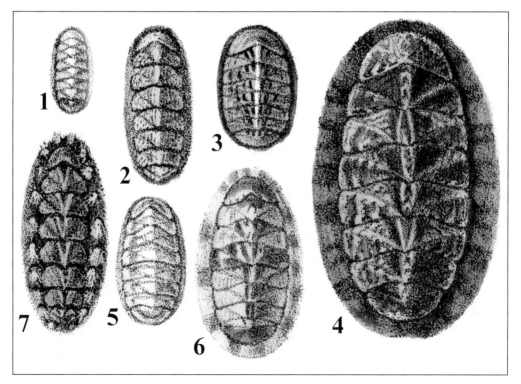

British chitons. 1 = *Leptochiton*; 2 = *Hanleya*; 3 = *Leptochiton*; 4 = *Tonicella*; 5 = *Ischnochiton*; 6 = *Callochiton*; 7 = *Acanthochitona*

overlapping plates that run down their back. They adhere to solid surfaces using a strong muscular foot (like a limpet), are slow moving and are herbivorous, browsing on algae. There are 17 species known from the British region, some of which are very rare. For a detailed guide to the known British species see *Molluscs: Caudofoveata, Solenogastres, Polyplacophora and Scaphopoda* (Jones, A., and Baxter, J., Linnean Society of London, 1987).

Sea Slugs (Nudibranchs)

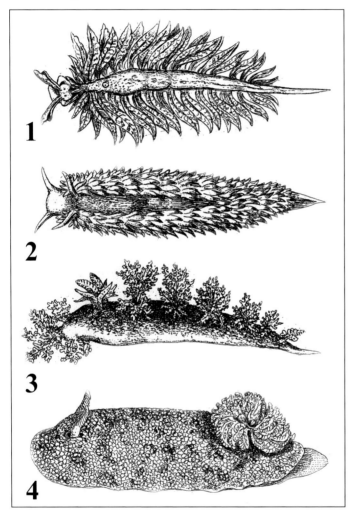

Some British nudibranchs. 1 = *Hermaea*; 2 = *Aeolidia*; 3 = *Dendronotus*; 4 = *Archidoris*

Sea slug is a general term that is used for any soft-bodied mollusc but here I mean it to mean members of the Order Nudibranchia (meaning 'naked gills') within the Subclass Opistho-branchia (see Chapter 6). In tropical seas the nudi-branchs are famed for their striking colours and intri-cate body forms. The British species are no less beautiful but they are generally small and rather shy, preferring to live offshore often in asso-ciation with a particular types of sponge, ascidian or hydroid, on which many of them feed. Because they lack a shell which could be collected and placed in a cabinet, the nudibranchs were not as widely studied as the gastropods and bivalves. In fact, the first wide-ranging studies of the British species did not occur until the 1840s when Joshua Alder (1792-1867) and Albany Hancock (1806-1873) produced a series of monographs on the subject. There are approximately 130 British species, many of which are known from only one or two specimens dredged up in Victorian times. The recent popularity of SCUBA diving has seen an increase in reports, especially by underwater photographers who are attracted to their bright colours. For more information on the British species see *Benthic Opisthobranchs* (Thompson, T., Linnean Society of London, 1988).

Cephalopods

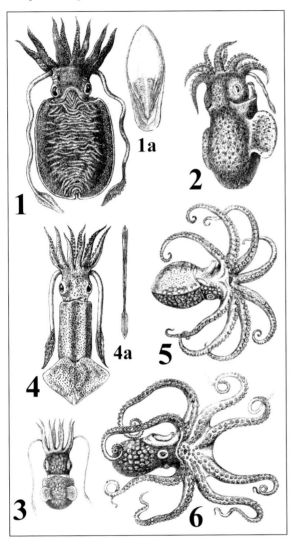

Some British cephalopods.
1 = cuttlefish (*Sepia*) and cuttlebone;
2 = *Sepiola*; 3 = *Rossia*; 4 = squid (*Logio*) and
pen; 5 = *Eledone cirrhosa*;
6 = *Octopus vulgaris*

The Class Cephalopoda (= 'foot-headed') contains such familiar (and edible) animals as the cuttlefish, squid and octopus. These animals are generally large, swimming, predatory animals that are rarely seen on the seashore, except when stranded or dead. Most cephalopods have a thin internal shell (e.g. the 'pen' inside a squid) which does not survive long after death, the exception being the thick, foam-like cuttlebone from inside a cuttlefish which may commonly be found washed up on the beach and which is sometimes placed inside aviaries for birds to peck at.

There are around 40 British cephalopod species, most of which live offshore and will only be seen by SCUBA divers or fishermen. An exception could be the octopus, of which there are two British species, the small northern curled octopus (*Eledone cirrhosa*; arm spread = 60cm) and the larger southern common octopus (*Octopus vulgaris*; arm spread of 300cm). The latter is worth mentioning because, starting in about 1899, it would form into vast plagues that invaded the southern coast of England, destroying local shellfish stocks. During these plague years hundreds of octopus would be found on the seashore where desperate fishermen would catch tonnes (literally) of the animals and dump them on local fields for use as fertiliser. Then, in 1962, the plagues stopped and the octopus became a very rare animal indeed with only a handful of British reports in any one year. This was a puzzle until it was discovered that the common octopus does not breed in British waters but instead reproduces in the Gulf of St Malo region in Brittany and afterwards swarms across the Channel to southern England. However, the Brittany coast represented the common octopus' extreme northern breeding limit and it is thought that the severe winter of 1961/62 wiped out the local stock, a situation from which the animal has not recovered. It is thought that the absence of the common octopus has permitted the traditionally northern curled octopus (which was probably preyed upon by the common octopus) to move its range southwards into areas where it was once rare or absent, such as Cornwall and the Channel Islands. There are no specific books detailing British cephalopods but the common species are covered by most seashore guides including *The Marine Fauna of the British Isles and North-West Europe* (Hayward, P., and Ryland, J., Clarendon Press, 1990. Vol.2).

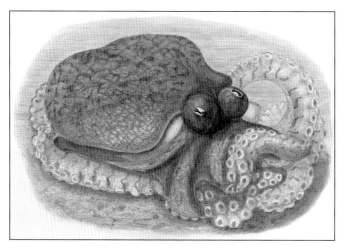

The common octopus (*Octopus vulgaris*)

A Checklist of British Seashells

THIS CHAPTER PROVIDES a systematic list of the all the seashell species featured in this book. For each species in the list the following information is provided:

The entry number in the main body of text

Its scientific name (in italics)

Its British distribution (see Introduction for more details)

Where on the beach it is likely to be found (see Table 1, below)

The substrate on which it prefers to live (rock, sediment, etc.)

Abbreviation Height	Explanation	Example of Tide
SZ	splash zone	area above highest tide
HWEST	high water extreme (equinox) spring tide	10m
HWST	high water neap tide	8.8m
HWST	high water spring tide	7.0m
MTL	mid-tide level	5.3m
LWNT	low water neap tide	3.5m
LWST	low water spring tide	1.0
LWEST	low water extreme (equinox) spring tide	0m
SL	sub-littoral (recreational SCUBA range)	0 to 30m deep
OS	offshore (below 30m)	>30m deep

Table 1. An explanation of the beach zones used in this chapter. The figures in column three are based on a hypothetical maximum tidal range of 10m and should not be used to calculate local tides: use a tide table to work out local tidal ranges before setting foot on a beach.

Phylum Mollusca

Class Polyplacophora (Chapter 17)

Class Gastropoda (Part One)

SUBCLASS PROSOBRANCHIA
Order Archaeogastropoda (Chapter 1)
Superfamily Haliotidacea
1 – *Haliotis tuberculata*; CI; LWEST to SL; rock
Superfamily Pleurotomariacea
2 – *Anatoma crispata*; N, NE, NW; SL to OS; rock
Superfamily Fissurellacea
3 – *Diodora graeca*; NE, SE, S, SW, W, NW, CI; LWST to OS; rock
4 – *Emarginula fissura*; all coasts; LWEST to OS; rock
5 – *Emarginula crassa*; N, SW, W, NW; LWST to OS; rock
6 – *Emarginula rosea*; SW, W, CI; SL to OS; rock
7 – *Puncturella noachina*; N, NE, E, NW; OS; rock
Superfamily Trochacea
8 – *Tricolia pullus*; S, SW, W, NW, CI; LWST to SL; rock
9 – *Margarites helicinus*; N, NE, E, NW; LWST to SL; rock
10 – *Calliostoma granulatum*; N, SE, S, SW, W, NW, CI; SL to OS; rock
11 – *Calliostoma zizyphinum*; all coasts; LWST to SL; rock
12 – *Gibbula cineraria*; all coasts; LWST to OS; rock
13 – *Gibbula magus*; N, S, SW, W, NW, CI; LWEST to OS; rock
14 – *Gibbula umbilicalis*; N, SW, W, NW, CI; HWNT to LWST; rock
15 – *Gibbula pennanti*; SW, CI; MTL to SL; rock
16 – *Gibbula tumida*; all coasts; SL to OS; sediment
17 – *Jujubinus exasperatus*; S, SW, W, CI; LWST to OS; rock
18 – *Jujubinus miliaris*; N, NE, S, SW, W, NW, CI; LWST to OS; rock
19 – *Jujubinus montagui*; N, NE, S, SW, W, NW, CI; SL to OS; sediment
20 – *Jujubinus striatus*; S, SW, W, CI; LWNT to SL; sediment
21 – *Osilinus lineatus*; S, SW, W, CI; HWNT to LWNT; rock
22 – *Dikoleps cutleriana*; SW, W, CI; SL to OS; rock
23 – *Dikoleps pusilla*; S, SW, W, CI; LWEST to OS; rock
24 – *Skenea serpuloides*; all coasts; LWEST to SL; rock

Order Patellogastropoda (Chapter 2)
Superfamily Patellacea
25 – *Tectura testudinalis* ; N, NE, NW; LWNT to OS; rock
26 – *Tectura virginea*; all coasts; LWST to OS; rock
27 – *Helcion pellucidum*; all coasts; LWST to SL; rock
28 – *Patella depressa*; S, SW, W, CI; LWNT to SL; rock
29 – *Patella ulyssiponensis*; all coasts; LWNT to SL; rock
30 – *Patella vulgata*; all coasts; HWNT to LWST; rock
31 – *Iothia fulva*; N, NE, E, W, NW; SL to OS; rock
32 – *Lepeta caeca*; N, NE, NW; OS; rock

Order Mesogastropoda (Chapter 3)
Superfamily Cerithiacea
33 – *Bittium reticulatum*; S, SW, W, NW, CI; LWST to SL; sediment
34 – *Bittium simplex*; SW, CI; SL; sediment
35 – *Turritella communis*; all coasts; LWEST to OS; sediment
36 – *Cerithiopsis barleii*; SW, W, CI; LWEST to OS; rock

37 – *Cerithiopsis pulchella*; SW, W, CI; SL; rock
38 – *Cerithiopsis tubercularis*; N, NE, S, SW, W, NW, CI; LWST to SL; rock
38 – *Cerithiella metula*; SW, W, NW; OS; rock

Superfamily Littorinacea

39 – *Lacuna crassior*; all coasts; LWST to OS; rock
40 – *Lacuna pallidula*; all coasts; LWNT to LWEST; rock
41 – *Lacuna parva*; all coasts; LWST to SL; rock
42 – *Lacuna vincta*; all coasts; LWNT to SL; rock
43 – *Littorina littorea*; all coasts; MTL to LWNT; rock
44 – *Littorina arcana*; N, NE, SW, W, NW, CI; HWNT to MTL; rock
45 – *Littorina saxatilis*; all coasts; HWNT to MTL; rock
46 – *Littorina saxatilis* var. *rudis*; all coasts; HWNT to MTL; rock
47 – *Littorina saxatilis* var. *tenebrosa*; all coasts; HWNT; rock
48 – *Littorina neglecta*; all coasts; MTL to LWST; rock
49 – *Littorina nigrolineata*; all coasts; HWST to MTL; rock
50 – *Littorina mariae*; all coasts; MTL to LWST; rock
51 – *Littorina obtusata*; all coasts; MTL to LWST; rock
52 – *Melarhaphe neritoides*; all coasts; HWNT to HWST; rock
53 – *Skeneopsis planorbis*; all coasts; LWNT to SL; rock
54 – *Eatonina fulgida*; S, SW, W, NW, CI; LWNT to SL; rock and sediment

Superfamily Rissoacea

55 – *Barleeia unifasciata*; NE, S, SW, W, NW, CI; LWNT to SL; rock
56 – *Alvania abyssicola*; N, NE, NW; OS; sediment
57 – *Alvania beanii*; all coasts; LWEST to OS; rock
58 – *Alvania cancellata*; N, S, SW, W, NW, CI; LWEST to SL; rock
59 – *Alvania carinata*; S, SW, W, NW, CI; LWNT to SL; rock
60 – *Alvania cimicoides*; N, NE, SW, W, NW, CI; SL to OS; rock
61 – *Alvania jeffreysi*; N, SW, NW; OS; sediment
62 – *Alvania lactea*; N, SW, NW, CI; LWST to SL; rock
63 – *Alvania punctura*; all coasts; LWEST to SL; rock
64 – *Alvania semistriata*; all coasts; LWEST to SL; rock
65 – *Cingula cingillus*; all coasts; MTL to SL; rock
66 – *Manzonia crassa*; all coasts; LWST to SL; rock
67 – *Manzonia zetlandica*; N, NE, E,S, SW, W, NW, CI; SL to OS; rock
68 – *Onoba aculeus*; N, NE, NW; LWST to OS; rock
69 – *Onoba semicostata*; all coasts; LWST to SL; rock
70 – *Pusillina inconspicua*; all coasts; LWEST to SL; rock
71 – *Pusillina sarsi*; all coasts; LWST to SL; sediment
72 – *Rissoa guerini*; S, SW, W, CI; LWST to OS; rock
73 – *Rissoa lilacina*; N, S, SW, W, NW, CI; LWST to OS; rock
74 – *Rissoa membranacea*; all coasts; LWST to SL; rock and sediment
75 – *Rissoa interrupta*; all coasts; MTL to SL; rock
75 – *Rissoa parva*; all coasts; MTL to SL; rock
76 – *Setia pulcherrima*; CI; LWST to SL; rock and sediment
77 – *Ceratia proxima*; SW, W, NW, CI; SL to OS; sediment
78 – *Hyala vitrea*; all coasts; SL to OS; sediment
79 – *Caecum clarkii*; SW, CI; SL to OS; sediment
80 – *Caecum glabrum*; all coasts; SL to OS; sediment
81 – *Caecum imperforatum*; SW, W, NW, CI; SL to OS; sediment
82 – *Tornus subcarinatus*; SE, S, SW, W, NW, CI; LWEST to SL; rock

83 – *Hydrobia ulvae*; all coasts; MTL to LWST; sediment
84 – *Hydrobia neglecta*; all coasts; HWNT to SZ; sediment
85 – *Ventrosia ventrosa*; all coasts; HWNT to SZ; sediment
86 – *Potamopyrgus antipodarum*; all coasts; HWNT to SZ; sediment
87 – *Truncatella subcylindrica*; S, SW, CI; HWNT to HWST; rock
88 – *Paludinella litorina*; S, SW, CI; HWNT to SZ; rock

Superfamily Strombacea

89 – *Aporrhais pespelecani*; all coasts; SL to OS; sediment
89 – *Aporrhais serresianus*; N, NE, NW; OS; sediment

Superfamily Calyptraeacea

90 – *Calyptraea chinensis*; S, SW, W, NW, CI; LWST to SL; rock
91 – *Crepidula fornicata*; E, SE, S, SW, W, CI; LWNT to SL; sediment
92 – *Capulus ungaricus*; all coasts; SL to OS; rock
93 – *Trichotropis borealis*; N, NE, NW; SL to OS; rock

Superfamily Cypraeacea

94 – *Simnia patula*; SW, W, NW, CI; SL; parasitic

Superfamily Lamellariacea

95 – *Erato voluta*; all coasts; SL to OS; rock
96 – *Trivia arctica*; all coasts; LWEST to OS; rock
97 – *Trivia monacha*; all coasts; LWEST to OS; rock
98 – *Lamellaria latens*; all coasts; LWST to SL; rock
99 – *Lamellaria perspicua*; all coasts; LWST to SL; rock
100 – *Velutina plicatus*; N, NE, E, S, SW, W, NW; LWST to SL; rock
101 – *Velutina velutina*; all coasts; SL to OS; rock

Superfamily Naticacea

102 – *Amauropsis islandicus*; N, NE, NW; SL to OS; sediment
103 – *Euspira catena*; all coasts; LWST to OS; sediment
103 – *Euspira pallida*; N, NE, NW; OS; sediment
104 – *Polinices fuscus*; S, SW, W, NW, CI; SL to OS; sediment
105 – *Polinices montagui*; N, NE, S, SW, W, NW, CI; SL to OS; sediment
106 – *Polinices pulchellus*; all coasts; LWEST to SL; sediment

Superfamily Tonnacea

107 – *Charonia lampas*; SW, CI; OS; sediment
108 – *Cymatium cutaceum*; CI; LWEST to OS; rock

Superfamily Triphoracea

109 – *Cheirodonta pallescens*; SW, W, CI; LWST to SL; sediment
110 – *Marshallora adversa*; N, NE, S, SW, W, NW, CI; SL to OS; rock
111 – *Metaxia metaxa*; S, SW, W, CI; SL to OS; rock
112 – *Monophorus perversus*; all coasts; LWST to SL; sediment

Superfamily Epitoniacea

113 – *Epitonium clathratulum*; all coasts; SL to OS; sediment
114 – *Epitonium clathrus*; all coasts; LWEST to SL; sediment
115 – *Epitonium trevelyanum*; all coasts; OS; sediment
115 – *Epitonium turtonis*; all coasts; SL to OS; sediment
116 – *Janthina janthina*; SW, W, NW, CI; OS; pelagic
117 – *Aclis ascaris*; N, SW, W, NW, CI; SL to OS; sediment
118 – *Aclis gulsonae*; N, SW, W, NW, CI; SL to OS; sediment
119 – *Aclis minor*; N, NE, SW, W, NW, CI; SL to OS; sediment
119 – *Aclis walleri*; N, SW; OS; sediment
120 – *Graphis albida*; all coasts; SL to OS; sediment

Superfamily Eulimacea
121 – *Crinophtheiros collinsi*; SW, W, NW, CI; OS; sediment
122 – *Eulima bilineata*; all coasts; LWST to OS; sediment
123 – *Eulima glabra*; N, S, SW, W, NW, CI; SL to OS; sediment
124 – *Melanella alba*; all coasts; SL to OS; sediment
125 – *Melanella frielei*; N, SW, W, NW, CI; SL to OS; sediment
126 – *Melanella lubrica*; SW, CI; SL to OS; sediment
127 – *Polygireulima polita*; all coasts; SL to OS; sediment
128 – *Vitreolina curva*; CI; SL to OS; sediment
129 – *Vitreolina philippi*; N, NE, S, SW, W, NW, CI; LWEST to OS; sediment

Order Neogastropoda (Chapter 4)
Superfamily Muricacea
130 – *Nucella lapillus*; all coasts; LWST to SL; rock
131 – *Ocenebra erinacea*; S, SW, CI; LWEST to OS; rock
132 – *Ocinebrina aciculata*; SW, CI; LWEST to OS; rock
133 – *Urosalpinx cinerea*; SE, S, CI; LWEST to SL; sediment
134 – *Trophon muricatus*; SW, W, NW, CI; OS; sediment
135 – *Trophon truncatus*; N, NE, NW; LWEST to OS; sediment
136 – *Beringius turtoni*; N, NE, E; OS; rock
137 – *Buccinum humphreysianum*; N, NE, NW; OS; sediment
138 – *Buccinum undatum*; all coasts; LWEST to OS; rock and sediment
139 – *Chauvetia brunnea*; S, SW, W, CI; LWEST to SL; rock
140 – *Colus gracilis*; all coasts; SL to OS; sediment
141 – *Colus islandicus*; all coasts; OS; rock and sediment
142 – *Hinia incrassata*; all coasts; LWEST to SL; sediment
143 – *Hinia pygmaea*; N, SW, W, NW, CI; SL to OS; sediment
144 – *Hinia reticulata*; all coasts; LWEST to SL; sediment
145 – *Neptunea antiqua*; all coasts; OS; rock and sediment
Superfamily Conacea
146 – *Comarmondia gracilis*; SW, W, NW, CI; SL; sediment
147 – *Haedropleura septangularis*; S, SW, W, NW, CI; LWEST to SL; sediment
148 – *Mangelia attenuata*; all coasts; SL to OS; sediment
149 – *Mangelia brachystoma*; all coasts; SL to OS; sediment
150 – *Mangelia coarctata*; all coasts; LWEST to SL; sediment
151 – *Mangelia nebula*; N, S, SW, W, NW, CI; LWEST to OS; sediment
152 – *Mangelia powisiana*; SW, W, CI; LWEST to SL; sediment
153 – *Mangelia rugulosa*; SW, CI; SL to OS; sediment
154 – *Mangelia smithii*; SW, W, NW, CI, SL, sediment
155 – *Oenopota rufa*; all coasts; LWEST to SL; sediment
156 – *Oenopota turricula*; all coasts; LWEST to SL; sediment
157 – *Raphitoma boothii*; N, S, SW, W, NW, CI; LWEST to OS; rock and sediment
158 – *Raphitoma echinata*; N, SW, W, NW, CI; SL; sediment
159 – *Raphitoma linearis*; all coasts; LWEST to OS; rock
160 – *Raphitoma purpurea*; E, SE, S, SW, CI; LWST to OS; sediment

Order Heterostropha (Chapter 5)
Superfamily Rissoellacea
161 – *Rissoella diaphana*; N, SW, W, NW, CI; MTL to LWST; rock
162 – *Rissoella globularis*; N, SW, W, NW; MTL to LWST; rock

163 – *Rissoella opalina*; N, SW, W, NW, CI; MTL to LWST; rock
164 – *Cima minima*; N, SW, W, NW, CI; LWEST to SL; sediment
165 – *Ammonicerina rota*; N, S, SW, W, NW, CI; LWST to SL; rock and sediment
166 – *Omalogyra atomus*; N, S, SW, W, NW, CI; MTL to SL; rock
Superfamily Pyramidellacea
167 – *Brachystomia carrozzai*; N,SW, W, NW, CI; LWEST to OS; rock
168 – *Brachystomia eulimoides*; all coasts; LWEST to SL; parasitic
169 – *Brachystomia lukisii*; N, SW, W, NW, CI; LWEST to OS; rock
170 – *Brachystomia scalaris*; all coasts; LWEST to SL; rock
171 – *Chrysallida decussata*; N, SW, W, NW, CI; SL to OS; sediment
172 – *Chrysallida indistincta*; N, SW, W, NW, CI; LWEST to OS
173 – *Chrysallida interstincta*; all coasts; LWST to SL; rock
173 – *Chrysallida terebellum*; CI; LWST to OS; sediment
174 – *Eulimella laevis*; N, NE, SW, W, NW, CI; SL to OS; sediment
175 – *Eulimella ventricosa*; N, SW, W, NW, CI; SL to OS; sediment
176 – *Folinella excavata*; SW, W, CI; SL to OS; sediment
177 – *Jordaniella nivosa*; N, SW, W, NW, CI; LWST to SL; rock
178 – *Jordaniella truncatula*; SW, W, CI; SL to OS; sediment
179 – *Liostomia clavula*; SW, CI; SL to OS.; sediment
180 – *Megastomia conoidea*; N, SW, W, NW, CI; SL to OS; sediment
181 – *Megastomia conspicua*; N, SW, W, NW, CI; SL to OS; sediment
182 – *Noemiamea dolioliformis*; N, SW, W, NW, CI; LWEST to SL; sediment
183 – *Odostomia acuta*; N, SW, W, NW, CI; SL to OS; sediment
184 – *Odostomia plicata*; N, NE, S, SW, W, NW, CI; LWST to SL; rock
185 – *Odostomia turrita*; N, NE, S, SW, W, NW, CI; LWST to SL; rock
186 – *Odostomia unidentata*; all coasts; LWST to SL; parasitic
187 – *Ondina diaphana*; N, NE, SW, W, NW, CI; SL to OS; parasitic
188 – *Ondina divisa*; all coasts; SL to OS.; parasitic
189 – *Ondina obliqua*; S, SW, W, NW, CI; SL to OS.; parasitic
190 – *Ondina warreni*; N, NE, S, SW, W, NW, CI; SL to OS.; parasitic
191 – *Partulida pellucida*; all coasts; LWST to SL; rock and sediment
192 – *Tragula fenestrata*; SW, CI; SL to OS; sediment
193 – *Turbonilla lactea*; all coasts; LWST to SL; sediment
194 – *Turbonilla pumila*; S, SW, W, NW, CI; SL to OS; sediment
195 – *Turbonilla pusilla*; SW, W, CI; LWST to SL; sediment
196 – *Ebala nitidissima*; N, NE, SW, W, NW, CI; SL to OS; sediment

Subclass Opisthobranchia (Chapter 6)
Order Cephalaspidea
    Superfamily Acteonacea
    197 – *Acteon tornatilis*; all coasts; LWST to OS; sediment
    Superfamily Philinacea
    198 – *Scaphander lignarius*; all coasts; LWEST to OS; sediment
    199 – *Cylichna cylindracea*; all coasts; LWEST to SL; sediment
    200 – *Philine aperta*; all coasts; LWST to OS; sediment
    201 – *Philine catena*; all coasts; LWEST to OS; rock
    202 – *Philine pruinosa*; all coasts; SL to OS; sediment
    203 – *Philine punctata*; all coasts; LWEST to OS; rock
    204 – *Philine scabra*; all coasts; SL to OS; sediment
    205 – *Diaphana minuta*; all coasts; LWEST to SL; sediment

206 – *Haminoea hydatis*; S, SW, CI; LWEST to SL; sediment
207 – *Haminoea navicula*; S, SW, W, CI; LWEST to SL; sediment
208 – *Retusa obtusa*; all coasts; LWEST to OS; sediment
209 – *Retusa truncatula*; all coasts; LWEST to SL; sediment
210 – *Retusa umbilicata*; all coasts; SL to OS; sediment
210 – *Rhizorus acuminatus*; all coasts; SL to OS; sediment

Order Nudibranchia (Chapter 17)
Class Scaphopoda (Chapter 7)
　　Order Dentaliida
211 – *Antalis entalis*; all coasts; SL to OS; sediment
212 – *Antalis vulgaris*; S, SW, W, CI; SL to OS; sediment

Class Pelycopoda (Part Two)

Order Nuculoida (Chapter 8)
　　Superfamily Nuculacea
213 – *Nucula hanleyi*; S, SW, W, CI; SL; sediment
214 – *Nucula nitidosa*; all coasts; LWEST to OS; sediment
215 – *Nucula nucleus*; all coasts; SL to OS; sediment
216 – *Nucula sulcata*; SW,NW, CI; SL to OS; sediment
217 – *Nuculoma tenuis*; N, NE, E, W, NW; SL to OS; sediment

Order Arcoida (Chapter 9)
　　Superfamily Arcacea
218 – *Arca tetragona*; all coasts; LWEST to OS; rock
219 – *Bathyarca pectunculoides*; N, NW; OS; rock
220 – *Striarca lactea*; S, SW, W, CI; LWST to OS; sediment
221 – *Glycymeris glycymeris*; all coasts; LWEST to OS; sediment

Order Mytiloda (Chapter 10)
　　Superfamily Mytilacea
222 – *Adipicola simpsoni*; N; OS; parasitic
223 – *Crenella decussata*; all coasts; LWST to OS; rock
224 – *Crenella pellucida*; SE, S, CI; LWEST to SL; sediment
225 – *Modiolarca tumida*; all coasts; LWEST to SL; rock
226 – *Modiolula phaseolina*; all coasts; LWNT to SL; rock
227 – *Modiolus adriaticus*; SW, CI; SL to OS; rock
228 – *Modiolus barbatus*; S, SW, W, CI; LWNT to SL; rock
229 – *Modiolus modiolus*; all coasts; LWNT to OS; rock
230 – *Mytilus edulis*; all coasts; LWNT to SL; rock
231 – *Mytilus galloprovincialis*; all coasts; LWNT to SL; rock
232 – *Musculus costulatus*; N, NE, S, SW, W, NW, CI; LWEST to SL; rock
233 – *Musculus discors*; all coasts; LWST to SL; rock
234 – *Musculus niger*; N, NE; SL to OS; rock
235 – *Rhomboidella prideauxi*; S, SW, CI; LWNT to OS; rock

Order Pterioida (Chapter 10)
    Superfamily Pteriacea
        236 – *Pteria hirundo*; S, SW, W, NW, CI; SL to OS; sediment
        237 – *Atrina fragilis*; S, SW, CI; SL to OS; sediment

Order Limoida (Chapter 11)
    Superfamily Limidae
        238 – *Limaria hians*; S, SW, W, CI; LWEST to SL; rock
        239 – *Limaria loscombi*; S, SW, W, NW, CI; SL to OS; rock
        240 – *Limaria gywni*; N; OS; rock
        241 – *Limatula subauriculata*; SW, W, NW, CI; OS; sediment
        242 – *Limatula subovata*; NW; OS; rock
        243 – *Limatula sulcata*; N, SW, W, NW, CI; SL to OS; sediment
        244 – *Limea sarsi*; N, NE; OS; sediment

Order Ostreoida (Chapter 12)
    Superfamily Ostreacea
        245 – *Ostrea edulis*; all coasts; LWEST to SL; sediment
        246 – *Crassostrea gigas*; SW, CI; LWNT to SL; cultured
    Superfamily Pectimacea
        247 – *Aequipecten opercularis*; all coasts; SL to OS; sediment
        248 – *Chlamys distorta*; all coasts; LWEST to SL; rock
        249 – *Chlamys islandica*; NW; OS; rock and sediment
        250 – *Chlamys varia*; all coasts; LWST to SL; rock and sediment
        251 – *Palliolum striatum*; N, SW, W, NW, CI; SL to OS; sediment
        252 – *Palliolum tigerinum*; all coasts; SL to OS; sediment
        253 – *Pecten maximus*; all coasts; SL; sediment
        254 – *Pseudamussium septemradiatum*; N, NE, NW; OS; sediment
        255 – *Cyclopecten greenlandicus*; N; OS; sediment
        256 – *Hyalopecten parvulinus*; NW; OS; sediment
        257 – *Propeamussium lucidum*; W; OS; sediment
        258 – *Similipecten similis*; all coasts; SL to OS; sediment
    Superfamily Anomiacea
        259 – *Anomia ephippium*; all coasts; LWNT to OS; rock
        260 – *Heteranomia squamula*; all coasts; SL to OS; rock
        261 – *Pododesmus patelliformis*; all coasts; SL to OS; rock

Order Veneroida (Chapter 13)
    Superfamily Lucinacea
        262 – *Loripes lucinalis*; SE, S, SW, W, CI; SL to OS; sediment
        263 – *Lucinella divaricata*; S, SW; LWEST to OS; sediment
        264 – *Lucinoma borealis*; all coasts; LWEST to OS; sediment
        265 – *Myrtea spinifera*; N, S, SW, W, NW, CI; SL to OS; sediment
        266 – *Thyasira croulinensis*; N, NE; SL to OS; sediment
        267 – *Thyasira equalis*; all coasts; OS; sediment
        268 – *Thyasira ferruginea*; N, NE, W, NW; OS; sediment
        269 – *Thyasira flexuosa*; all coasts; SL; sediment
        270 – *Thyasira gouldii*; N, NW; OS; sediment
        271 – *Thyasira obsoleta*; N; OS; sediment
        272 – *Thyasira pygmaea*; N; OS; sediment

273 – *Thyasira subtrigona*; N; OS; sediment
274 – *Diplodonta rotundata*; S, SW, W, CI; SL; sediment

Superfamily Galeommatacea

275 – *Galeomma turton*; SW, CI; LWEST to SL; rock
276 – *Kellia suborbicularis*; all coasts; LWST to SL; sediment
277 – *Lasaea adansoni*; all coasts; HWNT to LWST; rock
278 – *Semierycina nitida*; all coasts; SL to OS; sediment
279 – *Lepton squamosum*; S, SW, W, CI; LWEST to SL; sediment
280 – *Devonia perrieri*; N, NE, E, S, SW, W; LWEST to SL; sediment
281 – *Epilepton clarkiae*; S, SW, W, NW, CI; LWEST to SL; sediment
282 – *Montacuta donacina*; N, NE; SL to OS; sediment
283 – *Montacuta substriata*; all coasts; LWEST to SL; sediment
284 – *Mysella bidentata*; all coasts; LWEST to OS; sediment
285 – *Mysella dawsoni*; NE; OS; sediment
286 – *Tellimya ferruginosa*; all coasts; SL to OS; sediment

Superfamily Cymiacea

287 – *Arculus sykesi*; SW, CI; SL to OS; sediment
288 – *Neolepton obliquatum*; W; OS; sediment
289 – *Neolepton sulcatulum*; SW, W, CI; LWEST to SL; rock

Superfamily Astartacea

290 – *Astarte crebricostata*; N; OS; sediment
291 – *Astarte sulcata*; all coasts; SL to OS; sediment
292 – *Goodallia triangularis*; all coasts; SL to OS; sediment
293 – *Tridonta borealis*; N, NE; OS; sediment
294 – *Tridonta elliptica*; N, NE, E, NW; OS; sediment
295 – *Tridonta montagui*; N, NE, E, NW; OS; sediment

Superfamily Cardiacea

296 – *Acanthocardia aculeata*; S, SW, CI; LWEST to OS; sediment
297 – *Acanthocardia echinata*; all coasts; LWEST to OS; sediment
298 – *Acanthocardia tuberculata*; S, SW, CI; LWEST to OS; sediment
299 – *Cerastoderma edule*; all coasts; MTL to OS; sediment
300 – *Cerastoderma glaucum*; SE, S, SW, W, NW; MTL to LWST; sediment
301 – *Clinocardium ciliatum*; N; SL to OS; sediment
302 – *Laevicardium crassum*; all coasts; LWEST to OS; sediment
303 – *Parvicardium exiguum*; all coasts; LWEST to OS; sediment
304 – *Parvicardium minimum*; N, NE, SW, W, NW, CI; SL to OS; sediment
305 – *Parvicardium ovale*; all coasts; SL to OS; sediment
306 – *Parvicardium scabrum*; all coasts; LWEST to OS; sediment
307 – *Plagiocardium papillosum*; SW, CI; LWEST to SL; sediment

Superfamily Mactracea

308 – *Lutraria angustior*; S, SW, CI; SL to OS; sediment
309 – *Lutraria lutraria*; all coasts; LWEST to OS; sediment
310 – *Lutraria magna*; SW, CI; SL to OS; sediment
311 – *Mactra glauca*; SW, CI; LWEST to SL; sediment
312 – *Mactra stultorum*; all coasts; LWEST to OS; sediment
313 – *Spisula elliptica*; all coasts; SL to OS; sediment
314 – *Spisula solida*; all coasts; LWST to SL; sediment
315 – *Spisula ovalis*; W, CI; SL to OS; sediment
315 – *Spisula subtruncata*; all coasts; LWST to OS; sediment
316 – *Donacilla cornea*; S, SW; LWST to OS; sediment

Superfamily Solenacea

317 – *Solen marginatus*; SE, S, SW, W, NW, CI; LWEST to OS; sediment
318 – *Ensis americanus*; SE, S; LWST to SL; sediment
319 – *Ensis arcuatus*; all coasts; LWEST to SL; sediment
320 – *Ensis ensis*; all coasts; LWEST to SL; sediment
321 – *Ensis siliqua*; all coasts; LWEST to SL; sediment
322 – *Pharus legumen*; SW, W, CI; LWEST to SL; sediment
323 – *Phaxas pellucidus*; all coasts; SL to OS; sediment

Superfamily Tellinacea

324 – *Angulus squalidus*; SW, CI; SL to OS; sediment
325 – *Angulus tenuis*; all coasts; LWNT to SL; sediment
326 – *Arcopagia crassa*; N, NE, SW, W, NW, CI; LWEST to OS; sediment
327 – *Arcopella balaustina*; SW, W, NW, CI; OS; sediment
328 – *Fabulina fabula*; all coasts; LWST to SL; sediment
329 – *Gastrana fragilis*; SW, W, NW, CI; LWEST to SL; sediment
330 – *Macoma balthica*; all coasts; MTL to LWEST; sediment
331 – *Moerella donacina*; SW, CI; SL to OS; sediment
332 – *Moerella pygmaea*; N, SW, W, NW, CI; LWEST to OS; sediment
333 – *Donax variegatus*; SW, CI; LWEST to SL; sediment
334 – *Donax vittatus*; all coasts; LWST to SL; sediment
335 – *Azorinus chamasolen*; SW, W, NW, CI; SL to OS; sediment
336 – *Gari costulata*; all coasts; LWEST to OS; sediment
337 – *Gari depressa*; SW, W, CI; LWEST to OS; sediment
338 – *Gari fervensis*; all coasts; LWST to OS; sediment
339 – *Gari tellinella*; N, S, SW, W, NW, CI; LWEST to OS; sediment
340 – *Solecurtus scopula*; S, SW, W, NW, CI; LWEST to SL; sediment
341 – *Abra alba*; all coasts; LWEST to SL; sediment
342 – *Abra longicallus*; NW; OS; sediment
343 – *Abra nitida*; all coasts; SL to OS; sediment
344 – *Abra prismatica*; all coasts; LWST to OS; sediment
345 – *Abra tenuis*; NE, E, SE, S, SW, W, CI; MTL to LWEST; sediment
346 – *Ervilia castanea*; SW, CI; OS; sediment
347 – *Scrobicularia plana*; all coasts; MTL to LWEST; sediment

Superfamily Arcticacea

348 – *Arctica islandica*; all coasts; SL to OS; sediment
349 – *Coralliophaga lithophagella*; CI; SL to OS; sediment

Superfamily Glossacea

350 – *Glossus humanus*; N, S, SW, W, NW; SL to OS; sediment

Superfamily Veneracea

351 – *Callista chione*; SW, W, CI; SL to OS; sediment
352 – *Chamelea gallina*; all coasts; LWEST to OS; sediment
353 – *Circomphalus casina*; all coasts; SL to OS; sediment
354 – *Clausinella fasciata*; all coasts; LWEST to OS; sediment
355 – *Dosinia exoleta*; all coasts; LWST to SL; sediment
356 – *Dosinia lupinus*; all coasts; LWEST to OS; sediment
357 – *Gouldia minima*; all coasts; SL to OS; sediment
358 – *Irus irus*; S, SW, W, CI; LWEST to SL; rock
359 – *Mercenaria mercenaria*; SE, S; LWST to SL; sediment
360 – *Tapes aureus*; all coasts; LWEST to OS; sediment
361 – *Tapes decussatus*; S, SW, W, NW, CI; LWST to SL; sediment

362 – *Tapes philippinarum*; S; MTL to LWEST; sediment
363 – *Tapes rhomboides*; all coasts; LWST to SL; sediment
364 – *Timoclea ovata*; all coasts; LWEST to OS; sediment
365 – *Venerupis senegalensis*; all coasts; LWST to SL; sediment
366 – *Venus verrucosa*; S, SW, W, CI; LWEST to OS; sediment
367 – *Turtonia minutum*; all coasts; MTL to SL; rock
368 – *Petricola pholadiformis*; SE, S; MTL to SL; borer
369 – *Mysia undata*; all coasts; SL; sediment

Order Myoida

SubOrder Myina (Chapter 14)
Superfamily Myacea
370 – *Mya arenaria*; all coasts; LWNT to SL; sediment
371 – *Mya truncata*; all coasts; LWST to OS; sediment
372 – *Sphenia binghami*; all coasts; SL to OS; rock
373 – *Corbula gibba*; all coasts; LWEST to OS; sediment
Superfamily Gastrochaenacea
374 – *Gastrochaena dubia*; S, SW, W, CI; SL to OS; sediment
Superfamily Hiatellacea
375 – *Hiatella arctica*; all coasts; LWST to OS; rock
376 – *Panomya arctica*; N, NE, E, NW; SL to OS; sediment
377 – *Saxicavella jeffreysi*; N, NE, E, S, SW, W, NW; SL to OS; sediment

SubOrder Pholadina (Chapter 15)
Superfamily Pholadacea
378 – *Barnea candida*; all coasts; LWEST to OS; borer
379 – *Barnea parva*; SE, S, SW, CI; LWEST to OS; borer
380 – *Pholas dactylus*; SE, S, SW, W, CI; LWEST to OS; borer
381 – *Pholadidea loscombiana*; SW, W; LWST to SL; borer
382 – *Zirfaea crispata*; all coasts; LWST to SL; borer
383 – *Xylophaga dorsalis*; all coasts; SL; borer
384 – *Xylophaga praestans*; E; OS; borer
385 – *Teredo navalis*; all coasts; LWST to SL; borer
386 – *Lyrodus pedicellatus*; SW, CI; SL to OS; borer
387 – *Nototeredo norvegica*; all coasts; LWST to SL; borer
388 – *Psiloteredo megotara*; all coasts; OS

Order Pholadomyoida (Chapter 16)
Superfamily Thraciacea
389 – *Thracia convexa*; all coasts; SL to OS; sediment
390 – *Thracia distorta*; all coasts; LWEST to OS; rock
391 – *Thracia phaseolina*; all coasts; LWEST to OS; sediment
392 – *Thracia villosiuscula*; all coasts; SL to OS; sediment
393 – *Thracia pubescens*; SW, CI; SL to OS; sediment
394 – *Cochlodesma praetenue;* all coasts (not CI); LWEST to OS; sediment
Superfamily Pandoracea
395 – *Lyonsia norvegica*; S, SW, NE, CI; SL to OS; sediment
396 – *Pandora inaequivalvis*; S, SW, CI; LWST to SL; sediment
397 – *Pandora pinna*; all coasts; SL to OS; sediment

Superfamily Poromyacea

398 – *Poromya granulata*; N; OS; sediment

Superfamily Cuspidariacea

399 – *Cuspidaria abbreviata*; N, NW; OS; sediment

400 – *Cuspidaria cuspidata*; all coasts; SL to OS; sediment

401 – *Cuspidaria rostrata*; N, NW; OS; sediment

402 – *Cuspidaria costellata*; N, NW; SL to OS; sediment

Class Cephalopoda (Chapter 17)

Appendix One

A Glossary of Terms

WHAT FOLLOWS is a short glossary of the more common scientific terms used in this book and especially those that refer to the morphology of molluscs.

acicular	– needle-shaped.
abapically	– away from the apex.
adapically	– towards the apex.
adductor muscles scar	– a depression inside a bivalve which marks where the adductor muscle was attached.
anterior	– the front region; nearer the head.
aperture	– the opening (or mouth) of a gastropod shell.
apex	– the pointed tip of a shell.
apical whorl	– a whorl near the top of a gastropod shell.
apophysis	– a strip-like projection underneath the beaks of piddocks.
axial	– ribs or colour bands that are longitudinal, not spiral.
body whorl	– the lowest (and largest) whorl on a gastropod.
bifurcated	– two branched; two stems or double-pronged.
brachiate	– arm-like.
byssus	– organic fibres that attach a shell to another object.
canal	– a spout-like feature at the base of the aperture in some gastropods.
cancellated	– latticed ornamentation on a shell formed by small interlacing bars.
cardinal teeth	– the teeth immediately below the umbo.
carinate	– angled or keeled.
cephalic	– relating to the head region.
cephalic shield	– a flattened area associated with the head region.
chondrophore	– the pit inside the beak where the ligament is attached (bivalves only).
columella	– the central pillar in gastropods; the axis of coiling.
conjugate	– joined in pairs.
coeloconoid	– whorls that are concave in profile.
costa/costae	– raised, rounded longitudinal ridges.
costate	– a pattern involving costa.

crenulated	– wrinkled, or scalloped margin of a shell.
cyrtoconoid	– whorls that are convex in profile.
decussate	– similar to reticulate; a net-like pattern caused by costae and striations crossing at acute angles.
dendritic	– branching or tree-like in shape.
dendroid	– bush-shaped.
depressed	– flattened from above or sunk.
dextral	– right-handed.
diffuse	– widely spread out.
digitiform	– finger-like.
divaricate	– diverging rows, forking off or branching out.
ears	– lateral projections on the shells of some bivalves (e.g. scallops).
epidermis	– the periostracum (now an invalid term).
epipodal	– relating to the side of the foot.
equivalve	– where two valves are of a similar shape and size (i.e. symmetrical).
falcate	– shaped like a crescent.
fasciculated	– clumps of fine hairs on the girdle area of chitons.
ferruginous	– coloured brownish or yellowish-red.
fimbricated	– a fringed edge or border.
foot	– the soft structure used for moving and burrowing.
gape	– the space between two valves when they are closed.
globose	– sphere-shaped or globular.
granulated	– ornamented with minute grains or small nodules.
granule	– a minute elevation.
hinge	– where two valves meet.
imbricated	– structures that overlap with one another (like roof tiles).
imperforate	– no umbilicus is present.
incised	– having deep notches.
inequivalve	– where two valves are of different shape or size.
inner lip	– the area on the inside of the aperture.
intercostate	– the area between ribs or ridges.
interstices	– a narrow space between two parts.
involute	– where the last whorl of a gastropod envelopes earlier ones.
keel	– a distinctive, longitudinal ridge.
labial varix	– a thickened ridge associated with the outer lip.
lacunose	– a small pit.
lamellate	– plate-like.

lateral teeth	– teeth on either side of the umbo.
latticed	– an interlaced pattern on the shell.
ligament	– the organic band that forms the hinge between two valves.
lirate	– fine raised lines or grooves on the shell surface.
lumule	– a depression in front the beaks in bivalves.
maculated	– blotches or spots of colour.
maculose	– covered with spots.
malleated	– a pattern that looks hammered.
mantle	– a fleshy part of the body wall which secretes the shell.
margin	– the edge of a shell.
marginate	– a edge or border that is thickened.
median	– in the middle area.
metapodial	– relating to the posterior part of the foot.
mucronate	– terminating abruptly in a short point or spine.
node	– a tubercule or swelling.
nodose	– having tubercules or nodes.
olivaceous	– olive coloured.
operculum	– a circular horny disc that is used to seal the aperture.
opisthocline	– ribs that incline to the right (relative to the apex).
oral	– relating to the mouth region.
orthocline	– ribs that are arranged in a vertical pattern (relative to the apex).
outer lip	– the area on the outside of the aperture.
pallets	– two paddle-shaped structures used by some species to close a burrow (usually in wood or rock boring molluscs).
pallial line	– the mark inside a bivalve shell that connects the adductor scars.
pallial sinus	– an indentation in the pallial line.
papillae	– a conical projection of soft tissue.
parapodial	– on the outside of the foot.
parietal region	– a smooth region surrounding the aperture of a gastropod.
pelagic	– a open ocean dweller.
pen	– the internal shell of a cephalopod (usually squid).
perforate	– possessing an umbilicus.
periostracum	– a fibrous, skin-like coating on the outside of a shell.
peristome	– the rim of the aperture.
periphery	– the widest part of the whorl.
pilose	– covered with fine hairs.
podal	– relating to the foot.

posterior	– the back area of the shell or furtherest away from the head.
prosocline	– ribs that incline to the left (relative to the apex).
protoconch	– the upper-most whorls (i.e. the first to be formed) on a gastropod which may differ markedly from those below.
punctate	– a pattern of dots or coloured spots over the surface.
quincunx	– five things in a square-like pattern.
radial	– radiating from the centre.
reticulate	– a net-like or squared pattern on a shell produced by the intersection of costae and striations.
rhinophores	– modified/rolled head tentacles.
serrate	– an edge with a toothed, saw-like pattern.
sinistral	– left-handed.
siphon	– a part of the mantle that forms into a tubular structure.
spatulate	– paddle-shaped.
spicule	– a fine needle-like projection.
spinulous	– possessing small spines.
spiral striations	– striations that travel around the whorls parallel to the suture line.
spire	– the whorls located above the body whorl.
squamate	– scale-shaped.
striations/striae	– fine lines across the surface of the shell.
strigate	– fine closely set grooves.
sulcata	– indented.
suture	– the seam along which two bodies meet (e.g. the point where two whorls meet).
teeth	– sharp, pointed projections; usually associated with the hinge area of bivalve.
teleoconch	– the lower whorls below the protoconch (i.e. the adult whorls).
tricostate	– having three ribs or ridges.
tubercule	– a small, discreet mound-like elevation such as knob or pimple.
tuberculated	– a pattern of tubercles.
umbilicus	– the navel-like depression on the underside of some gastropods.
umbo/umbones	– the area behind the beaks (on bivalves).
valve	– a detachable solid shell.
varix	– a thickened rib.
whorl	– a single coil on a gastropod shell.

Appendix Two

A List of Useful Associations and Institutions

WHAT FOLLOWS is a short list of institutions that may be of interest or assistance to amateur British conchologists.

British Molluscan Societies

Conchological Society of Great Britain & Ireland: www.conchsoc.org
The Malacological Society of London: www.malacsoc.org.uk
British Shell Collectors' Club: www.britishshellclub.org.uk

UK Museums and Public Galleries

ENGLAND

Alton, Gilbert White's House and Oates Museum: www.gilbertwhiteshouse.org.uk
Cambridge: University Museum of Zoology: www.zoo.cam.ac.uk
Cambridge: Sedgwick Museum of Earth Sciences: www.sedgwickmuseum.org
Chesil Beach Visitor Centre: www.chesilbeach.org/CBVC
Chester: Grosvenor Museum: www.grosvenormuseum.co.uk
Dorchester: Dorset County Museum: www.dorsetcountymuseum.org
London: Natural History Museum: www.nhm.ac.uk
Lulworth Cove Heritage Centre, Dorset: www.lulworth.com
Oxford: Museum of the History of Science, Oxford: www.mhs.ox.ac.uk
Oxford: Pitt Rivers Museum: www.prm.ox.ac.uk
Oxford University Museum of Natural History: www.oum.ox.ac.uk
Reading: Cole Museum of Zoology: www.colemuseum.rdg.ac.uk
Reading Museum: www.readingmuseum.org.uk
Salcombe: Maritime and Local History Museum: www.devonmuseums.net
Salisbury: Salisbury and South Wiltshire Museum: www.salisburymuseum.org.uk
Shoreham: Marlipins Museum: www.sussexpast.co.uk
Taunton: Somerset County Museum: www.somerset.gov.uk
Tring: Walter Rothschild Zoological Museum: www.nhm.ac.uk/tring
York: Yorkshire Museum: www.yorkshiremuseum.org.uk

SCOTLAND

Aberdeen Maritime Museum: www.aagm.co.uk
Arran: Rosaburn Heritage Museum: www.arranmuseum.co.uk

Banff Museum, Aberdeenshire: www.aberdeenshire.gov.uk
Isle of Bute: Bute Museum: www.butemuseum.org
Isle of Islay: Islay Museum of Life: www.islayinfo.com
Isle of Skye: Skye Museum of Island Life: www.skyemuseum.co.uk
North Berwick Museum: www.eastlothian.gov.uk
Stirling: Smith Art Gallery and Museum: www.smithartgallery.demon.co.uk

WALES
Cardiff: National Museum Wales: www.museumwales.ac.uk
Hiraethog: Llyn Brenig Visitor Centre: www.hiraethog.org.uk
Neath Museum: www.neath-porttalbot.gov.uk

NORTHERN IRELAND/IRELAND
Belfast: Ulster Museum: www.ulstermuseum.org.uk
Dublin: National Museum of Ireland (Natural History): www.museum.ie

CHANNEL ISLANDS
Jersey Museum: www.jerseyheritagetrust.org
Guernsey Museum: www.museum.guernsey.net

Bibliography

BELOW is a selection of the works that I have most commonly consulted during my years as an amateur conchologist. For a long while I had to use London libraries to look at the older Victorian publications in this list; I now notice that facsimile copies of many of these same volumes are available free on the internet (try Google's book page or www.archive.com).

Abbott, R.T., 1991. *Seashells of the Northern Hemisphere*. Gallery.

Alder, J., and Hancock, A., 1845-1855. *A Monograph of the British Nudibranchiate Mollusca*. Ray Society.

Allen, J.A., 1962. *The Fauna of the Clyde Sea Area*. Scottish Marine Biological Association.

Angel, H., 1975. *Seashore Life on Sandy Beaches*. Jarrold.

Beedham, G.E., 1972. *Identification of the British Mollusca*. Hulton Educational Publications.

Brown, T., 1835. *The Conchologists' Textbook*: Fullarton and Co.

Campbell, A.C., 1976. *Seashore & Shallow Seas of Britain and Europe*. Hamlyn.

Christensen, J.M., 1980. *Bivalves of the British and Northern European Seas*. Penguin.

Clark, W., 1855. *A History of the British Marine Testaceous Mollusca*, J. van Voorst.

da Costa, E.M., 1778. *The British Conchology*, The Author.

Dance, S.P., 1976. *Shell Collector's Guide*. David and Charles.

Dillwyn, L.W., 1817. *A Descriptive Catalogue of Recent Shells*. J & A Arch.

Donovan, E., 1799-1804. *The Natural History of British Shells*. F & C Rivington.

Duncan, F.M., 1943. *British Shells*. King Penguin.

Evans, I.O., 1962. *Observer's Book of Sea and Seashore*. Frederick Warne.

Forbes, E., and Hanley, S., 1853. *A History of the British Mollusca and their Shells*. van Voorst.

Graham, A., 1971. *British Prosobranch and other Operculate Molluscs*. Linnean Society of London.

Graham, A., 1988. *Molluscs: Prosobranch and Pyramidellid Gastropods*. Linnean Society of London.

Hanley, S., 1856. *An Illustrated and Descriptive Catalogue of Recent Bivalve Shells*. Williams and Norgate.

Hayward, P., Nelson-Smith, T., and Shields, C., 1996. *Sea Shore of Britain and Europe*. Collins.

Hayward, P.J, and Ryland, J.S., 1990. *The Marine Fauna of the British Isles and North-West Europe*. Oxford University Press.

Heppell, D., Smith, S.M., and Picton, B.E., 1997. 'Mollusca', in Picton, B.E. and Howson, C.M., *The Species Directory of the Marine Fauna and Flora of the British Isles and Surrounding Seas*. Marine Conservation Society, pp.213-250.

Jeffreys, J.G., 1860. 'A Synoptical List of the British Species of *Teredo*, with a Notice of the Exotic Species. *Annals and Magazine of Natural History*. Vol. 6: 121-127.

Jeffreys, J.G., 1862-1869. *British Conchology*. J. van Voorst, 5 vols.

Jones, A.M. and Baxter, J.M., 1987. *Molluscs: caudofoveata, Solenogastres, Polyplacophora and Scaphopoda*, Linnean Society of London.

Lister, M., 1685-1692. *Historiae sive synopsis Methodicae Conchyliorum quorum Omnium Picturae ad Vivum Delineatae, Exhibetur Liber Primus*. Author.

McKay, D. and Smith, S.M., 1979. *Marine Mollusca of East Scotland*. Royal Scottish Museum.

McMillan, N.F., 1968. *British Shells*. Frederick Warne.

Montagu, G., 1803. *Testacea Britannica*, J. Hollis.

Montagu, G., 1808. Supplement to *Testacea Britannica*. J. Hollis.

Reid, D.G., 1996. *Systematics and Evolution of Littorina*. The Ray Society.

Seaward, D.R., 1982. *Sea Area Atlas of the Marine Molluscs of Britain and Ireland*. Conchological Society.

Sinel, J., 1906. *An Outline of the Natural History of our Shores,*. Swan Sonnenschein and Co.

Smith, S.M. and Heppell, D., 1991. *Checklist of British Marine Mollusca*. National Museums of Scotland.

Smith, S.M., 1981. *How to Collect Marine Mollusca*. Conchological Society No.18.

Smith, S.M., and Heppell, D.H., 1991. *Checklist of British Marine Mollusca*. National Museums of Scotland.

Sowerby, G.B., 1859. *Illustrated Index of British Shells*. Simpkin, Marshall and Co. (1st edition).

Sowerby, G.B., 1887. *Illustrated Index of British Shells*. Simpkin, Marshall and Co. (2nd edition).

Tebble, N., 1966. *British Bivalve Seashells*. British Museum (Natural History).

Thompson, T.E., 1988. *Berthic Opisthobranchs*. Linnean Society of London.

Turk, S.M., 1971. *Seashore Life in Cornwall and the Isles of Scilly*. Barton.

Turton, W., 1819. *A Conchological Dictionary of the British Islands*. John Booth.

Turton, W., 1822. *Conchylia Insularum Britannicarum*, Cullum.

Winkworth, R., 1932. 'The British Marine Mollusca', *Journal of Conchology*. vol. 19(7), pp. 221–252.

Yonge, C.M., 1949. *Seashore*. Collins.

Index of Species Names

Index of Common (Vernacular) Names